DEDICATION

For my beloved wife, Susan, who passed away in 2021 –
The best wife, mother and grandmother that any man could ever hope
for – My precious partner in life and in law – She was the shining role
model for our children and grandchildren – Susan will live in our
hearts and minds forever –

AMERICA WHAT IS THE MATTER WITH US?

AMERICA WHAT IS THE MATTER WITH US?

A History of Presidential Lies - The Failures of our War Against Terror and our Policy of Democracy Promotion

STANLEY M. ROSENBLATT

CONTENTS

Dedication i
FOREWORD xi
INTRODUCTION xv
A BRIEF PREVIEW OF EVERY CHAPTER xxxv

1 AFGHANISTAN - THE TRAGEDY OF AMERICA'S FINAL DEPARTURE 1

2 PAKISTAN 42

3 IRAQ 62

4 IRAN – AND HOW AMERICA HAS DEALT WITH THIS STATE SPONSOR OF TERRORISM 97

5 THE PHENOMENON OF DONALD TRUMP 103

6 JANUARY 6, 2021 – HOW COULD WE HAVE BEEN UNPREPARED FOR THE ATTACK AT THE CAPITOL? 122

7 ROBERT CARO ON THE EXERCISE OF POLITICAL POWER IN A DEMOCRACY 130

8 HOW STORMY DANIELS BECAME FAMOUS – HOW MICHAEL AVENATTI BECAME INFAMOUS – 142

9	OTHER HIGHLY INTELLIGENT AND ACCOMPLISHED PEOPLE MAKING INCREDIBLY DUMB DECISIONS — 148
10	HAD HILLARY CLINTON WON IN 2016, SHE WOULD HAVE BEEN ONLY THE SECOND FEMALE PRESIDENT — 157
11	THE SUPER-RICH CONTROL AMERICAN POLITICS — 162
12	POVERTY AND INEQUALITY — 169
13	THE FALSE PROMISES OF INDEPENDENCE AND DEMOCRACY — 176
14	AFRICA – INDEPENDENCE YES – DEMOCRACY NO — 202
15	THE TOTALLY AVOIDABLE DEATH OF GEORGE FLOYD — 224
16	THE TRAGEDY AT THE ROBB ELEMENTARY SCHOOL IN UVALDE, TEXAS — 227
17	THE ME TOO MOVEMENT- THE DOWNFALL OF A HOLLYWOOD GIANT — 231
18	THE MYTH THAT AMERICANS ARE BASICALLY HONEST THE COLLEGE ADMISSIONS CHEATING SCANDAL — 242
19	THE DRUG OVERDOSE EPIDEMIC — 247
20	THE UKRAINE AND THE AMERICAN PUSH TO HAVE IT JOIN THE NORTH ATLANTIC TREATY ORGANIZATION — 255
21	AMERICAN INDIANS AND THE CRUEL POLICY OF FORCED ASSIMILATION — 264

22	STARBUCKS – A NATION OBSESSED WITH COFFEE IS NOT GOING TO WIN ANY WARS	273
23	THERANOS – ANOTHER EXAMPLE OF SMART PEOPLE MAKING STUPID DECISIONS –	279
24	HOW THE ULTRA-RICH AND MULTINATIONAL CORPORATIONS USE TAX HAVENS TO CHEAT THEIR FELLOW AMERICANS	283
25	THE ART OF TAX AVOIDANCE	288
26	ROOSEVELT AND TAFT – HOW TWO PRESIDENTS WENT FROM BEING BEST FRIENDS TO BECOMING ENEMIES –	298
27	SOME OTHER PRESIDENTIAL ELECTIONS – LANDSLIDES AND SQUEAKERS	305
28	ADDITIONAL REFLECTIONS ON PRESIDENTIAL ELECTIONS AND POLITICS	313

ABOUT THE AUTHOR   319

FOREWORD

When my wife, Susan, and I decided to sue the tobacco companies, every lawyer we knew said that we were crazy. The companies had never lost a case. We were told that it made no sense for a small firm to take on an industry with unlimited resources. My primary motivation was to cross-examine the CEOs and blast them for denying that cigarettes caused cancer or were addictive.

The industry brought in super star experts with impressive credentials to support those lies. The defense stressed the warnings about disease which appeared on every package of cigarettes. Congress had passed laws requiring that the tobacco companies post those warnings. Tobaccos argument was that everyone knew the risks associated with smoking and, therefore, smokers assumed those risks.

Susan and I embarked on a 2-year jury trial. Hard to believe but I questioned a total of 157 witnesses on both direct and cross-examination. Susan, as the appellate lawyer, handled by herself all the legal arguments and the thousands of objections and motions that flooded the courtroom on a daily basis.

Tobaccos strategy was to overwhelm the opponent with tactics designed to prevent a coherent presentation. It was me and Susan against a cast of some 40 defense lawyers. At times, tobacco would bring in a lawyer to handle a single witness or make a single legal argument. They inundated the court with voluminous legal briefs arguing that the case should be thrown out and why various witnesses should not be allowed to testify. Susan, facing a battalion of skilled lawyers on her own had to respond to this mountain of objections, and she did so brilliantly.

Tobacco's basic pitch was that they were selling a legal product - people had the right to choose to smoke. They had the audacity to preach about freedom.

Tobacco always contended that the cause of cancer was something in the environment or in various foods or bus fumes or exposure to an industrial site - anything except a 30-year history of smoking two packs a day. They also contended that all anyone had to do to quit smoking was will power. This approach enabled me to say to the jurors – "Doesn't it make you angry to have your intelligence insulted over and over again by these lawyers?"

After 7 days of deliberation, the jury returned a verdict of $145 Billion against all the tobacco companies – THE HIGHEST AWARD IN AMERICAN HISTORY.

It would be natural for a reader to wonder why a trial lawyer who took on Big Tobacco would be writing a book about Afghanistan, Iraq, Pakistan and the American political system. My primary motivation to sue the tobacco companies was to expose and punish the lies they had told us for generations about disease causation and addiction. There is a nexus between those lies and the lies we are told by our government.

I greatly value transparency – being direct, straightforward and honest. Not being evasive and cute and tricky and underhanded.

American politicians and members of Congress lie to the American people all the time. So do presidents. For years, our government lied to us about progress we were supposedly making in our 20-year wars in Afghanistan and Iraq. That's why Americans kept quiet, no protests, no demonstrations.

Biden lied when he said that the Afghan Army on its own could prevent a Taliban victory. Obama lied when he said that Iraq had become a stable, sovereign nation. Bush lied when he said that Iraq possessed weapons of mass destruction.

They all lied when they pretended that Afghanistan, Iraq and Pakistan would become functioning democracies. Donald Trump did not invent presidential lying. And there were never any consequences for those lies. Why did we invade in the first place? Because Bush got the country all hyped up about our war against terror. We were going to bring Al Qaeda and the other terrorists to justice. Politicians of both parties eagerly jumped on that bandwagon.

ISIS, the most blood thirsty of all terrorist organizations, did not exist on 9/11! Terror now is much more widespread than it was on 9/11. Throughout Africa affiliates of Al Qaeda and ISIS are attacking and killing on a daily basis. Our war on terror has been a tragic failure. The Taliban control the entire country of Afghanistan. At one time ISIS controlled one third of Iraq.

Our government never leveled with us about our fantasy policy goals and the unnecessary sacrifices of millions of young, patriotic, brave and naïve Americans. Our government lied to us on an almost daily basis during the years of the Vietnam War.

Need I mention the years of lying about President Bidens mental condition. His allies in the media played an active role in the fiction that Biden was sharp. Yes, he could be effective when reading a speech from a teleprompter. But in nearly every other circumstance when he spoke or answered questions his deficiencies were obvious.

And then came the debate of June 27, 2024 when all of his problems were exposed. Even his closest supporters had to admit his performance was a disaster. And it came after a week of preparation with about 15 coaches – not one of whom had the courage to tell the truth – that in 90 minutes of unscripted questions and back and forth with Trump his problems would be exposed.

President Bidens enablers will say – yes he had a bad night but he is capable of running the country. No, the debate exposed the core of the president's diminished capacity. How could his wife and friends have done that to him?

The public has become immune because the fabrications have become part of our political system. A strong motivating factor for this book is to get Americans to insist that our government be straight with us, that it tell us the truth at all times.

NOTE: I WILL UPDATE EVERY CHAPTER IN MY BOOK BY WAY OF MY WEBSITE AVAILABLE AT – WWW.STANLEYM-ROSENBLATT.COM.

INTRODUCTION

After reading my introduction, you will understand why the title of my book is –

WHAT IS THE MATTER WITH US? And you will be asking yourself the same question.

I begin with what may very well be the worst day in American history – September 11, 2001. That's the day when 19 Arabs hijacked four American passenger planes.

The plan was hatched by Osama Bin Laden, the leader of the terrorist organization – Al Qaeda. Two planes struck the gleaming skyscrapers – the Twin Towers of the World Trade Center in Manhattan. Both buildings collapsed killing nearly 3,000 Americans who were at their normal office jobs.

Many victims suffered horrific deaths jumping from the 60th or 70th floors to escape being burned to death, landing on the concrete pavements.

Many suffered deaths so severe that their remains could not be identified. Three hundred and forty-three firemen and women lost their lives on that awful day.

Another plane hit the Pentagon killing several hundred more patriotic Americans. The hijackers had another target in mind, our Capitol, which houses Congress. That plan was foiled by incredibly brave Americans, knowing that they were going to die, took action to divert the plane which crashed in a field in Shanksville, Pennsylvania.

Over the years, about 300 more firefighters and paramedics died from inhaling toxic dust as they searched for body parts. To this day there are hundreds of remains so obliterated that they could not be identified. Think of the agony suffered by their loved ones.

The United States was able to capture five of the Arabs who were involved in the planning and carrying out of this vile mission.

I AM WRITING THESE WORDS IN 2024 AND NONE OF THE FIVE HAVE EVER BEEN BROUGHT TO TRIAL! HOW COULD THAT BE?

YES – WHAT THE HELL IS THE MATTER WITH US?

They are all at Guantanamo, our naval base in Cuba where they have it pretty good. Their religious practices are respected, the food is decent, they can watch television and chat with their comrades.

How incredibly passive Americans have become! Never organized protests against the outrage of not bringing the mass murderers to trial 24 years after their crime.

We have become a nation obsessed with procedure. There have been a huge number of hearings at Guantanamo before a succession of military judges and prosecutors. Over time, the case has amassed well over 400,000 pages of filings and exhibits. Much of the focus has been on protecting the due-process rights of the defendants.

We have become a nation where people are fearful of being criticized. Fearful of being labeled racist. The hijackers took flying lessons in the United States, but they had no interest in learning how to land. None of the instructors reported this fact to the authorities. They were worried that they would be criticized for targeting Muslims.

There is no doubt in my mind that some of the security people at the airports were suspicious of these groups. They were amateurs, not seasoned spies or professionals. They would not have been acting in a normal, relaxed way. They would have been nervous, eyes darting. None of them were accompanied by wives or children. The security people said nothing. They knew that being labeled as prejudiced could destroy their careers.

On October 12, 2000, a group of Arab terrorists attacked the United States Destroyer Cole sitting in a port in Yemen which killed 17 sailors. The Saudi Arabian accused of leading this attack has been in United

States custody since 2002. Like the 9/11 killers, he has never been brought to trial.

We invaded Afghanistan a month after 9/11 to capture or kill Bin Laden.

AFGHANISTAN

It took us 10 years to find him. I will explain why it took so long when I get to Pakistan. President Bush II transformed that very limited objective into a generalized war against terror worldwide, the Global War on Terrorism. A war which lasted for over 20 years and did not accomplish its objective.

Terrorist organizations were much stronger and numerous at the end of the 20 years than at the beginning. ISIS, the strongest and most vicious of them all, did not exist on 9/11!

The passive American public accepted the longest war in American history without a peep. As 9/11 was the worst day in American history, our exit from Afghanistan was the most humiliating day in American history. Although our 100,000 plus combat troops had been removed by President Obama at the end of 2014, America still had a residual force of several thousand in Afghanistan during the Biden administration.

Biden made a decision to remove that entire residual force. For the first time in 20 years, Afghanistan was empty of American troops. When there was criticism that the Afghan security forces, on their own, would not be able to defeat the Taliban, Biden told the American people a huge lie –

"I TRUST THE CAPACITY OF THE AFGHAN MILITARY, WHICH IS BETTER TRAINED, BETTER EQUIPPED AND MORE COMPETENT THAN THE TALIBAN IN TERMS OF CONDUCTING WAR."

During August 2021, the Taliban captured 15 provincial capitals in 9 days. They captured the national capital of Kabul.

The Taliban accomplished this because – "the better trained" Afghan military simply refused to fight. We had spent billions training and equipping the 300,000-plus member security forces who refused to confront the Taliban as they marched toward victory.

For a time, we had 150,000 troops plus some 25 NATO countries in Afghanistan, and we couldn't defeat the Taliban. But Biden was telling us that the Afghan military, on its own, could accomplish that. Or at the very least could prevent the Taliban from taking over the entire country.

President Biden told another huge lie about our effort in Afghanistan when he said –

"We achieved our objectives."

When Obama was campaigning against Hillary Clinton in 2008, he said –

"Afghanistan was the war that we have to win."

And when he removed our combat troops at the end of 2014, he said our sacrifices led –

"To a responsible conclusion." More presidential lies which do not arouse fury in the American people.

The "conclusion" in 2021 was a humiliating defeat.

The United States has the most sophisticated weaponry in the world. Great planes and great pilots. And we lost to a terrorist organization which did not possess a single fighter jet. Our government has never explained to the American people how that could happen. The American people have never demanded an explanation. Many were too focused on their iPhones to even notice.

Robert Gates, our Secretary of Defense under both Bush and Obama, told the truth when he said –

"Our lack of understanding of Afghanistan, its culture, its tribal and ethnic politics, its power brokers and their relationship was profound."

Over 150 American and NATO military forces were murdered by the Afghanistan security forces. Yes, by our allies! It was so common, it had a label –

"Green on blue killings."

That should have been the signal for our leaders to say – we are getting the hell out of this dysfunctional, unappreciative country. Instead, our leaders told us to stay the course, and that was okay with the majority of Americans.

We knew nothing about the character of the man we installed as the leader of Afghanistan – Hamid Karzai, in December 2001. He remained in that position until September 2014.

How did Karzai show his appreciation for American sacrifices?

He called us – "demons – trespassers and occupiers for our own purposes."

He said that our presence caused more extremism and that we inflicted needless suffering on his people. In spite of the insults, our government (the perennial suckers) continued to pour in billions to the Karzai government year after year.

Nearly 3,000 American service members have been killed in Afghanistan. Young, healthy, patriotic volunteers. Over 20,000 were wounded – many with permanent injuries, paralysis, loss of limbs, brain traumas and mental illness. It has been estimated that $350 billion will need to be spent caring for the wounded – medical and disability payments. Costs will rise as the veterans age.

Bad decisions, a belief in fantasies and the acceptance of lying can have terrible consequences. Perhaps the biggest fantasy of all was that our sacrifices were going to be able to transform Afghanistan into a democracy.

PAKISTAN

America considered Pakistan to be a close ally in our "war against terror." Yet in many ways Pakistan was our enemy.

For years terrorists in Afghanistan killed American soldiers. They then crossed over the border into Pakistan where they were protected by the military and their all-powerful spy intelligence service. Our leaders knew this, and they tolerated it. We continued to give Pakistan billions of dollars in military and economic aid in spite of this treachery. Yes – perennial suckers!

President Clinton wrote a book 4 years after leaving office in which he said –

"Pakistan supported the Taliban and, by extension, Al Qaeda... and the Pakistan military was full of Taliban and Al Qaeda sympathizers." That also explains why the militaries of Afghanistan and Iraq are so ineffective against terrorists. Bush and Obama knew what Clinton knew – that Pakistan supported terror groups – yet they both tolerated it.

Zalmay Khalilzad had been America's ambassador to both Afghanistan and Iraq as well as our ambassador to the United Nations. He was part of the Bush II administration, and he tried to get our government to take a stand against Pakistan's treachery but with no success.

Quoting Khalilzad –

"Pakistan was playing a perfidious and dangerous double game and needed to be called on it . . . the resilience of the Taliban is primarily due to the military and intelligence services providing sanctuary and support." They could rest up, refresh themselves and prepare for a return to Afghanistan where they could kill more Americans.

Husaini Haqqani was Pakistan's ambassador to the United Nations 2008-2011. He confirmed that the Taliban received money, training and arms from Pakistan's Interservice Intelligence Directorate (ISI).

He said –"The United States was effectively arming a country that was in turn arming insurgents who were killing American troops in Afghanistan. The relationship between the United States and Pakistan embodies a history of failure."

Haqqani has been much more honest about that relationship than our presidents have been. In my Pakistan chapter I cite more instances of Pakistan's treachery.

In spite of all this, the United States designated Pakistan as a – "MAJOR NON-NATO ALLY." Some ally!

President Obama said the following – he – "reaffirmed that a mutual commitment to democracy is a key pillar of the United States-Pakistani partnership."

"DEMOCRACY?" Pakistan has been ruled by its military directly or indirectly throughout its history. Two political dynasties controlled the office of Prime Minister for decades – the Bhutto clan and Nawaz Sharif. Benazir Bhutto and Sharif had both been prime minister multiple times. Sharif was convicted on corruption charges and served time in prison. Benazir was accused of corruption and was in exile for many years. Sharif was also in exile after his release from prison. At times the military would allow them to return.

Benazir's father had been Prime Minister. The military had him executed in 1979. Benazir returned from exile in 2007 hoping to regain leadership. On December 27, 2007 she was assassinated. Nepotism is so strong that her husband became the leader in spite of the fact that he had served time in prison for crookedness. SOME DEMOCRACY MR. OBAMA!

When corruption is part of the fabric of a society it even infects science. A. Q. Khan was hailed as the Father of Pakistan's nuclear program. He sold plans, designs and technology to Iran and North Korea. Two enemies of the United States.

Think of the consequences if terrorists ever got their hands on Pakistan's vast supply of nuclear weapons.

"PARTNERSHIP?"

For years, Pakistan kept Bin Laden's secret from the United States. That's why it took us 10 years to finally find him and kill him. He had lived for years in a mansion in Pakistan along with several wives and children. In a mansion very close to the equivalent of Pakistan's "West Point."

Pakistan got a leader in 2018 who hates America.

Imran Khan was a beloved figure, having led Pakistan to victory in 1992, winning the cricket world cup. He was not a part of Pakistan's two traditional political dynasties.

He praised the Taliban for their "holy war" against the United States.

He said – "Pakistan has suffered enough fighting America's war."

America has – "caused disaster in Pakistan."

Khan celebrated the Taliban victory in Afghanistan, saying that they had – "broken the chains of slavery." When he first sought office, the military backed him. His popularity went to his head and at times he advocated policies of which the military disapproved. For that disobedience he was arrested on corruption charges in May 2023.

That was the usual playbook when the military wanted to get rid of a prime minister. They would be charged with corruption. Many of them were in fact corrupt – corruption that was tolerated so long as they did not defy the military. No prime minister ever served out the full terms to which they had been elected.

SOME DEMOCRACY MR. OBAMA!

Khan was replaced by the brother of Nawaz Sharif. Nepotism reigns supreme. Khan had promised to straighten out Pakistan's awful economy and to solve the deeply rooted corruption. He failed big time on both pledges.

Although Pakistan is rich in valuable minerals, natural gas deposits, and oil, it has never succeeded in translating that wealth into raising the standard of living for the population at large. The country survives on loans from the International Monetary Fund and the World Bank. Also on handouts from Saudi Arabia and the United Arab Emirates.

Can such a country really be called sovereign? Can we be confident that such a country can protect its nuclear assets?

This is not a country which young, patriotic American volunteers should die for!

When Khan crossed the military, he wound up in prison. His sentence was harsh – many years.

In May 2023 after Khan had been removed from office and arrested, his followers torched and ransacked several military installations. That had never happened before.

Khan was a prisoner during the parliamentary elections February 2024. His party was not permitted to participate. ONE HELL OF A DEMOCRACY MR. OBAMA!

Many of his followers ran as independents and many won. A youth movement backed Khan and they were very savvy about the internet and social media allowing them to get their message out.

The election result came as a shock – his followers gained the most seats in the parliament although still not enough to form a majority. A coalition will need to be formed.

Khan's party claimed vote rigging deprived it of many more seats and that if the election had been honest, they would have won a majority with no need to form a coalition.

His party will, I am sure, be excluded from any coalition. The likelihood is that any coalition will be led by Nawaz Sharif, a three-time former prime minister, or his brother Shehbaz. Their party won the second most seats in the February 2024 election.

On my website I will update developments. Developments like –

How long will any coalition last?

Will Khan be released from prison?

Will the military ease up or get even stricter?

Will there be protests and rioting by Khan's followers?

The economy remains in bad shape. Inflation is running at about 30%, they will need another huge loan from the International Monetary Fund. Whoever is in charge, Pakistan will remain dysfunctional.

Terror attacks against Pakistan itself have increased since the Taliban takeover in Afghanistan.

It is simply flat out dishonest to pretend that Pakistan is a democratic country or a reliable partner of the United States.

IRAQ AND IRAN

The United States invaded Iraq twice. Our first invasion was under the first President Bush in 1991.

Why did we invade? Saddam Hussein had invaded Kuwait, a country about which Americans knew nothing and cared nothing about. We did not invade Iraq because Bush cared about Kuwait – an Arab kingdom.

Bush gave his real reason in a book published several years after he left office – "A World Transformed." We invaded Iraq because Bush was worried that Iraq would invade Saudi Arabia.

Unbelievably, Bush sent a half-million troops to protect Saudi Arabia. Congress and the American people went along with it. It took us four days to defeat Iraq's military! Astonishing – a half-million troops sent to fight a 4-day war. Both Bushes were groupies for Saudi Arabia.

Bush's pitch to Congress and the American people was that we would rescue Kuwait and restore its democracy. That was a total fiction. Kuwait was a royal dictatorship, it had never experienced democracy.

President Bush believed that after suffering a humiliating defeat, the Iraqi people (the majority Shiite Muslims and the Kurds) would overthrow the dictator Hussein. That never happened.

Instead we left Hussein with helicopter gunships which he used to crush an uprising which Bush himself had actually encouraged. We left Saddam with the same absolute powers he had before our invasion for 12 more years. THAT'S NOT A MISPRINT – 12 MORE YEARS!

How could we have left him in power after he imprisoned 163 American hostages for 4 months? The American people passively accepted him remaining in power in spite of the fact that our troops suffered many deaths.

President Bush's son invaded in 2003. What was the rationale for that invasion?

We were told very dramatically that Saddam possessed weapons of mass destruction. After high-level inspections by qualified people, it was established conclusively that Iraq had no such weapons. But we stuck around in Iraq for 20 more years. And again the American people just went along.

I am convinced that the Bush Administration knew there were no weapons of mass destruction. Way back on June 7, 1981 the Israeli Air Force obliterated Iraq's Osirak nuclear reactor. Instead of applauding that action, both the United States and Europe condemned Israel for daring to disrespect Iraq's treasured sovereignty.

I believe the real reason for our 2003 invasion was for Bush (the son) to redeem his father's terrible decision to allow Saddam to remain in power. We captured him in the second invasion and executed him.

Another reason for the invasion was Bush's belief in a fantasy. He believed that Iraq could be part of –

"The global democratic revolution."

He actually said that. Just how naïve can our leaders be?

President Obama indulged another fantasy as he pulled out our combat troops (leaving a small residual force) at the end of 2011.

He said – "We're leaving behind a sovereign, stable, self-reliant Iraq."

He could not possibly have believed that!

In 2014 the Iraqi military melted away before the onslaught of ISIS. Just as the Afghan Army melted away before the onslaught of the Taliban. America had spent billions training and equipping both the Iraqi military and the Afghan military.

A parliamentary election was held in Iraq in October 2021. A Shiite cleric, Muqtada Al Sadr, won the largest block of seats. During the civil war between Shiite Muslims and Sunni Muslims Sadr commanded an army that killed hundreds of Americans.

A finance minister, Ali Allawi, resigned from a dysfunctional government with this going away blast –

"Vast underground networks of senior officials, corrupt businessmen, and politicians that dominate entire sectors of the economy and siphon off literally billions of dollars from the public purse."

Endemic corruption and nepotism are a way of life in all of our allies – Iraq, Afghanistan and Pakistan. These are not countries that America's youth should be fighting for or dying for.

Iran-backed militias are the most powerful military and political force in Iraq. Former Prime Minister Maliki said in April 2009 –

"Today we face a new war of subversion, sedition and suspicion."

Prime Minister Abadi said –

"No one can control them – (Iran's militias). It is a very dangerous cocktail of militias and mafia."

No Obama we did not leave behind – "a sovereign stable self-reliant country."

Instead Obama and his Secretary of State, John Kerry, negotiated with Iran for many months to end sanctions believing their lie that their nuclear activities were never intended to develop a bomb. Just how naïve can our "leaders" be?

Biden bought into the Obama/Kerry fiction. He relaxed enforcement of sanctions on Iran's oil sales, he sought to reinstate the Obama deal with Iran which Trump had scuttled, he agreed to hand Iran $6 billion as part of a trade for five American hostages. Billions that would be used to advance terrorist goals by Iran's numerous proxies.

America's relations with Iran constitute a national disgrace, a national embarrassment. Iran has been very clever by advancing its terrorist aims through proxies. Proxies that they supply with advanced weapons and professional training. Proxies that include Hamas, Hezbollah in Lebanon, and the Houthis in Yemen. Also their militias that attack American troops stationed at bases in Iraq and Syria. The United States often responds to these attacks. These tit for tat exchanges are nonsense. Our government has never said to Iran – "Stop these attacks or we will attack you." No, the American mantra has always been to avoid escalation.

It is utterly disgraceful how the Houthis of Yemen have humiliated us. They have for months fired missiles, drones and rockets at ships traversing the Red Sea – navy vessels and commercial shipping. In spite of numerous airstrikes the attacks on shipping continued disrupting the flow of global trade.

Saudi Arabia, Iran's chief rival in the region, backed the government of Yemen in its civil war against the Houthis. Saudi Arabia bombed incessantly for several years, but they could not defeat the Houthis who remain the dominant force in Yemen. The so-called government is weak and poses no threat to the Houthis.

American airstrikes will be as effective as those of Saudi Arabia. Recognizing this, the Saudis stopped bombing and sought a peace deal. A ceasefire has been in effect since 2022.

When Hamas attacked Israel on October 7, 2023, murdering men, women, and children – burning, raping, beheading babies – they also killed some Americans and took Americans hostage.

This is what Biden should have said to Iran – "Your proxy Hamas has killed Americans and taken Americans hostage. If the Americans are not freed in 48 hours we will attack Iran with massive force. We will destroy your capacity to produce a nuclear bomb.

And remember that we possess an array of nuclear weapons. Nothing is off the table. We never avenged your murder of 241 sleeping American marines in Lebanon as we never avenged your kidnapping of American hostages that you held captive for over 400 days. American civilians who never did your country any harm. And don't bother telling us the lie that Hamas is independent and will not listen to you."

Yes, let the world know that if you kill Americans or take Americans hostage there will be actual consequences instead of meaningless threats.

I am well aware that all the policymakers, the pundits and the editorial writers will severely criticize my recommendation to attack Iran. They will accuse me of oversimplification, they will wring their hands about escalation and a wider war.

No, I am not guilty of oversimplification. It is they who are guilty of overcomplication. That is their game – if everything is complicated, they are viewed as being smart since they are addressing the complexities.

On January 28, 2024, an Iran-backed militia launched a drone from Iraq which struck an American military base in Jordan. Three of our service members were killed, over 40 were injured some very seriously including brain traumas.

Way less than 1% of Americans had any idea that we have troops in Jordan which shares borders with Iraq and Syria. Overall we have about 2,000 troops in Jordan – Army and Air Force. They are there to fight ISIS. We also have troops in Iraq and Syria. So a quarter of a century after 9/11, we are still engaged in our war against terror.

President Biden said, "we know the attack was carried out by radical Iran-backed military groups operating in Syria and Iraq."

OK – SO WHAT ARE WE GOING TO DO ABOUT IT?

The political and military party line answers that question!

President Biden said – "We will hold all those responsible to account at a time and in a manner of our choosing."

Over and over gain the administration made it clear that we would not hold Iran to account—

General Charles Brown Jr. Chairman of the Joint Chief of Staff – "We don't want to go down a path of greater escalation that drives to a much broader conflict."

Those are his marching orders from the Commander in Chief.

This in spite of the fact that Iran's Revolutionary Guard Quds Force is spread throughout the region training and equipping its proxies with drones, rockets and missiles.

Defense Secretary Austin said – "The President and I will not tolerate attacks on U.S. forces."

REALLY?

During the several months preceding February 2024, there had been over 165 attacks by Iran-backed militias against our troops in Iraq and Syria. Beyond humiliating!

Why did Trump call the Obama/Kerry deal "The worst deal ever negotiated?"

In many circles, both in the United States and Europe, the agreement finalized in July 2015 was hailed as a great accomplishment.

Trump removed America from the "deal" in May 2018. He reinstated sanctions and added to them choking off Iran's oil exports which was their greatest source of revenue.

Iran obtained tangible benefits from the agreement. Many sanctions were removed, we released about $100 billion in frozen assets. And all we got in return was a promise which was a lie.

The promise being that their enrichment of uranium was only directed toward peaceful purposes, that their underground Fordow nuclear site was in no way directed toward producing a nuclear weapon.

Obama told us that –

"They cannot create a nuclear weapon." That "Iran has agreed to unprecedented inspections of its programs." Obama and Kerry believed the Iranians would cooperate with the inspectors.

President Obama had been able to close the deal without the necessity of getting congressional approval. By not referring to the deal as a "deal," he was able to bypass that requirement. Good old political gimmickry at work.

In January 2018, Israel obtained access to secret Iranian nuclear archives which proved that their goal was of course a nuclear weapon. Only the befuddled naive could have believed otherwise.

The deal placed no restrictions on Iran's missile programs. Since then, Iran's advancement in missile technology has made giant strides.

General Kenneth McKenzie, Jr. who had been the head of U.S. Central Command said -

"They have over 3,000 ballistic missiles of various types. Their missiles have significantly greater range and significantly enhanced accuracy."

The missiles are precision guided. They would be capable of carrying nuclear warheads. Iran's stockpile of highly enriched uranium continues to grow. I would not be surprised if they already have a bomb. If not, they are very close.

Iran manufactures thousands of drones, selling many to Russia.

President Biden had allowed the international embargo on Iran's missile programs to lapse. Because of his policies, there was a surge in oil exports which resulted in billions pouring into Iran's hands.

In November 2023 our State Department reissued a sanctions waiver that gave Iran access to over $10 billion. Billions that could be used to fund and equip Iran's terrorist proxies in Syria, Iraq, Lebanon, and Yemen. Yes – what the hell is the matter with us?

Our ever-gullible Secretary of State Blinken was not embarrassed to say that the $6 billion "will be available only for humanitarian purposes."

He followed that up with the assurances that we have always handed to Iran – "The United States does not seek conflict with Iran."

After the Obama/Kerry deal, Iran's leaders continued to call America -

"The Great Satan." And we just took it.

Both the United States and Europe spent a year begging Iran to reinstate the awful Obama deal. In spite of all the concessions we were willing to make, Iran said "no." No matter what they did we never threatened them with an attack. Iran was supremely confident that in a Biden/Blinken administration, they had nothing to worry about.

Our leader feeds us this tired party line about Iran not directly controlling its proxies. That's a dangerous lie because it contains an element of truth. I don't think Iran gets involved in the details of individual attacks or decides on the dates of attacks or their precise targets. But if Iran tells its militias or other proxies to do something specific, or refrain from doing something, they will obey. They are subordinate to the "great power."

Of course, the Iranian leadership (Ayatollah Khamenei) pushes the idea that their proxies are independent, and the United States plays along.

Hundreds of ships avoid the Suez Canal to escape Houthis attacks causing them to go an extra 4,000 miles around southern Africa. The added expense causes prices to rise for everyone. The canal lies at the northwest end of the Red Sea. America and the rest of the world simply puts up with this outrage.

In November 2023, the Houthis hijacked a commercial vessel taking the 25-member crew hostage. The Unites States has used air strikes and missiles against the Houthis but they continue to attack. Just like they continued to attack in their civil war in spite of incessant bombing by Saudi Arabia and the United Arab Emirates. By the way, America without getting directly involved was a strong ally of the Saudis in their war against the Houthis.

Everything changed and didn't really change on January 28, 2024. That's the day when Iran's most prominent militia, Kataib Hezbollah, struck a remote military outpost in Jordan with drones, killing three American soldiers. Two of those killed were very young female soldiers.

Iran peddled their so called "plausible deniability" crap and again, America played along. But President Biden knew we had to react in a forceful way and we did. A few days after January 28, our planes struck 85 targets in Iraq and Syria, plus 36 strikes on Houthi targets in Yemen.

We hit zero targets in Iran. Iran's great fear is that if the United States struck forcefully their regime would likely collapse. That's why they pray that Trump does not become president again. Iran has many internal enemies – separatists and terrorists. Sunni secularists who despise the authoritarian Shiite theocracy. In January 2024, a suicide bomber killed over 100 Iranians. ISIS claimed responsibility.

That's why we still have troops in Iraq and Syria – to continue our battle against ISIS. So 23 years after 9/11, America is still fighting ISIS and other terrorist groups. Yes, 23 years after Bush's "Global War on Terrorism" which we lost and for which Bush, Cheney and Rumsfeld were never called to account. It's worth repeating – ISIS did not exist on 9/11.

There have been protests against the government which are ruthlessly suppressed. The economy is weak, unemployment is high, corruption is everywhere. Yes – Iran would have a lot to worry about if America removed the shackles of misplaced restraint and ferociously attacked.

Our threats are meaningless when everyone knows Iran has sanctuary guarantees from America. Defense Secretary Austin said – "Iran's support for Houthis attacks on commercial vessels must stop."

Well, the attacks did not stop. Nor will the attacks by other proxies stop. The solution is staring all of us in the face. STRIKE IRAN!

Instead, we have been protecting Iran during its march toward a nuclear weapon. A policy that is unworthy of us as a nation.

Now I am going to address two American tragedies. Tragedies that could have been avoided with the exercise of commonsense, normalcy and courage. I have chapters on these tragedies.

THE DEATH OF GEORGE FLOYD

George Floyd bought a pack of cigarettes with a counterfeit $20 bill. It was never established that Floyd even knew the bill was counterfeit. A teenage clerk reported it. A different clerk might have laughed it off. It deserved to be laughed off. Unbelievably, four cops arrived to deal with this "crime." We are talking about a lousy pack of cigarettes.

Floyd offered no resistance at all, yet he ended up face down on concrete with Derek Chauvin's' knee on his neck for 9 minutes. The cops wanted him to get into their police car, Floyd explained that he was claustrophobic. He was 6 feet, 4 inches and feared that he would have a panic attack if stuffed into the vehicle. For not immediately following that "command," he was punished on the ground. Floyd repeatedly said that he was unable to breathe, but Chauvin did not lift his knee until Floyd was dead.

No one in the crowd that had gathered shouted –

"Get your damn knee off his neck, you are killing this guy. You are being filmed on dozens of cell phones, and look around at all these witnesses – you will be prosecuted." These cops might have arrested the yeller for daring to interfere.

That indelible and unforgettable picture led to protests and riots in all 50 states.

THE MURDER OF FOURTH GRADERS

On May 24, 2022, an 18-year-old killer entered Robb Elementary School, in Uvalde, Texas with a high-powered AR-15 style rifle and murdered 19 fourth graders and two teachers. This happened exactly 2 years after the Floyd tragedy.

Law enforcement personnel were on the scene almost immediately. Yet 77 minutes elapsed from the time the killer entered the school until a United States border control agent went into the classrooms and killed the killer. During the 77 minutes, there were nearly 400 law enforcement personnel, from various agencies, at the school. For 77 minutes, none of them confronted the shooter. These are macho Texas tough guys. Texas is a gun culture; many of those roaming the schools hallways were expert marksmen.

They were engaged in moronic debates about –

Who was the incident commander –

About the need for a command post –

Whether they were dealing with an active shooter situation or a barricaded subject situation –

The need to establish a command structure.

We have become a country which embraces meaningless chatter when immediate action is required. I repeat – we have become a country obsessed with procedure and technicalities and fear of being criticized.

MY WEBSITE – www.stanleymrosenblatt.com

Many months can pass between the time a book is completed and the actual publication date. A book like mine which deals with current events needs to be updated. MY UPDATES WILL BE LAID OUT IN MY WEBSITE.

For example, my book was completed months before the presidential election of November 2024. It was completed while the Russian/Ukrainian war was ongoing. Those subjects, as well as many others, will be updated on my website.

By scanning my Table of Contents you will know every topic that I have covered.

A BRIEF PREVIEW OF EVERY CHAPTER

AFGHANISTAN – THE LONGEST WAR IN AMERICAN HISTORY AND WE WERE DEFEATED BY A TERRORIST ORGANIZATION –

The Al-Qaeda attack on September 11, 2001 was probably the worst day in American history. The most humiliating day in American history occurred in August 2021.

America had removed well over 100,000 of her combat troops at the end of 2014. We left a residual force of a few thousand in Afghanistan to prevent a terrorist takeover. President Biden removed that residual force in its entirety, saying that the Afghan military on its own could prevent a Taliban victory. As the Taliban were marching toward victory in August 2021, the Afghan military refused to confront them.

The Taliban just rolled in and took over. So after our 20-plus-year involvement in Afghanistan, a terrorist organization became the ruler of the country. Yes – a humiliating defeat!

As President Biden lied about the superiority of the Afghan forces, he told this additional lie –"We achieved our objectives."

PAKISTAN – A PERFIDIOUS "ALLY" WHO PROTECTED TERRORISTS WHO KILLED AMERICANS – AND THEY PROTECTED BIN LADEN –

Our leaders call Pakistan a – "major non-NATO ally." President Obama had called Pakistan a "democracy," knowing that the military, through several dictators, had controlled Pakistan throughout its history. He has told America that Pakistan is a valuable "partner," knowing that it provided a sanctuary for the Taliban who were killing thousands of American troops in Afghanistan. All our "leaders" knew this and accepted it. Pakistan knew of Bin Laden's location for years in their country but kept it secret from the United States.

The leader Imran Khan who was elected with the military's blessing in 2022 hates America and praised the Taliban victory in Afghanistan. The leader that we chose in Afghanistan, Hamid Karzai, also blames America for his country's problems. Nothing like gratitude, is there?

IRAQ – WE INVADED BECAUSE PRESIDENT BUSH II TOLD US IRAQ POSSESSED WEAPONS OF MASS DESTRUCTION. THAT WAS NOT TRUE. PRESIDENT OBAMA'S LIE –

President Bush II invaded Iraq in 2003 because he told the American people that Saddam Hussein possessed weapons of mass destruction. Exhaustive inspections established that was not true.

The truth is we invaded to redeem his father, who allowed Hussein to remain in power for 12 more years following our victory in the first Gulf War in 1991. That invasion was also predicated upon a falsehood. President Bush I admitted that his main concern was Saudi Arabia not Kuwait.

When we pulled out 95% of our troops at the end of 2011, President Obama told us that we were leaving behind a stable, sovereign, self-reliant Iraq. How could he have said that with a straight face?

After our troops left, ISIS took over one-third of the "self-reliant" country, and our troops had to return to do battle with ISIS. The Iraqi military upon whom we had lavished billions refused to confront ISIS, just as the Afghan military refused to confront the Taliban.

IRAN – WE SPENT 20 YEARS FIGHTING FOR IRAQ – AT THE END OF THOSE YEARS OUR WORST ENEMY – IRAN – WAS THE DOMINANT POWER IN IRAQ –

The world's leading state sponsor of terrorism has become the dominant player in the "sovereign" nation of Iraq. Iran-backed militias with links to Iran-backed political parties are in control.

I discuss the deal that the Obama/Kerry team made with Iran, believing their lies that their nuclear activities were conducted strictly for peaceful purposes.

President Biden begged Iran to reinstate the deal that Trump had scuttled, but Iran said "no." They can be arrogant because Biden has made it crystal clear that we will never attack Iran directly even though their proxies attack and kill our military personnel at bases in Iraq and Syria. Our military is there to fight ISIS, which didn't exist on 9/11. Iran and its proxy, Hezbollah, killed 241 sleeping marines in Beirut, Lebanon – an atrocity that America never avenged. I discuss why our marines never should have been there in the first place.

THE PHENOMENON CALLED DONALD TRUMP

Donald Trump was never a governor or a senator or a mayor. He never held any political office and he never served in the military. Yet in 2016 he became president by defeating the most recognizable woman in the world - Hillary Clinton.

The Trump haters cannot understand the affection and loyalty of his followers - his base which numbers in multiple millions. Nor can they understand that their unrelenting and vicious insults simply increase the loyalty of that base.

No president or aspiring president in the history of our country has ever been subjected to such abuse. My chapter details that abuse. Day after day, night after night. A couple of samples out of thousands –

"He is a lawless, immoral, terrifying president."

"He is a malignant fraudster, a demagog, a thug who engages in nonstop mendacity."

And, of course, he is a "wannabe dictator who is a threat to our democracy." He persists in spite of the attacks and after being abandoned by former allies such as the Wall Street Journal, the New York Post, and that beacon of the conservative movement - The National Review. Plus, of course, the four criminal cases against him. Over ninety felony counts.

Millions love him because he is seen as a fighter, a man who refuses to surrender or walk away. His backers say every other politician would have folded long ago.

Even during his Presidency he was attacked non-stop. The impeachments, the special counsel Robert Mueller who spent nearly two years investigating him.

Trump's opponents love to preach about togetherness, bringing the country and its diverse factions together. Surely, they must understand that their over the top attacks create the opposite - divisiveness. Do they not understand that by insulting Trump they likewise insult millions of his followers? Not a great way to promote togetherness.

JANUARY 6, 2021 – HOW COULD WE HAVE BEEN UNPREPARED FOR THE ATTACK AT THE CAPITOL?

Had the National Guard been present, there would have been no attack. Why wasn't the National Guard there?

The attack was entirely predictable. Trump's followers believed what he had been telling them for months – that the election had been stolen. If you believe that, you are very angry and on that very day, Congress was going to certify that Joe Biden was the new president. How could anyone be surprised that Trump's followers would try to prevent that from happening?

It was obvious from social media posts and threats on pro-Trump web sites that there would be violence, particularly after Trump got the crowd worked up.

Comments like – "It's going to be wild."

"Storm the Capitol."

Talk about a second civil war. Talk about all hell is going to break loose.

The Proud Boys and the Oath Keepers, having reputations for violence, would be there in full force. Radical groups were coordinating with each other.

Congress is responsible for the security of the Capitol. Both the House and Senate have Sergeants at Arms responsible for that security. Pelosi and Schumer, the leaders of both branches, did nothing except the usual – telling the world what a terrible person Donald Trump was. All they had to do was demand the presence of the National Guard during Trump's speech. The media never criticized them for their flagrant dereliction of duty.

What about the FBI, the Department of Homeland Security, and the Capitol Police Force, which has an intelligence division? They were all asleep. There actually were some discussions about calling in the Guard after Trump's speech. Hard to believe, but some Generals were opposed to doing so. There were moronic debates about – "how would it look to have a military presence on this sacred ground?" Nonsense talks about public relations.

The word that was tossed around more than any other was – "optics." No one was normal enough to say – the hell with optics, get the National Guard out there. By the time the Guard finally arrived hours later, the rioters were out of the Capitol Building.

There is a time for debate and there is a time for action. Americans have lost sight of that distinction. They have become immersed in procedure and stalled because of their fear of being criticized.

Robert Caro on the Exercise of Political Power in a Democracy

Robert Caro is a brilliant writer, researcher, and interviewer. He has written books about two individuals that demonstrate how political power can function. Lyndon Johnson and Robert Moses.

Moses was the most powerful individual in the history of municipal and state governments. Yet, he was never elected to anything. He dominated every field of public works in New York City and in the state of New York. Any company that wanted a contract with the city or state had to deal with Moses. He was all-powerful for 44 years– from 1924 until 1968, during the terms of six governors and five mayors. He headed 12 government entities at both the state and city level. I explain how this brilliant and manipulative man was able to acquire so much power.

He built seven bridges, which linked the boroughs together, 15 expressways, apartment buildings, and numerous parks. He accomplished great projects, but he was not a nice guy. Caro calls him an– "utterly ruthless person." He would evict thousands from where they had lived for generations if their buildings were in the way of one of his expressway projects.

Caro on Johnson

In his five-volume work on President Johnson, he makes it clear that Johnson, just like Moses, was– "ruthless and cruel." You will definitely agree with that assessment as you read this chapter.

Caro makes it clear that Johnson stole the election which made him a United States Senator and started him on his path to power.

The thing Caro admires most about Johnson was his ability to pass groundbreaking legislation during his tenure as majority leader of the United States Senate.

Caro on Johnson and Vietnam

In 1964, Johnson crushed the Republican candidate for president, Barry Goldwater. By 1968, he was so unpopular because of the Vietnam War that he declined to seek reelection. That was the year that Nixon defeated Johnson's vice president, Hubert Humphrey, by a whisker.

Johnson had sent half a million troops to Vietnam in the hope of securing victory for South Vietnam against the North. Why? Because he believed in the discredited– "domino theory." A theory which contended that if our ally lost to the communist North, other countries in the region would fall to communism like dominoes. President Kennedy had also believed in the domino theory, but it was only after his assassination that Johnson sent massive numbers of American troops (draftees) to the region.

An anti-war movement developed and Nixon removed hundreds of thousands of our troops, but we continued bombing. Congress put an end to funding South Vietnam in June 1973. By April 30, 1975, the North was totally victorious. There was no avalanche of dominoes. Vietnam became a valued trading partner of the United States. In many ways we became allies, both fearing the rising power of China.

Tragically, over 55,000 brave and patriotic Americans died because of a fantasy. Beware of hyped-up slogans that call for great sacrifices unnecessarily. Americans were so disgusted by the war and its aftermath, that we were cold to returning and wounded veterans.

STORMY DANIELS AND HER LAWYER MICHAEL AVENATTI, WHO IS IN PRISON HAVING BEEN CONVICTED OF MULTIPLE CRIMES –

The media disgraced itself by giving Avenatti hundreds of hours of free airtime to repeat endlessly that his client really did have sex with Donald Trump. The worst offenders were CNN and MSNBC. No one with a normal I.Q. believed Trump's denial and anyone with a normal I.Q. said – "who cares?"

The media always referred to an "affair" between Stormy and Trump. No, idiots – an affair implies a relationship, not a one-shot deal devoid of meaning. They also referred to her as an "actress." No, idiots – pornography does not require acting lessons.

Stormy very clearly said it was a one-shot consensual deal. Trump paid her $130,000.00 not to reveal it. I think that decision was flat out stupid. Had he simply admitted it and apologized to his wife and children, I don't think it would have hurt him one bit in terms of votes. Men would have laughed it off, a ton of locker room jokes. Just another example in Trump's long line of self-inflicted wounds.

On April 4, 2023, a Manhattan grand jury indicted Trump on 34 felony counts of falsifying business records to hide the payment. Millions of Trump haters pretend that this is normal. The truth is that it is anything but normal.

The previous District Attorney (Vance) refused to bring criminal charges. The present District Attorney (Bragg) refused to bring charges – but he changed his mind. He realized that he would become famous prosecuting a former president on these charges. He knew the media would have a field day as the trial progressed and everyone in New York would know his name. I knock the grand jury system in this chapter.

By the way, Michael Avenatti is in prison, having tried to blackmail Nike, having stolen from his own clients, and even having stolen from Stormy. And this is the guy Anderson Cooper and Rachel Maddow brought into your homes, night after night for months.

INTELLIGENT PEOPLE MAKING VERY DUMB DECISIONS WHICH HAVE DESTROYED CAREERS

The very best example of this title is President Nixon. His decision to install a taping system. Absent that system, he would not have resigned nor would he have been impeached. His own words sealed his fate. The obsession with his legacy and his ego did him in.

Nixon made another dumb decision. Once Congress started to investigate the Watergate break-in and knowing of his own complicity in its aftermath, he should have destroyed the tapes. He would have been severely criticized for doing so, but he would not have faced impeachment on the naked word of John Dean. The tapes were his own property.

Just two years before his resignation, Nixon was reelected in a landslide victory over the Democratic candidate, Senator George McGovern. Nixon won every state except for Massachusetts.

In this chapter, I detail awful decisions made by other presidents, prominent politicians and generals. Here's just one stark example – how could President Kennedy not have understood that the Bay of Pigs invasion was doomed to fail? Castro had a well-trained, loyal military which crushed the rebellion easily. That victory is the main reason why Castro was able to remain in power for over a half-century. Dumb decisions have consequences.

HAD HILLARY CLINTON WON IN 2016, SHE WOULD HAVE BEEN ONLY THE SECOND FEMALE PRESIDENT

Who was the first? Edith Bolling Galt, Woodrow Wilson's second wife, whom he married on December 18, 1915. His first wife had died. Galt was the 42-year-old widow of a wealthy jeweler. She had no background or education in affairs of state.

After World War I, President Wilson became obsessed with America joining the League of Nations. He was all for spreading democracy and independence and self-determination. He naively believed that the League could accomplish the end of warfare. There was opposition in the Senate to the League because there was a fear that such an international body could infringe upon American sovereignty.

Wilson went on a speaking tour to sell the League – 42 speeches in 22 days during September 1919. That schedule took its toll.

On October 2, 1919, Wilson suffered a major stroke caused by a cerebral thrombosis that caused blockage of blood flow to the brain. He was unconscious for several days. He became paralyzed on his left side, he needed a wheelchair, he was blind in one eye, his speech was impaired. Obviously, Article II, Section 1 of the Constitution should have been involved – dealing with the –

"Inability [of the President] to discharge the Powers and Duties of said office."

The public and the media had no idea about how serious Wilson's condition was. The usual lies emanated from his doctors that at most he was suffering from nervous exhaustion brought on by his efforts on behalf of the League. They said his mind was unimpaired. Anyone spending 5 minutes with him knew that was not true. In addition to the paralysis, Wilson was struck with a case of influenza and a serious urinary tract infection.

Two amazing things in the aftermath of the stroke. The failure of Vice President Thomas Marshall to assert himself and the failure of anyone in Congress or the Cabinet to insist upon an independent medical examination.

Mrs. Wilson did not allow the Vice President to visit and he took it. She decided who could see the President, and for how long. She decided what matters would be brought to his attention. She was functioning as the de facto president, and she got away with it during the remainder of her husband's second term. How could that have been tolerated by the entire nation? Yes – what is the matter with us? For the most part history has ignored her takeover!

Wilson remained President until his second term expired on March 4, 1921. Back then, even though a president was elected in November, he did not actually take office until March 5 of the following year. Years later, that date was changed by an Amendment 20 to the Constitution so that a president would take office on January 20. Wilson died on

February 3, 1924. There is no doubt that Wilson's wife was devoted to him. How about her devotion to the country and the Constitution?

THE SUPER-RICH CONTROL AMERICAN POLITICS

There is a great fiction in our political system. The super-wealthy can contribute to non-profit organizations which do not have to disclose the identity of their donors. Our tax code calls these organizations social welfare organizations.

Many of them are, in reality, political machines which engage in promoting a party or cause without naming a specific candidate. The rule which is evaded by the schemers is that if they are directly engaged in politics, they would have to disclose the names of donors. They play the game of being good guys –

"Promoting the common good and general welfare of the community as a whole."

That makes them tax exempt.

Super PACs (political action committees) provide another avenue for wealthy control. There's no limit to the amount of money that can be donated to these PACs. PACs identify with specific candidates, but the fiction is that they are not allowed to coordinate campaigning or spending.

PACs receive nearly all their funds from financial services executives, bankers, hedge fund, private equity people and, of course, from over-the-top wealthy individuals. Shell companies, limited liability companies can mask the identity of donors. Dark money can be funneled through non-profits. The crooks are way ahead of the cops. The prohibition against coordination is, in practical terms, unenforceable and the Federal Election Commission is both undermanned and toothless.

The favored candidate has all that money at his disposal for advertising, paying the salaries of staff, etc. Unlike non-profits, the identity of the millionaires and billionaires who contribute must be disclosed. But the schemers can avoid that requirement.

The United States Supreme Court added to the power of the super-rich in its 5 to 4 –

2010 decision in *Citizens United*. The majority held that corporations and unions have the same first amendment rights as individuals, meaning there is no limit on how much money they can spend to advance their political agendas. The Court said that restrictions on corporate and union expenditures are unconstitutional. In reaching that conclusion the Court had to ignore its own precedents.

There was a recall movement against California governor, Gavin Newsom, which failed. He raised $70 million to defeat it. Several in the Hollywood crowd contributed a half-million dollars. Zuckerberg's wife contributed $750,000. They gave that kind of money because they knew that Newsom would do their bidding. He demonstrated his friendship in the past. If you don't find the $70 million or the $1 billion spent by Bloomberg to be obscene you have been brainwashed.

Poverty, Inequality, and Homelessness

In 1964, President Johnson declared– "an unconditional war on poverty."

Another war that America has lost.

Janet Yellen, Treasury Secretary under Biden, a former head of the Federal Reserve, said in 2021–

"We have 24 million adults and 12 million kids that are going hungry every day."

A Federal Reserve survey of household economics released in May 2021, said that nearly one-third of adults were–

"Struggling to get by or just getting by."

The United States Department of Agriculture reported that in 2021, over 41 million Americans were on food stamps. Many Americans have such low-paying, lousy jobs that they need food stamps– "to get by."

Millions of Americans live paycheck to paycheck. They have no savings. Poor people have to deal with pawn brokers, loan sharks, and the payday loan industry, which charges outrageous levels of interest.

Nationwide, there were over 650,000 homeless Americans in 2022 and 2023. Including veterans and students. Bezos, Musk, Soros, Zuckerberg, and Gates could solve homelessness overnight if they gave a damn. What can be more humiliating than having your meager belongings tossed on the sidewalk after being evicted? Or having to sell your blood in order to be able to feed your children.

Couple the above with how great the banks, hedge funds, and private equity firms are doing. You've all heard of the investment guru Warren Buffett and his conglomerate Berkshire Hathaway, whose net earnings in 2023 were $97 billion – its highest ever annual profit. Its investments in American Express, Coke, Geico Insurance, and Occidental Petroleum have done great. Hooray for free markets and free enterprise.

America will be truly great when poverty and homelessness are eradicated, and when 1% of the population, having greater wealth than 95% of the rest of us, will no longer be tolerated. When concrete steps are taken to make the distribution of wealth fairer.

THE FALSE PROMISES OF INDEPENDENCE AND DEMOCRACY

More wars have been fought to promote or prevent independence movements than for any other causes.

After World War I, President Woodrow Wilson was a strong advocate for independence movements, for self-determination.

India had been the crown jewel of the British Empire. It was granted independence after World War II. Independence led to a blood bath between its majority Hindu and Muslim populations. The Muslims split off from India forming a new independent country - Pakistan. In time, part of Pakistan split off to become a new independent country - Bangladesh. The birth of these three independent nations caused millions of deaths.

There once was a country named Yugoslavia, consisting of six republics including Serbia, Croatia and Bosnia. All the republics were bitten by the independence bug leading to wars between them and hundreds of thousands of deaths.

None of the former republics became a democracy. The Soviet Union fell apart by the end of 1991. It had consisted of 15 republics including the Ukraine, Georgia, Armenia and Lithuania. All the republics became independent, several were ruled by dictators - none of them became a democracy.

The so-called Arab Spring occurred in Tunisia in 2011 when a fruit peddler set himself on fire protesting the injustices of Arab rule. In response, protests flooded the Arab world against the misrule of their own governments. The long-time ruler of Egypt, Mubarak, fell - so did other dictators in Yemen, Tunisia and Libya. Qadaffi of Libya was killed by his own people - he had ruled for 42 years.

Many Americans expected democracy to flourish as they had the same expectation when Yugoslavia and the Soviet Union disintegrated. Egypt is ruled by a military dictator. Only Tunisia came close to imitating a democracy, but it was hardly a real democracy. By 2021, Tunisia had a new dictator in place. I am astonished that so many Americans expect democracy to take hold in countries that have never experienced democracy. Democracy promotion is one of the most persistent myths of our political system.

My chapter deals with several other countries thirsting for independence. Will China go to war over Taiwan? Sri Lanka, a Buddhist nation, fought a war against the Hindu Tamils which lasted for 26 years; the Tamils lost. The Kurds have been fighting for independence for generations. Quebec and Scotland have sought independence in referendums which they lost, but they did not engage in terror or warfare to achieve their goals.

To the everyday citizen, the only thing independence eventually means is that there is a new group of insiders who are in charge. I offer solutions to the tragedies that independence movements usually cause. For instance, broad and meaningful autonomy where minority rights are respected.

AFRICA - INDEPENDENCE YES - DEMOCRACY NO

The European colonial powers had dominated the continent of Africa for generations. Britain, France, Portugal, Belgium, and Germany. By the 1960s the colonial era was over, nearly every African country had become independent.

Many thought democracy was just around the corner. In most instances, the new black leaders were worse than the Europeans. They got Idi Amin of Uganda, Robert Mugabe of Zimbabwe, Omar Bashir of Sudan - the list is a long one.

The Africans got black dictators who remained in power forever.

In 2016 at age 92, Mugabe was celebrating 36 years as president of Zimbabwe -

In Uganda, Yoweri Museveni was the leader for 40 years -

In Angola, 38 years - in Cameroon, 40 years -

I recite many more examples of decades in office.

What else has characterized Africa since independence?

Civil wars, military coups, corruption and fraudulent elections -

I discuss the histories of many individual countries. In Rwanda, Hutus carried out a genocide against Tutsis, murdering close to a million. Black Africans killing other black Africans. America knew nothing about either group.

Our people have no idea about how deeply America is involved in Africa. We have troops there, we have drone bases there, we have an Africa Command. We are there to fight terrorism. Boko Haram and Al Shabab, an affiliate of Al Qaeda are very powerful having inflicted many thousands of deaths on their fellow Africans.

America's policy under President Biden and his Secretary of State, Blinken, is democracy promotion - an embarrassing fantasy.

At one time, we got involved in Somalia when 18 American military heroes were savagely murdered by the troops of a notorious warlord. Hollywood made this tragedy into a movie - "Black Hawk Down."

For decades, the main interest of Americans about Africa was focused on criticism of South Africa and its Apartheid regime. Nelson Mandela was a genuine hero of the resistance, having served 27 years in prison. South Africa is always cited as a democracy, but it has hardly been a success story. It is a country run by insiders, and by oligarchs. Corruption has reigned at the highest levels of government. The gap between the masses and the wealthy elite is wider than in almost any other country. There are a few bright spots on the continent but in my chapter, I leave them to the optimists.

THE TRAGIC DEATH OF GEORGE FLOYD

George Floyd died because of the horrible judgment of the police who interacted with him. Floyd had gone to a neighborhood convenience store in Minneapolis, Minnesota to buy a pack of cigarettes. A teenage clerk reported that Floyd paid for the cigarettes with a counterfeit $20 bill. That call led to a chain of events which impacted American history.

Hard to believe, but four cops arrived to deal with this – "crime." The police officer in charge was Derek Chauvin, who had been on the Minneapolis force for 19 years.

Floyd was frightened to be confronted by four cops who wanted to place him in a police vehicle. He told the cops that he was claustrophobic, but they did not care. Floyd was 6 feet 4 inches and would have been scrunched in the police car. Chauvin gave a command about getting into the car, and Floyd did not immediately obey. That is a grave sin to the police mentality nationwide.

Floyd did not have a weapon, he was never aggressive, he was not even verbally aggressive, he was not going anywhere. But that's how Floyd ended up face down on the concrete roadway with Chauvin's knee on his neck for over 9 minutes. Floyd pleaded again and again and again – "I can't breathe." Not one of the other cops was normal enough or sympathetic enough to say – "This is ridiculous, this guy is not a criminal, get your damn knee off his neck."

A crowd had gathered, yet they remained silent while watching a murder in progress. All someone had to yell was – "You are murdering a helpless man, you are being filmed and this will be on the news nationally." When that video circulated online, a revolution was born. You would expect protests in Minneapolis – but not all over America. The protests occurred in over 2,000 cities and towns across all 50 states.

A jury found Chauvin guilty of murder, and he was given a 21-year sentence. A smidgen of common sense, and normalcy would have avoided the tragedy.

A smidgen of common sense and normalcy could have saved the lives of 19 fourth graders in an elementary school in Texas.

L – A BRIEF PREVIEW OF EVERY CHAPTER

THE TRAGEDY AT THE ROBB ELEMENTARY SCHOOL IN UVALDE, TEXAS

An 18-year-old killer walked into the school, armed with a high-powered AR-15 style rifle and murdered 19 fourth graders and 2 teachers.

From the time the killer entered the school until he was killed, 77 minutes elapsed. By the time the shooter was killed, nearly 400 law enforcement personnel were at the school. NOT ONE OF THEM TOOK THE INITIATIVE TO KILL THE KILLER.

First on the scene were officers from the Uvalde School District Police Force, and its chief, Pete Arredondo. His officers assumed that he was the "incident commander," but he said that he was not. To hell with the label, confront the killer and kill him.

During the 77 minutes, officers from these other agencies arrived –

The United States Border Control – the Texas Department of Public Safety, which includes rangers – state troopers – the local sheriff's office.

During the 77 minutes, there were moronic debates about – who was the "incident commander"? Were they dealing with an active shooter situation or a barricaded suspect situation? The inaction was a dramatic demonstration of how our culture has become obsessed with procedure and a fear of being criticized. So many of the cops were brave and very familiar with weapons yet they were frozen into inaction.

They could hear gunshots. How could it have been anything other than an active shooter situation? The situation obviously demanded immediate action, not a discussion. After 77 minutes the killer was finally confronted and killed but by then 19 precious 4th graders were dead.

THE ME-TOO MOVEMENT OUTED A SCANDAL THAT HAD CONTINUED FOR GENERATIONS

The scandal was the mistreatment of American women by American men. Over the years millions of women had been harassed and assaulted, and millions of men got away with it. Women were afraid to come forward - they would be ridiculed - some who did were criticized even ostracized.

The abuse was pervasive. It occurred at universities, in the media, in the military. The "Me Too" movement lifted the lid of secrecy - it ensnared Bill O'Reilly, the superstar of Fox News - Leslie Moonves, the chief executive of CBS - Matt Lauer of the Today Show - Bill Cosby - Charlie Rose, etc. Thousands of upstanding citizens, many wealthy and educated, engaged in this behavior.

The man responsible for the explosion of exposure was Harvey Weinstein, a Hollywood giant. He was accused by over 90 women, which demonstrates how long his assaults were tolerated and how women simply lived with the shame and kept silent. A few brave women came forward and the movement became a revolution.

The best example of silence about decades of abuse is the hierarchy of the Catholic Church. The second-best example is the Boy Scouts organization where pedophiles flourished.

Lawrence Nassar was at Michigan State University and for two decades he was the team physician for USA gymnastics.

He had molested young girls for many years doing totally unwarranted examinations, yet the girls kept silent until "Me Too." Surely many of them told their parents who also remained silent. The mentality of silence was that the Institution had to be protected.

But keeping quiet protected criminals and guaranteed new victims. Think of the traumas, the lifelong effects. My chapter provides example after example of how silence abetted abuse.

THE MYTH THAT AMERICANS ARE BASICALLY HONEST - THE COLLEGE ADMISSION CHEATING SCANDAL

Parents paid bribes to get their children admitted to prestigious universities. All these parents were educated and wealthy - nearly all came from the worlds of finance, hedge funds, real estate, law firms and medical practices. I guarantee you that all thought of themselves as basically honest.

So how did the scheme work? The middleman was a guy named William Rick Singer, who advertised himself as a private admissions consultant. Coaches would be bribed to designate their kids as skilled athletes in sports such as volleyball, water polo, soccer and tennis. The truth was that the admittees had no such skills, their resumes were faked.

In some instances, test administrators, those monitoring college entrance exams - SAT, ACT - would be bribed to make these kids appear smarter than they actually were. Fifty-two parents were criminally charged, most pled guilty. Singer, too!

In my chapter I lay out dishonesty and fraud in many other areas - such as millions claiming unemployment insurance benefits to which they were not entitled - banks - for profit schools - massive fraudulent schemes during the pandemic - internet crime. It is not a pretty picture and the extent of it is always downplayed.

THE DRUG OVERDOSE EPIDEMIC AND THE HEARTLESS CHASING AFTER PROFITS –

Did you ever hear of the Sackler family or their company, Purdue Pharma, which manufactured a painkiller – Oxycontin? A painkiller which made them billionaires. A painkiller which caused thousands of overdose deaths. There were other manufacturers and distributors who accomplished the same thing with other opioids.

Of course, the strategy was to downplay the risk of addiction and stress that the killer drugs were a vital part of the landscape of a new era of pain management. The Sacklers and others could not have become billionaires without the active and enthusiastic participation of thousands of doctors.

American doctors prescribed painkillers way more heavily than doctors in any other country. Some succumbed to outright bribery. Others simply got free, first-class travel for them and their families to exotic locations. The finest hotels, restaurants, the most expensive wines. The doctors ignored the first commandment of medical schools –

"FIRST, DO NO HARM."

In 2021, there were over 100,000 overdose deaths in America. Well over a half-million such deaths to date. The authorities took note. There were guilty pleas to the federal felonies of defrauding health agencies and drug enforcement officials. There were multiple billion-dollar settlements to cities and states. There were bankruptcies. Purdue went through bankruptcy, but not the Sacklers personally; they remained billionaires even after settling for billions.

Pharmacy chains at Walgreens, CVS and Walmart paid out billions for failing to investigate and curtail obvious over-prescribing.

An interesting footnote – McKinsey, the most successful consulting company in the world, was fined heavily because of their advice to Purdue and others on how to turbo-charge sales. Sad to say, but pure greed remains part of the American fabric alongside millions of do-gooders who are not focused on the accumulation of wealth.

THE UKRAINE – THE RUSSIAN INVASION COULD HAVE BEEN EASILY AVOIDED

Had the Ukraine told Putin it had no interest in becoming a member of NATO, the North

Atlantic Treaty Organization, Russia would not have invaded. Many blamed America for the invasion because it was American presidents who strongly encouraged the idea of the Ukraine's membership. What motivated these politicians was their naïve and dangerous idea of spreading democracy. Probably the strongest proponent of that fantasy was President Bush II.

Fiona Hill worked in the Bush administration. She was regarded as brilliant, a Russian specialist on the National Intelligence Council. She told Bush that advocating for NATO membership for Ukraine was a bad idea that would provoke Russia. He did not follow her advice.

President Clinton was all for Ukraine joining NATO. His Secretary of Defense, William Perry, told him that Ukrainian membership would be a profound strategic blunder. Clinton did not follow that advice.

George Kennan was a legendary figure in American diplomacy whose specialty area had been the Soviet Union. He had served as our ambassador to the Soviet Union. Kennan very clearly said that NATO's expansion into Russia's sphere would be –

"A tragic mistake."

Our "leaders" did not listen. Myths die hard.

Robert Gates who had been Secretary of Defense under both Bush and Obama said –

"Trying to bring the Ukraine into NATO was truly overreaching and an especially monumental provocation."

It was a "provocation" directed at Russia because the Ukraine had been part of Russia for centuries, for centuries before the Soviet Union even existed.

Gates and the others all knew how Russia would react. William Burns had been our ambassador to Russia and later, the director of the Central Intelligence Agency, and he pointed out that NATO membership would be a terrible decision.

Thousands of Russian troops had been on the border of Ukraine for months. Putin's intentions could not have been clearer, yet some of our geniuses said he would not attack.

Russia invaded in February 2022. As I am writing these words during March 2024, the war is ongoing. The great irony in all this is that thus far, NATO has not invited the Ukraine to join. The Ukrainians have fought bravely but they have suffered thousands upon thousands of deaths and permanent injuries. The physical damage to their country has been astounding – it will take decades and hundreds of billions of dollars to rebuild. And of course, America will be asked for billions in that effort.

Nearly everyone predicted a short war in which Russia would be victorious. Few understood the resolve, tenacity and competence of the Ukrainian Armed Forces.

The warnings were clear and on target but they were ignored. The idea of Ukraine coming into America's orbit, of joining the west was intolerable both to Putin and most Russians.

AMERICAN INDIANS – WHAT WE DID TO THEM WAS UNFORGIVEABLE

What does our revered Declaration of Independence call Indians? – "merciless Indian savages."

They were here first. It is well known how we stole their lands, pushed them onto reservations, and violated our treaty obligations and promises.

Less well known was the cruel policy of assimilation, which lasted for over a century. Children, some as young as 4 or 5, were forcibly removed from their families and placed in hundreds of boarding schools. The purpose of the policy was to Americanize the children. They were punished if they spoke their native language or adhered to any native traditions. Most never saw their parents again.

The policy of assimilation led to generations of poverty, alcohol and drug abuse, violence, greatly reduced life expectancy, crime, and domestic abuse. Because of the multiplicity of tribes, the Indian people were never able to organize an effective civil rights movement. Indian leaders were not invited to appear on *Meet the Press*, etc. to air their grievances. America lost a great talent pool because of the misguided policy of assimilation.

STARBUCKS – A COUNTRY OBSESSED WITH EXOTIC COFFEES IS NOT GOING TO WIN ANY WARS –

By mesmerizing millions, Howard Schultz became a multi-billionaire. Amazing to me, millions bought into his propaganda, such as –

"Starbucks is like a second home where everyone takes care of each other."

"Starbucks is an inclusive gathering place for all." –

Yeah, you are getting so much more than a cup of coffee. You are getting love and togetherness. We are manipulated so easily.

And then there are the relentless full-page ads for –

New ultra-caramel frappuccino or a mocha cookie crumble Frappuccino – or

A cold-foam cascara cold brew... find yourself happy –

Or a caramel brulee latte –

An American should be embarrassed to order one of these drinks.

The workers (baristas) bought into this nonsense until they didn't. Schultz referred to them as PARTNERS until a few said – don't insult my intelligence.

Thousands eventually decided that they wanted a union to represent them. Schultz was stunned by that demand; he was very anti-union and punished many activists.

The National Labor Relationships Board found – "egregious and wide-spread misconduct" – by management against their own employees.

During strikes, former partners would carry signs calling Schultz – "Union Buster in Chief."

That's his real legacy, not his home-away-from-home pitch.

THERANOS PROVES BILLIONAIRES CAN BE VERY DUMB

How did 19-year-old Elizabeth Holmes become a billionaire? She started a company called Theranos which claimed that by drawing a couple of drops of blood from a pinprick to a finger, it would be possible to scan for scores of diseases. She claimed that early detection would save millions of lives.

To a normal person, that sounded too good to be true. Why wasn't this miracle developed at a prestigious medical school or research institution? Did the billionaire investors consult with legitimate experts? I doubt it.

But they sure as hell bought into it, investing over $900 million. Why not – she was on the cover of business magazines, referred to as some kind of genius visionary.

Here are some of the investors –

The heirs of Walmart –

Rupert Murdoch, the owner of Fox News and the Wall Street Journal –

Larry Ellison of Oracle –

Robert Kraft, the owner of the New England Patriots football team.

Henry Kissinger was on the board of Theranos, so was another former Secretary of State, George Shultz, who didn't take his grandson's advice that it was all a scam.

Walgreens and Safeway installed her devices in their stores. Elizabeth hid the many failures of the magical machines. She blocked peer review.

The engineers and scientists employed by the company kept quiet, the pay was too good to pass up.

The Wall Street Journal did some investigating, and the truth eventually emerged. Elizabeth Holmes was convicted by a federal jury in California on January 3, 2022 of defrauding investors and received an eleven-year sentence. The focus of the trial was on investor losses when the focus should have been on the victims who relied on the accuracy of the testing.

HOW THE ULTRA-RICH AND MULTINATIONAL CORPORATIONS USE TAX HAVENS TO CHEAT THEIR FELLOW AMERICANS

They cheat their fellow Americans by not paying their fair share of taxes. Their fellow Americans who do not have access to the strategies of the wealthy.

The very rich know how to shift profits to subsidiaries in low tax, foreign countries. There is a trick called inversion which allows an American company to merge with a foreign company and by relocating its headquarters to a lower tax country.

Offshore shell companies are set up to buy luxury real estate and keep ownership secret.

America's beloved companies - Apple, Amazon, Google, Facebook and Twitter (renamed by Musk to X), etc. all have expertise at utilizing these and other gimmicks to make their shareholders richer. Our Internal Revenue Service is no match for the lawyers, accountants, lobbyists and consultants who advise the honchos of these companies on how to navigate the very complex system of taxing international corporate income.

There is a law firm in Bermuda called Appleby which specializes in tax avoidance strategies and shelters. The firm has over 30,000 American clients. I call it the cheaters hall of fame.

The big four accounting firms have close relations with the Treasury Department. Many work for Treasury and then join the accounting firms as partners when they leave. These are the guys and gals who invent the loopholes and shelters. That's why they are so valuable to the clients of these firms. They know how to avoid audits.

If the multinationals paid what they truly owed, America would be a much better country - a much fairer country with greatly reduced poverty and inequality.

The real scandal is that these strategies for the most part are legal and utilized by some of the most respected people in the country. The 30,000 clients of the Appleby firm all view themselves as honest. They are wrong!

THE ART OF TAX AVOIDANCE

The art has been very successful because there are highly respected lawyers and accountants who run circles around hardworking agents of the Internal Revenue Service who are simply overwhelmed. The former Commissioner of the Internal Revenue Service, Charles Rettig, said that - "The actual tax gap could approach and probably exceed one trillion dollars per year." Rettig is saying that if the cheaters paid what they actually owed the Treasury would have an additional trillion dollars every year. Think of what that money could do to improve the lives of Americans.

Rettig went before the Senate Finance Committee asking for billions of dollars so that he could hire many more auditors. He admitted that his employees were "outgunned" by the lawyers and accountants employed by the super-rich.

The IRS needs sophisticated auditors who can spot the cheaters behind an intricate web of partnerships and subsidiaries. The cheaters and their lawyers and accountants love the complexity and that's why hardworking IRS agents are "outgunned." Political contributions to Congress and lobbyists are behind that complexity.

The IRS receives millions of phone calls because regular people who want to do the right thing are confused. Because the Service is understaffed most of these calls are never returned.

President Biden would like to catch the cheaters but his proposal to do so is absurd. He asked for $80 billion to add 87,000 employees to the service. Several secretaries of the Treasury when they leave government join hedge funds and private equity firms. They are not looking out for the little guy or girl.

This chapter gives examples of how individuals who live like kings pay zero in certain years like Donald Trump. How about Leon Black of the private equity firm Apollo Global Management? He paid Jeffrey Epstein (yes that Jeffrey Epstein) $150 million for tax advice which enabled him to avoid $2 billion in taxes. That kind of thing should infuriate normal taxpayers and members of Congress. But it doesn't.

Real estate gurus like Trump claim hundreds of millions of dollars in losses which are not real losses. They all love depreciation gimmicks. Trump once claimed as a business expense for his "Apprentice" television program $70,000 for hair styling.

THE SOLUTION TO THE ABUSES IS TO GREATLY SIMPLIFY THE TAX CODE WHICH CONSUMES OVER 70,000 PAGES INCLUDING LEGAL DECISIONS.

ROOSEVELT AND TAFT - HOW TWO PRESIDENTS WENT FROM BEING BEST FRIENDS TO BITTER ENEMIES

Theodore Roosevelt had to be persuaded to accept the vice-presidency. He was an energetic activist who knew he would be bored in that position. And, he was bored, but that didn't last long since President William McKinley was assassinated in September 1901. After serving out the remainder of McKinley's term, Roosevelt won his own election in 1904.

He accomplished great things and that's why he is on Mount Rushmore along with Washington, Lincoln and Jefferson. He was responsible for the building of the Panama Canal – He reformed the Civil service – pushed for the development of our superb national parks – and won the Nobel Peace Prize for his mediation of the Russian-Japanese War.

In 1904, Roosevelt announced that he would not seek another term, which he came to regard as the worst decision of his life. He would have won easily in 1908 - instead, he campaigned very hard for his best friend, William Howard Taft, who did win in 1908. Taft defeated William Jennings Bryan whom the Democrats nominated a total of three times. Bryan lost all three attempts to become president.

As it turned out, Roosevelt strongly disagreed with many of Taft's policies and sought to replace him in 1912 - which turned out to be a terrible decision. He felt that Taft did not push hard enough for progressive causes and believed he had become too cozy with the old Republican Guard which had always catered to Wall Street. The Republicans nominated Taft for re-election, so Roosevelt ran as a third-party candidate with the "Bull Moose Party." The former best friends had become political enemies. Their nasty fight made Woodrow Wilson president in 1912 - the first Democratic President in 20 years.

The combined vote of Roosevelt and Taft exceeded Wilson's total by over a million. Roosevelt won only six states - Taft did worse; winning only two and even losing his home state of Ohio.

In 1921, President Warren Harding appointed Taft to be Chief Justice of the Supreme Court. Taft said -

"This is the greatest day of
my life."

Roosevelt and Taft were polar opposites in terms of their temperaments. They eventually reconciled. Roosevelt's brother was the father of Eleanor, who married the four-term Franklin Roosevelt. Bitter disputes over the years developed between the two Roosevelt branches. Franklin never appointed Teddy's sons to any important positions.

SOME OTHER PRESIDENTIAL ELECTIONS - LANDSLIDES AND SQUEAKERS

I deal with two presidents who experienced great success as well as great failures. Nixon defeated Lyndon Johnson's vice president Hubert Humphrey in 1968 by less than 1%. He also lost a squeaker to President Kennedy in 1960.

Many believed that by virtue of Mayor Daley's machine and Joe Kennedy's fortune, his son won Illinois which handed him the victory. Nixon never got credit for not contesting that outcome. He lost to Kennedy 49.7% against 49.5%.

In 1962 Nixon lost his bid to become governor of California but six years later he was president. Nearly all the political gurus, the commentators, the so-called experts predicted that Nixon's career was over after the California loss.

In 1972 Nixon had a landslide victory against Senator George McGovern. Nixon won everything except for Massachusetts and the District of Columbia. Less than two years later - on August 9, 1974 - Nixon had to resign because of the Watergate scandal. His own tapes sealed his fate.

Let me hop over to President Johnson. Of course he became president when President Kennedy was assassinated. When he ran for president in 1964, he crushed Barry Goldwater by the largest popular margin in US history.

His terrible decisions extending our involvement in the Vietnam war made him so unpopular that he declined to run in 1968. So both Johnson and Nixon went from the ecstasy of victory to the agony of failure. Johnson loved being President.

Reagan crushed Carter, winning all but six states. When he ran for re-election against Carter's vice president, Walter Mondale, his victory was even greater. Mondale only won his home state of Minnesota. Mondale was the first presidential candidate to put a woman on his ticket as vice president – Geraldine Ferraro. It didn't help.

I discuss presidential elections during the 1920s as well as President Roosevelt's four victories. When Roosevelt ran for his fourth term in 1944, he was a very sick man and it showed.

As Woodrow Wilson's doctors lied about his condition after a massive stroke, Roosevelt's doctors also lied asserting that he was in good shape. He was re-elected in November 1944 and died on April 12, 1945. Truman became president and it was his decision to drop atomic bombs on two Japanese cities.

In 1948, when Truman ran against New York Governor Thomas Dewey, Dewey was heavily favored. Truman pulled a huge upset. Dewey also lost to Roosevelt in 1944. The most controversial election result of all time was Bush vs. Gore in 2000 – the winner decided by a 5 to 4 vote of the U.S. Supreme Court. Bush became president even though Gore received a half-million more votes.

Politicians love to prattle over the cliché that we are a nation of laws not men. Gore only needed one vote - there were four dissenters on the Supreme Court. Had the makeup of the Court been different Gore would have become president. It is men and women who interpret the laws and pass the laws. Had Gore won his home state of Tennessee he would have become president.

ADDITIONAL REFLECTIONS ON PRESIDENTIAL ELECTIONS AND POLITICS

Two terrible things can happen to a candidate who is nominated for president.

1. He can lose in a landslide.
2. He can lose his home state.

I have previously mentioned that Al Gore, Clinton's vice president, lost his home state of Tennessee to Bush in the 2000 election.

Al Smith had been the governor of New York. When he ran against Herbert Hoover in 1928, he lost New York.

Alf Landon had been the governor of Kansas. When he ran against Franklin Roosevelt in 1936, he lost his home state and had the additional humiliation of winning only two states - Maine and Vermont.

Adlai Stevenson had been the governor of Illinois. When he ran against Dwight Eisenhower in 1952, he lost his home state. He ran against Eisenhower a second time in 1956 and lost again. When Kennedy won in 1960, many in the political hierarchy expected that Stevenson would be appointed Secretary of State. Instead, that position went to Dean Rusk. Many were surprised that Stevenson accepted the position of Ambassador to the United Nations. The Ambassador simply carries out policies made by others.

George McGovern was a United States senator from North Dakota. When he ran against Nixon in 1972, he lost his home state and suffered the additional humiliation of winning only a single state - Massachusetts. I would think he said to himself – "Why the hell did I fight so hard to get the nomination."

Sometimes one screw-up can doom a candidate. Michael Dukakis was the governor of Massachusetts, a staunch liberal strongly opposed to the death penalty. He was asked a very unusual but penetrating question by a seasoned interviewer.

If your wife was raped and murdered, wouldn't you want the killer to be executed?

Had he said – "I would want to strangle that bastard myself" - he might have become president instead of the senior George Bush. Instead he gave a weak, long-winded answer as though he was teaching a class in constitutional law. Sometimes honest emotion is called for instead of a dubious lecture.

Bush received 426 electoral votes to Dukakis's 111 in 1988.

Four years later, Bush lost to Clinton, with 44.9 million votes to his 39.1 million. A third-party candidate named Ross Perot, very rich and very strange, was in the race as well. He received a huge number of votes - 19.7 million - but zero in the Electoral College. Even Teddy Roosevelt could not win as a third-party candidate with the Bull Moose Party.

The 22nd amendment limits a president to two terms. Franklin Roosevelt's accomplishment can never be duplicated.

Eight presidents have died in office.

I list 15 vice presidents who became president. Among the most recent ones - Biden, the senior Bush, Ford, Nixon and Johnson. That's the main incentive to accept the vice presidency - an ill-defined position which often results in fulfilling a menial role. You do what the president tells you to do and that's it.

I mention some tough political ads - many call them vicious - which have been effective. There is often glory in being president, often much heartache as well. There is always an avalanche of critics and second-guessers ready to pounce.

CHAPTER 1

AFGHANISTAN - THE TRAGEDY OF AMERICA'S FINAL DEPARTURE

The United States invaded Afghanistan in October 2001. Unbelievably we remained for 20 years, and even more unbelievably the American public passively accepted this involvement. I begin this chapter at the end of our involvement – our defeat in August 2021. And yes, that's what it was – a DEFEAT.

Thousands upon thousands of Afghans were at the airport hoping to be evacuated to almost anywhere because they did not want to live or be killed under a Taliban government.

The Taliban controlled the route to the airport, but they did not spot an ISIS suicide bomber. On August 26, 2021 the bomber killed 170 including 13 U.S. service members – mostly 20-year-old marines.

The airport tragedy was followed by yet another tragedy 3 days later, this one having been caused by well-intentioned Americans. Intelligence analysts and drone operators at a Qatar base unleashed a Hellfire missile from a Reaper drone on a vehicle they thought belonged to an ISIS operative. They could not have been more wrong.

What they struck was a Toyota being driven by Zemari Ahmadi. Mr. Ahmadi was an electrical engineer who had worked for an American aid organization for some 15 years. His whole focus was helping his fellow Afghans.

Ahmadi was on his way home when several children rushed out to greet him. Our missile killed him along with nine others, including seven children, all blown to bits.

For over 2 weeks our military denied the error, implying that the vehicle contained explosives and may have been on its way to the airport. Chairman Milley referred to it as - "a righteous strike." Finally, on September 17, the Pentagon admitted the truth.

August 29, the day of the strike, was the same day that 13 caskets arrived at Dover Air Force Base in Delaware.

When President Biden was criticized for not leaving a residual force of 3,000 to 4,000 troops, he said -

"I trust the capacity of the Afghan military, which is better trained, better equipped and more competent than the Taliban in terms of conducting war."

Biden would have a lot of competition but that is one of the most absurd statements ever made by any American President. The Taliban totally defeated the Afghan military.

That was always the lie that was told to the American people when we downsized our military presence in both Afghanistan and Iraq. That their own militaries would be capable of preventing a terrorist victory. When we left Iraq under Obama, ISIS took over a third of the country and declared an Islamic Caliphate. American forces had to return to battle a terrorist organization that did not exist on 9/11.

In 9 days during August 2021, the Taliban captured 15 provincial capitals culminating in the takeover of Afghanistan's capitol – Kabul – on August 15.

"The better trained, better equipped and more competent" – Afghan forces simply melted away. The naïve suckers of all time (our government) for two decades had spent more than $80 billion training and equipping the Afghan military and police.

In an op-ed piece, former Lieutenant General and former National Security Advisor (briefly under Trump) McMaster wrote about "self-delusion" leading to the disaster of our retreat. He said –

"The gap between fantasy in Washington and reality in Afghanistan explains how we have arrived at this point. The Taliban didn't defeat us. We defeated ourselves. More than 20 US-designated terrorist organizations call this region home."

Even Biden acknowledged that – "the terrorist threat has metastasized across the world." Proof that the American war against terror had failed.

Biden's Secretary of State, Antony Blinken, wrapped himself in another fantasy – that by keeping our embassy open we would be achieving some type of moral victory. Blinken said in June 2021 -

"We are not withdrawing. We are staying. The embassy is staying."

A State Department spokesman, Ned Price, said – "Let me be very clear about this. The embassy remains open."

Open to do what? Price continued – "The Taliban must stop this ongoing violence, they must stop it."

Our embassy in Kabul had 4,000 employees, about 1,400 Americans – on a beautiful 15-acre compound. The embassy personnel lived in Afghanistan. Presumably they had some understanding of the country's dynamics, some understanding of the corruption which permeated every level of society, both civilian and military. Did any one of our diplomats tell Biden that the security forces would fold during the Taliban advance? The Afghan army had a history of folding in previous battles with the Taliban.

America's No. 1 military leader Mark Milley, Chairman of the Joint Chiefs of Staff, said no one predicted that -

"A security force of 300,000 would evaporate in 11 days."

The consensus of our intelligence agencies was that the Afghan security forces could hold off the Taliban for 1 to 2 years. How could the CIA, the Defense Intelligence Agency, the Director of National Intelligence and the State Department Intelligence Bureau all have been so wrong?

Defense Secretary Austin and Milley concurred with that estimate. Before the Taliban victory, Blinken had said -

"We do have deep concerns that the Taliban may be trying to take the country by force. But for that to happen Afghanistan would be a pariah state."

Just how naïve can our "leaders" be? Of course, the Taliban wanted to take over the entire country. Any well-informed ninth grader would have known that. And the "pariah state" comment is simply silly.

The deputy leader of the Taliban was warmly welcomed in China by their foreign minister. China, Russia, Iran and other nations want access to Afghanistan's vast minerals, they want to do business and could care less about the Taliban's serial violations of human rights.

Biden lied about his decision to remove all our military personnel saying that he was following the military's recommendations. All of the military leadership favored leaving a small residual force. The Afghan security forces were dependent on American air support, intelligence, surveillance and logistics.

There was no end to Blinken's fantasizing -

"A new chapter of America's engagement with Afghanistan has begun. It's one in which we will lead with our diplomacy." More examples of fantasizing –

Biden – "The truth is this did unfold more quickly than we had anticipated. We went to war with clear goals. We achieved those objectives." We went to war with only one goal – to get Bin Laden. It took ten years to accomplish that. Later our goals became winning the war against terror and nation building and we never – "achieved those objectives."

Bush – "We will not waver, we will not falter and we will not fail." What happened during August 2021 was the very definition of "failure."

President Ghani of Afghanistan – "Our security forces are fully capable of defending its people."

Biden said that we went to Afghanistan for the express purpose of getting rid of Al Qaeda.

In a June 2021 report the United Nations said that Al Qaeda was present in at least 15 provinces. Also that – "The Taliban and Al Qaeda remain closely aligned and show no indication of breaking ties."

In 2023, Al Qaeda even has affiliates in Africa.

President Bush was a strong advocate of nation building. The United States spent billions building hospitals, roads and bridges.

Biden made one true-statement when he said that America could never deliver a – "stable, united, secure Afghanistan."

That conclusion was echoed by General Petraeus –

"You can't take a country from the seventh century which is where Afghanistan was under Taliban rule to the 21st century in 20 years."

Petraeus pointed out that we were dealing with an Afghan military that had to be taught remedial skills like reading, writing, adding and subtracting. That fact led to many miscommunications with American pilots which resulted in misguided bombs that killed thousands of civilians. These errors caused the countries we were fighting for to hate us.

In addition to taking over the entire country, the Taliban acquired billions of dollars-worth of sophisticated American weapons – airplanes, helicopters, assault weapons, rockets, machine guns, Humvees.

Our guy, President Ghani, fled Afghanistan to the United Arab Emirates on the very day that the Taliban took over Kabul.

When the Taliban won, they played the public relations card to a certain extent, issuing a general amnesty order that would protect government workers, military officials, and pilots from being punished. Blinken and Price probably believed that.

Instead, the Taliban killed scores of former members of the security forces. A report from Human Rights Watch documented over 100 murders in four separate provinces. Disappearances and executions were plentiful. The Taliban engaged in a spree of assassinations against journalists, government, military, and civilian leaders.

By the end of August, America had evacuated over 120,000. In spite of that very impressive number, thousands of Afghans who wanted to leave were unable to. Interpreters and anyone else who partnered with

America were in danger of being hunted down. Scores of Afghan pilots had fled to Tajikistan or Uzbekistan.

One of the biggest myths sold and bought by the American public was that Afghanistan is a sovereign country. Karzai in particular, president for over a decade, was always quick to condemn any slight to Afghanistan's precious sovereignty.

Over 70%of the revenue of the deposed government came from international aid-from donors such as the International Monetary Fund and the World Bank. Foreign donors covered about 75% of the government's spending. Even with all that aid Afghanistan's economy remained dismal. It is a perversion of language to pretend that such a country is truly independent and sovereign.

Up until now I've dealt with the end of America's 20-year misadventure in Afghanistan. Now I'm going back to the beginning when no one dreamed that our war would last so long.

HOW IT ALL BEGAN

Why did we invade? To capture or kill Osama bin Laden the leader of al-Qaeda and the "mastermind" of the murder of over 3,000 Americans on September 11, 2001. Unbelievably the media often referred to him as a "mastermind." Like you really have to be a mastermind to fly planes into buildings.

Had the Taliban, who were in charge in Afghanistan in 2001, turned Bin Laden over to us we never would have invaded. We did not invade because the Taliban were evil violators of human rights. The effort to get Bin Laden was transformed into a generalized war against terror. No American ever voted for that transformation.

Why did it take America so long to kill Bin Laden? President Clinton (1992-2000) knew that he was a mortal threat and gave the order for him to be killed. In a book Clinton wrote four years after leaving office he said – ..." Bin Laden had issued a fatwa calling for attacks on American military and civilian targets anywhere in the world...by this time we had been following him for years...in January 1996, the CIA had established a station focused exclusively on his network...after the

African slaughter I became intently focused on capturing or killing him and with destroying Al Qaeda."

Clinton labeled Bin Laden as "perhaps the preeminent organizer and financer of international terrorism in the world today." Clinton never got Bin Laden nor did Bush in his 8 years in office.

"The African Slaughter" Clinton refers to was the attack on American embassies in Kenya and Tanzania in 1998 which resulted in 257 deaths. In spite of the Iranian takeover of our embassy in 1979 and Saddam Hussein taking hostages in 1990, America remained adamant about the symbolism of embassies even in countries where we were despised. Our embassies are always the primary targets for those who hate us.

It took the United States ten years to finally get Bin Laden who was in Pakistan. We were so distrustful of the Pakistani military and their intelligence service that we told them nothing about our plan to raid Bin Laden's compound. We went into Abbottabad with four helicopters and 79 Navy Seals, killed Bin Laden and removed his body to be thrown into the sea. We came in undetected and left undetected. Obviously, this was a huge embarrassment to Pakistan's military and intelligence establishments.

Bin Laden had been living in a three-story mansion for at least five years. The mansion was surrounded by 12-foot-high concrete walls topped by barbed wire plus two security fences. The structure was about eight times the size of other homes in the neighborhood. The only thing missing was a sign saying – "Bin Laden lives here." Not only Bin Laden but three of his wives and several of his children.

Abbottabad is home to an elite military academy which sits about one mile from the residence. The city is loaded with active and retired military officers, military intelligence, and local police. It is impossible that insiders in the military did not know who was living in that house. And of course, Pakistan was our close ally in our war against terror, a country to which we gave billions in military and economic aid.

Within a couple of months after September 11, the United States could have killed Bin Laden. He was in Tora Bora, a mountainous region in eastern Afghanistan. There were only about 100 U.S. military personnel in the area and we knew additional troops were needed to block the mountain paths leading into Pakistan. The request was made for additional troops, and in one of worst decisions of the entire war, the request was denied.

Years later (November 30, 2009) the Senate Committee on Foreign Relations whose chairman was John Kerry issued a report on - "How we failed to get Bin Laden" – in Tora Bora years earlier. The report said –

"The decision not to deploy American forces to go after Bin Laden or block his escape was made by Secretary of Defense Donald Rumsfeld and his top commander, General Tommy Franks… Even when his own commanders and senior intelligence officials in Afghanistan and Washington argued for dispatching more U.S. troops, Franks refused… "

Kerry continued –

"When we went to war less than a month after the attacks of September 11, the objective was to destroy Al Qaeda and kill or capture its leader Osama Bin Laden, and other senior figures in the terrorist group and the Taliban, which had hosted them. Today more than eight years later, we find ourselves fighting an increasingly lethal insurgency in Afghanistan and Pakistan that is led by many of these same extremists. Our inability to finish the job in late 2001 has contributed to a conflict today that endangers not just our troops and those of our allies, but the stability of a volatile and vital region."

That failure has never been thoroughly investigated nor explained to the American public. A passive public has never demanded an explanation.

The Obama "surge" in 2010 was going to turn everything around. The additional American troops (about 33,000) would bring victory nine years after our invasion.

The focus of the surge was Helmand Province, the largest of Afghanistan's 34 provinces. The most intense fighting occurred in two districts of the province – Sangin and Marja.

American soldiers and Marines as well as British troops fought valiantly in these districts. More Americans and Britons lost their lives in

Sangin than in any other district. The public was told we had pacified Helmand.

By 2015 Sangin and Marja were again in Taliban hands. United States and NATO forces would eventually leave, but the Taliban would remain. That's where they were born, where they grew up, where they were indoctrinated to hate and kill infidels in thousands of madrassas and mosques.

Congress requires the Pentagon to issue periodic reports – "on progress toward security and stability in Afghanistan." The Pentagon report of December 2012 said that only a single Afghan brigade out of 23 was capable of operating on its own – yes, one brigade after billions of dollars and thousands of dead and maimed Americans. The report also found that violence was higher than it had been before the hyped "surge."

In 2014 and 2015 the Taliban were conducting mass attacks on government sites, military installations and police stations. On August 30, 2014 the Taliban attacked the headquarters of the Afghan intelligence service (the National Directorate of Security) in the city of Jalalabad. The Afghan government couldn't protect itself let alone the population at large. Our "leaders" knew this early on yet continued to perpetuate the myth (the lie) that the Afghan forces on their own could prevent a Taliban victory.

The success of Taliban attacks was astonishing. They were able to get through heavily fortified government compounds, they got past armed guards and checkpoints and rings of security. They have been able to hit the American embassy and NATO headquarters in Kabul, they have struck the Afghan Defense Ministry. And this was happening when we had over 100,000 troops in the country.

There were instances when the Afghan army melted away. In nearly every head-to-head encounter with the enemy, the Afghan security forces greatly outnumber the Taliban, yet the terrorists usually prevail and do so even when United States airstrikes support the Afghan forces.

The army is plagued by desertions and corrupt leadership. There have been many instances where soldiers in the field have been without adequate food, water or ammunition.

The Afghan Special Forces numbering about 11,000 out of some 350,000 security personnel (army and police) have been effective. Although not their role, they are often called upon to replace or assist conventional forces. This takes them away from operations they were trained to conduct such as nighttime commando raids. It is extraordinary that there are still so many brave Afghans willing to fight, particularly in view of their horrendous losses -- losses which have increased greatly since the American pullout in 2014. 2015 was their worst year since the start of the war with nearly 8,000 soldiers and police deaths.

Many civilian deaths are inadvertently caused by American airstrikes and drone strikes. To cite one striking example --

On October 3, 2015 an American AC130 gunship mistakenly hit a hospital in Kunduz. This was not just any hospital, it was one run by that superb organization, "Doctors Without Borders" -- and contained a fully-equipped trauma center and intensive care unit. There was confusion and poor communication between the Afghans on the ground and the American pilots. The attack continued for over an hour, resulting in 42 deaths – doctors, patients and medical workers. Such tragedies did not cause America to rethink its position. No – we were committed to our war against terror!

Afghanistan is very much a third-world country meaning that seriously wounded civilians, soldiers and police do not get the medical care and follow up that they need. Nor do the fighters get the benefits to which they are entitled. So many end up homeless with disabilities that make employment impossible. The economy is in terrible shape and unemployment is very high even for the able bodied. That explains in part why so many are willing to risk their lives for a paycheck while serving in the military or police.

Afghanistan has significant oil and gas reserves. It is loaded with minerals -- iron, copper, gold, cobalt, lithium. Why can't they be self-supporting? The reason is corruption and the fact that Afghanistan is a dysfunctional country at every level. There are many wonderful individuals in Afghanistan -- educated, selfless and cultured -- but they don't run the country. It is run by tribal leaders, by warlords with their own militias, by the usual insiders.

The ever-gullible American public assumed that after 2014 there would be no more deaths, no more disabled young, patriotic Americans. After 13 years America was finally done. President Obama said our effort had come – "to a responsible conclusion." Trump often lied with bombast, Obama lied quietly and during his eight years in office he was almost never challenged. Sure – "a responsible conclusion" – our well-trained Afghan military would be able to handle the Taliban.

A debate began as to how many troops America would leave in Afghanistan after 2014. Because of the false promises made about no more combat after 2014 the administration had to come up with a new fiction which was that the remaining troops would only be engaged in training, advising and assisting Afghan security forces. The United States told the same lie when we left Iraq at the end of 2011.

When our troops accompanied the Afghans after 2014 they were using their weapons just as they did prior to "the end of their combat mission." In particular our elite special operations forces were doing so. The United States continued to use air strikes and drones armed with missiles.

In January 2016, Lieutenant General John Nicholson, our top commander in Afghanistan, told the Senate Armed Services Committee that the security situation was "deteriorating." After all those years, after all our sacrifices of American deaths and crippling injuries, after multiple billions of dollars, the ability of the Afghan forces to defend themselves was "deteriorating."

With American and coalition forces mostly gone, Afghanistan would have to do without our sophisticated, modern weaponry. Our aircraft have sensors that can locate the enemy in hiding and have the ability to send live video feeds – flying gunships using cannon fire that can spread that fire for over 100 yards – helicopters with precision guided missiles – drones which can fire missiles. They would have to do without our intelligence intercepts, artillery, tanks, logistic support, spy satellites and advanced communications.

With all those advantages plus over 100,000 American troops we were still unable to defeat a terrorist group which lacked a single aircraft. We also had over 30 NATO countries assisting us. Including NATO forces, at one period there were over 140,000 troops on our side.

Guerilla fighters spurred by religious fervor and possessing total familiarity with the landscape were able to defeat our massive coalition, as they were able to defeat the Soviets 30 years earlier. Once we left, a Taliban victory became inevitable.

A GREAT GENERAL IS FIRED

Because of a self-inflicted wound, the United States lost the services of the commander of all United States and NATO forces in Afghanistan, a superb combat General – Stanley McChrystal. Favorable media coverage is important to gain public support for spending billions of dollars and sacrificing thousands of lives in a foreign country – a country that 99% of Americans have never visited or had any desire to visit. The same percentage of Americans have never had a conversation with an Afghan or Pakistani. The need to cooperate with the media turned out to be responsible for ending a brilliant military career. McChrystal allowed a reporter from Rolling Stone Magazine to embed himself in his activities and those of his staff so that an in-depth article could be written.

McChrystal let his guard down; he didn't understand or he forgot that the reporter's mission was to get a good story with juicy quotes. The media loves controversy. McChrystal and his aides spoke critically of nearly every member of President Obama's national security team. He was quoted as saying that Obama appeared "uncomfortable and intimidated" during their first meeting. How could he have not understood what Obama's reaction would be when he read the article?

Under our system of government a community organizer from Chicago who is elected president becomes McChrystal's boss. A governor of Arkansas who never served in the military becomes Commander in Chief with the authority to issue orders to generals and admirals who have devoted their lives to military service. The generals know they have to play the game and be respectful to their "superiors," but how much respect can combat veterans have for politicians without military experience? President Obama fired General McChrystal in June 2010.

Defense Secretary Robert Gates called General McChrystal – "one of the finest men at arms this country has ever producedover the past decade no single American has inflicted more fear and more loss of life on our country's most vicious and violent enemies than General McChrystal."

McChrystal was replaced by General David Petraeus. Petraeus played the media even better than Kissinger did in his day, the journalists gushed over him as did most politicians. Although his accomplishments in Iraq and later in Afghanistan were exaggerated and short-lived, the media made him the most famous general of his generation. There was speculation that he would go into politics and have a realistic shot at becoming president. He had commanded coalition forces in Iraq (2007-08) and in Afghanistan (2010-11). After retirement, Obama selected him as Director of the Central Intelligence Agency.

Petraeus had agreed to be interviewed by a woman who planned a book glowing with praise about his personal and professional qualities. Although married for decades with a reputation as a solid family man, Petraeus and his "biographer" (also married with children) began an affair which in time became known.

While he was at the helm of the CIA, he handed over highly classified materials to "that woman." He was forced to resign in 2012 after which he pled guilty to the misdemeanor of mishandling classified information.

Sound familiar?

McChrystal and Petraeus were both advocates of the doctrine of counterinsurgency. This was particularly ironic in the case of McChrystal because for many years as the leader of our Joint Special Operations Command he was in the business of killing terrorists.

For years, the basic American strategy in the war was counterterrorism – a straightforward doctrine meaning locate and kill as many terrorists as possible. At some point our leaders became mesmerized by the doctrine of counterinsurgency the focus of which was to protect the population — to clear territory, to hold it and then build on it. The doctrine is often referred to as "nation building" as though it is the job of America to create out of a tribal, clan-based, decentralized society functional institutions as part of an effective central government (something Afghanistan has never had). In 2009 President Obama spoke of a "civilian surge of agricultural specialists and educators, engineers and lawyers" who would teach Afghans how to create a modern country.

The Joint United States Army – Marine Corps Field Manual entitled "Counterinsurgency" says – "Soldiers and Marines are expected to be nation builders as well as warriors." They are expected to protect civilian populations and develop expertise in reconstruction and development aid. We have sent cultural experts, governance experts, development specialists and conflict managers into rural areas of Afghanistan.

The United States military has carried out thousands (yes thousands) of development projects since our invasion in 2001. We have built hundreds of miles of highways; we build schools and public buildings, we repair and replace bridges, we dredge canals. We build water treatment facilities – we spend billions on education, health care and economic development. Aren't we wonderful? Still we are seen as occupiers who support a corrupt, ineffective government that does not provide basic services. For all our naïve sucking, up we are not winning hearts and minds.

Good intentions that are divorced from reality can end up being a one-way ticket to a tragedy. Take the tragic case of Paula Loyd. There is something called the Human Terrain System which has some 20 teams in Afghanistan; it is an Army program that sends social scientists into Afghanistan to help soldiers understand their culture.

Paula Loyd, an Army veteran with degrees in anthropology and diplomacy, who attended Wellesley and Georgetown, was a valued member of such a team. On November 4, 2008 she was interviewing a civilian who, out of the blue, doused her with gasoline and set her ablaze. After months of suffering Paula died.

Yes—boys and girls, by all means learn about their culture. But never admit that part of that culture is killing those who disagree with their religious, ethnic or tribal beliefs. A lot of our heavy American thinkers gather together to brainstorm—"how can we understand these people and get them to like us?" Yet they refuse to talk straight about the differences in values, beliefs and customs which are unbridgeable. And they downplay the visceral hatred that many Muslims have for western values.

General Karl Eikenberry has said that if the basic doctrine of counterinsurgency is the establishment of a legitimate government able to deliver essential human services, then the doctrine has clearly failed.

James Jeffrey who served as our Ambassador to Iraq (2010 to 2012) has said that "counterinsurgency was a recipe for defeat." Jeffrey says it makes no sense for politicians to give military leaders "broad goals of social transformation."

The economies of our "allies" (Afghanistan and Pakistan) are in shambles. If not for American money, if not for the United States Agency for International Development, if not for the International Monetary Fund, the World Bank and other international donors both countries would sink into total chaos.

There are huge electric power shortages in both countries. Both have corrupt tax collection systems accompanied by massive evasion. Education, healthcare, traffic, roads, pollution, sewage, garbage collection are to cite only a few of the areas which are substandard.

An American could spend months or even years in Afghanistan and still know next to nothing about Pashtuns, Tajiks, Uzbeks, Hazaras, Turkmens or Baluchis. The same applies to Pakistan tribes – Punjabi, Sindhi, Pashtun, Baluchi, Mohajirs. Here are a couple of instances of social attitudes that prevail in Afghanistan. In 2016 in Kabul (not in some primitive rural village), a mob lynched a female Islamic scholar over false rumors that she had burned some pages in the Koran. Zero due process, zero rule of law.

In February 2017, an armed mob stormed a police station to kill two young lovers. The 18-year-old girl dared to elope without her family's permission. Her brothers were part of the mob. Many young women have been killed by family members for daring to escape an arranged, ill-suited, unhappy marriage.

There are hatreds and rivalries and jealousies between tribes and ethnicities that outsiders cannot begin to fathom. America was shocked when black Africans killed other black Africans in the hundreds of thousands. And the reason for the shock was because we were ignorant of the conflict between Hutus and Tutsis in Rwanda or the mindset of a people who can kill their neighbors on a massive scale. Americans were likewise ignorant of the hatred between Sunni Arab Muslims and Shiite Arab Muslims. When it comes to ethnic, tribal, and religious hatreds, mankind has made no progress since we lived in caves.

I live in South Florida. Dade County contains over 20 cities including Miami, Miami Beach, Coral Gables, North Miami and Hialeah. There are residents of Coral Gables who have lived in that city for 40 years and have never set foot in Hialeah even though the cities are 20 minutes apart by car. Vice versa applies as well. Coral Gables is the home of the University of Miami including its medical school and law school. It is very suburban and wealthy, containing beautiful homes, manicured lawns, high rise office buildings, golf courses and very expensive restaurants. Hialeah is for the most part industrial, working class, and loaded with warehouses and newer Latin immigrants. There are plenty of wealthy and cultured individuals living in Hialeah, yet those cities are two different worlds and there is little social interaction between them. Yet we engage in the fiction that through good will and cultural sensitivity, we can relate to and understand the Pashtuns, the Uzbeks and the Tajiks. America learned nothing from the disastrous experience of the Soviets in Afghanistan.

The Soviets invaded Afghanistan in December 1979 and remained for a decade. The chief opponents of the puppet communist regime were the Mujahedeen - radical Islamic fundamentalists who were fierce fighters. We did not have a clue as to the true mind set of our newly found "friends."

The United States needed Pakistan's help in training the Mujahedeen. We had a very solid relationship with Pakistan's dictator - General Muhammad Zia-ul-Haq, who was our key liaison with them. Haq was a fervent Islamic militant and was instrumental in the passage of the blasphemy laws which provided the death penalty for those who dared insult the Prophet or Islam.

We supported the Mujahedeen with sophisticated weaponry capable of downing Soviet aircraft (Stinger anti-aircraft missiles, Kalashnikovs, etcetera) and tons of cash. The Soviets, with a force of 140,000 troops, could not prevent guerilla attacks on their convoys and bases. By 1989 the Mujahedeen had forced the Soviets to withdraw. Thirty-one years later they forced America to withdraw; they had become the Taliban.

The Soviets had tried their hand at winning hearts and minds. They engaged in large infrastructure projects, they built an engineering school, there was a Soviet house of science and culture. The Soviet leadership believed they could transform a backward, agricultural society into a modern state. They were wrong, and America was even more wrong, having the Soviet failure staring it in the face.

It was one thing to be rid of the Russians and the local communists; it was quite another to form a stable national government. The inevitable occurred - myriad factions, competing warlords vying for power resulted in a four-year civil war. America lost interest once the Soviets were defeated. We became obsessed with Iraq's invasion of Kuwait in August 1990.

The Mujahedeen (Taliban) won the civil war and controlled the country from the mid-1990s until the American invasion in 2001. A report by the Afghan Human Rights Commission said 180 mass graves resulted from the civil war, with a total of one million dead and another 1.3 million disabled.

Amazingly in light of our subsequent experience, we defeated the Taliban very quickly (within a few weeks) during our initial invasion. We had CIA operatives on horseback calling in precision strikes from B52 bombers. We were able to accomplish this with only about 10,000 special operations forces. We were aided enormously by brave Afghans who comprised the Northern Alliance - members of the Uzbek, Tajik and Hazara tribes - all of whom were opposed to the Taliban's harsh version of Islam.

TERROR IN AFGHANISTAN – A MERE SAMPLING

One can generalize about the Taliban, the Haqqani network, Al Qaeda, etc. They are all volunteers; they are dedicated fanatics who beyond a couple of sound bites could not articulate why they have killed thousands of their fellow Muslims. They are not looking to get rich or have productive careers, or go on family vacations. Most of them have no fear of death; they welcome martyrdom – that's what makes them so dangerous and so effective.

In 2011 there was a sharp increase in political assassinations – assassinations of provincial governors and other officials. General Daoud was a heroic figure in the fight against the Soviets; he became the regional police chief of north Afghanistan and was murdered May 28, 2011. In April 2011, the police chief of Kandahar was killed by a suicide bomber in his own headquarters. In the first half of 2011 among those murdered were three police chiefs, the mayor of Kandahar and senior advisor to the president. These officials were often murdered by close associates, people they trusted.

On September 20, 2011 there was a meeting in the home of the leader of the Afghanistan High Peace Council, a former president of Afghanistan. President Rabbani had been a leader of the anti-Taliban Northern Alliance. The Rabbani home was crowded with peace seekers, when a "supporter" embraced him, and then exploded the bomb in his turban.

Rabbani trusted the killer as did his security people. Rabbani knew Afghanistan like you know your block, your neighborhood – yet he was fooled.

In October 2018, a teenager who was trusted entered the governor's compound in Kandahar province where he managed to kill the police chief, the provincial intelligence chief and wound an American general. Raziq Abdul, the police chief, was feared by the Taliban because he had been so effective against them. Two of his predecessors had also been murdered.

Here's another example of a very savvy Afghan being murdered by a supposed ally. I speak of President Karzai's half-brother, Ahmed Wali Karzai, perhaps the most powerful man in Afghanistan. Ahmed had greater control over Kandahar and the south than his brother had over the rest of the country. Kandahar is both the Taliban heartland and the Karzai family heartland. On July 12, 2011, Ahmed was murdered by a trusted friend who was also a police official. Yet the American political and military establishment expect 19 or 20-year-olds from Newark or Birmingham or Grand Rapids to be able to distinguish the good guys from the bad. It is an irrational expectation.

On May 19, 2011, an Afghan construction crew working on a road project was attacked leaving 35 dead – security guards, laborers and engineers.

In late June 2011 nine suicide bombers attacked the Intercontinental Hotel in Kabul. In spite of this very up to date hotel being heavily fortified with several rings of security, the bombers were able to shoot guests at the swimming pool and in the dining room. They would have killed many more absent the arrival of NATO helicopters. The Haqqani Network, the strongest arm of the Taliban, proudly claimed responsibility.

On February 21, 2011, a suicide bomber killed 31 Muslims who were waiting in line to receive identification cards at a census office. Also in February a police headquarters was attacked in Kandahar, killing nineteen.

On June 25, 2011, the terrorists blew up a hospital leaving 20 dead including children and midwives. They target weddings, funerals, mosques – any venue where crowds gather. The Taliban have specialized in attacking and burning schools, killing both students and teachers. They are opposed to the education of females and have sprayed girls and their teachers with acid leaving many with permanent disfigurement and blindness.

On August 6, 2011 there occurred the single largest loss of American lives during the war. The Taliban using a rocket propelled grenade struck a Chinook helicopter killing 40 –

including 22 members of an elite Navy Seal team – the bravest of the brave.

America's failure in Afghanistan, NATO's failure in Afghanistan was laid bare on Sunday, April 15, 2012. The Haqqani Network carried out synchronized attacks at seven different secured targets in four different provinces. Suicide bombers and gunmen were able to strike Parliament and the diplomatic quarter in the Afghan capital. Amazingly the United States and NATO had no clue that these attacks were on their way.

These sophisticated, coordinated attacks had to have been planned weeks, probably months in advance. The terrorists crossed hundreds of miles to hit seven spread out well-guarded targets. Weapons and ammunition had to be brought to diverse locations and sat there until they were ready. Hundreds of terrorists had to be involved in the planning, logistics and transport. Yet America was taken by surprise. We have embassies, but we don't have a great spy network. We are ignorant of how many Taliban have infiltrated government ministries.

In late June 2012 seven Taliban suicide bombers attacked a popular lakeside resort outside of Kabul. They targeted this hotel because it allowed dancing and may have been frequented by prostitutes. The attackers went into the dining room where guests were eating, and killed twenty.

In late October 2012 a 15-year-old suicide bomber in Afghanistan killed 45 of his fellow Muslims as they emerged from a mosque after celebrating a major holiday. Among the dead were 25 members of Afghanistan's national security forces including two police chiefs – the very people who are trained to thwart terrorist attacks.

What follows is a sampling of terrorist acts committed by the Taliban and ISIS in more recent years. Yes, ISIS had a strong presence in Afghanistan. In April 2017 some ten Taliban suicide bombers infiltrated Afghanistan's largest Army base killing some 160 soldiers. Grasp that number, grasp the date - how could that happen? America has spent billions training and equipping the Afghan Army and Police and yet a military base was that vulnerable.

The Taliban overran another Afghan military base in October 2017, murdering 43 soldiers.

On May 31, 2017, a truck bomb exploded in Kabul at the entrance to the Green Zone killing approximately 150 civilians going about their everyday tasks. The Green Zone is the most fortified, supposedly the best protected area in all of Afghanistan. It is home to the Coalition Military Headquarters, the Presidential Palace and several foreign embassies.

In July 2016, an ISIS suicide bomb killed 80 Shiite Hazaras in Kabul. Oh you didn't know that ISIS hates Hazaras even though they are Muslims and they also hate and kill Shiite Muslims?

In March 2017, ISIS struck the Army's main hospital in Kabul killing dozens of Afghan soldiers being treated for their wounds.

In October 2017, ISIS struck two Shiite mosques in Kabul killing 88. In late December 2017, ISIS hit a Shiite cultural center killing 41.

An ISIS suicide bomb killed over 40 teenagers taking a course to prepare themselves for university entrance examinations. I could go on and on giving more specific examples of senseless killings, but what would be the point?

I have cited several attacks in 2011 and 2012 just to demonstrate they occurred while over 100,000 American troops were in the country. No member of Congress said then or before or after – "let's get the hell out of that country and simply admit that we have made a terrible mistake and also admit that Bush's global war against terror has been a horrible failure."

AMERICANS BEING KILLED BY OUR AFGHAN ALLIES

How have we been getting along with our allies, the security people we are training (military and police), the people Americans are dying for? On April 27, 2011 an Afghanistan Air Force officer, a trained pilot, murdered eight United States Air Force personnel and one U.S. contractor at Kabul International Airport. In December 2009, seven high ranking United States intelligence officers were murdered at a major CIA base by our "ally." These were not isolated atrocities.

Well over 150 American and NATO military members have been killed by our so called "allies." The attacks have been given a label – "green on blue killings." The killers' salaries, uniforms, and weapons have been paid for by American taxpayers.

On February 17, 2020, an Afghan soldier killed two American sergeants.

The victims were both members of the Army's 7th Special Forces Group.

Antonio Rodriguez had served ten tours in Afghanistan, first as an Army Ranger then as a member of the Special forces. Can you believe ten tours?

Javier Gutierrez was a Green Beret and the father of four.

Yes, the American victims have identities. Identities that are unknown to their fellow Americans. Brave, patriotic Americans who were suckered to buy into false promises of extending democracy and defeating terror. That's why they volunteered.

In late May 2012, United States Air Force trainers were carrying rifles and wearing body armor to protect themselves from the very men they were training. Not even this record persuaded our political or military leaders to demand that we extricate our patriotic volunteers from this hopelessness.

In April 2014, an Afghan police officer killed three Americans at a hospital, a hospital where they were helping to care for sick and wounded Afghans - do-gooders all. One of the victims was a superbly trained pediatrician, a nine-year volunteer in a killing zone who treated Afghan babies. He trained Afghan physicians to do the same, but he was murdered because a heartless fiend had some fiery sermon or slogan swimming around in his befuddled head.

So many of our "allies" hate our values, our cursing, our jokes, our comments about women and sex. We didn't understand them and they didn't understand us, and a mountain full of sensitivity lectures will never change that very basic fact.

Bad enough to lose a loved one in battle, but to lose a son or husband or father or daughter to a bullet from a supposed ally – how can one cope with that? Our own government inflicts punishments on our patriotic young men and women. Because of the other war (Iraq) we don't have enough volunteers, so we send our soldiers back again and again.

Overall across the military, 160,000 plus service members have done four or more combat tours in Afghanistan or Iraq. The United States Army admits that in the year 2010 over 320,000 soldiers sought treatment for mental health reasons. Many of the veterans have abused drugs and alcohol; some have committed terrible crimes. It is mind shattering for a veteran to see his marriage dissolve or to have his home foreclosed when his non-serving neighbors of the same age are pursuing their private interests, obsessing about their investment strategies.

The aftermath of Afghanistan and Iraq will continue for decades. In April 2012 the Department of Veterans Affairs announced plans to hire about 1600 additional psychiatrists and social workers to reduce long wait times for diagnosis and treatment. Many suicides have occurred while waiting to see a mental health expert; the system is overwhelmed by the huge number of returning military personnel who need help.

What follows is just one horrible example of a soldier's mental breakdown.

United States Army Staff Sergeant Robert Bales, on the night of March 16, 2012, killed 16 sleeping Afghan civilians in their homes including nine children. He went into three separate houses and set fire to several of the female children. He did this in a poor rural area after leaving his base in Kandahar province. Bales, age 39, was an eleven-year veteran with a solid record. This was his fourth deployment in a war zone.

Let's look at the Afghan local police or village defense forces who have been trained by American Special Operations troops for the purpose of protecting their communities— mainly rural areas which do not have a national police presence. Many of these local cops were former

Taliban and some had criminal records. They were seen as one of the cornerstones of the American exit strategy.

On March 30, 2012 one cop drugged his colleagues and killed nine of them as they slept shooting them all in the head. The killer had been accepted by the elders of the town despite his previous links to the Taliban. They knew him and his family and believed his conversion was genuine. Another Afghan local policeman cooperated with the Taliban by allowing them entrance on March 7, 2012 to kill nine more local police.

CORRUPTION

Whenever a scholar or seasoned journalist describes Afghanistan and deals with the subject of corruption the word that is universally used to describe it is "endemic"— which means that corruption is chronic, it is part of the everyday fabric of life on a national level, a local level and an individual level. When corruption reigns, it is the insiders who prosper, while the rest of the population is exploited – hatreds build and a fractured society results. And it is into this mix that the starry-eyed American government has poured nearly a trillion dollars. For a long time we (our government) paid the salaries of thousands of fictitious soldiers. Some corrupt commanders would pocket the money paid to these ghost soldiers.

Finally in January 2017, the United States wiped more than 30,000 names of suspected ghost soldiers from our payroll. This fraud was discovered by John Sopko, America's Special Inspector General for Afghan reconstruction. Sopko said – "we still don't know how many police and how many soldiers we are paying salaries for. We don't even know how many Generals.

Congress created that office to monitor the progress or lack thereof of the Afghan government and its military. Inspector Sopko said in his report of January 2019, that the American government views Afghanistan as –

"Consistent with a largely lawless, weak and dysfunctional government."

Kept secret from the American public is how much of Afghanistan's territory is controlled by the Taliban and the number of deaths inflicted on Afghan security forces.

By early 2019, the Taliban controlled or contested more territory than at any time since our invasion.

Also secret are U.S. performance assessments of the Afghan army and police as well as progress on anti-corruption efforts. The public was not complaining about being in the dark; they were not demanding this information. Rather their focus was on the impeachment circus and the Democratic debates.

Sopko makes it clear that in 2019 corruption remained endemic.

He put much of the blame on the United States –

"It would take years for the United States to realize that it was fueling corruption with its excessive spending and lack of oversight."

Sopko uncovered evidence of Afghan soldiers selling weapons and vehicles to the enemy.

His report said that training classes for Afghan pilots were shut down after more than 40% of the student pilots went absent without leave.

The United States supports an army of private contractors and security firms. We have outsourced to the private sector duties that were previously performed by the military. Many Afghan companies with ties to terrorists have obtained United States contracts; some companies were discovered to be providing bomb-making materials to the terrorists. They could easily trick American inspectors through well-disguised subsidiaries and through secret relations with politicians and the military.

Security contracts are very lucrative. Fortunes have been made running a protection racket for the American supply chain which involved thousands of trucks. Owners of trucking companies which carried supplies to hundreds of American bases became multi-millionaires. Politically connected American companies have made fortunes building roads, bridges and schools. Whichever way America turns, it gets taken.

The State Department under Secretary Pompeo cut $100 million in aid that was to go for a hydroelectric project to provide power to the cities of Kandahar and Ghazi. Why?

Because of government corruption and financial mismanagement, and because of the government's inability to transparently manage American resources. Pompeo also announced the cessation of funding for an Afghan anti-corruption committee calling it -

"Incapable of being a partner in the international effort to build a better future for the Afghan people."

The United States hired two global auditing firms (KPMG and Ernst & Young) to see how taxpayer money was being spent. Their conclusion – Afghanistan cannot be trusted to be honest and this applies to all its ministries.

Admiral Mike Mullen was paying one of his many visits to Afghanistan in August 2011 when he said – "Criminal patronage networks ... are woven into the fabric of how things get governed, ... how decisions get made." In February 2014, a report of the Joint Chiefs of staff said the same thing referring to the country as a collection of "criminal patronage networks."

There cannot be anything approaching true democracy in a society which is corrupt from top to bottom. It is inevitable that in such a society the political process will also be corrupt. In every election there have been credible claims of fraud.

The Kabul Bank is Afghanistan's largest private financial institution. It became a veritable candy store for the well-connected. It was disclosed in 2010 that the bank had lost about $900 million because of an outrageous loan policy. Many of the loans were made interest free, requiring no collateral and lacking any concrete repayment obligation.

The bank lent a brother of President Karzai $6 million so that he could purchase a townhouse in Dubai. Dubious loans were made to the brother of Afghanistan's first vice president, to members of Parliament, to government ministers. Bank management maintained two sets of books in order to disguise reality.

Sometimes corruption causes deaths. For example, corruption at Dawood National Military Hospital in Kabul – Afghanistan's main military hospital, where wounded soldiers arrive for treatment. The families of these unfortunates were solicited for bribes to receive food, medicine and basic care. And who was doing the soliciting? Educated and trained doctors and nurses! The commanding general of the hospital was one of the worst violators; some patients died from starvation and simple infections because they could not afford the bribes. The former Surgeon General of Afghanistan stole tens of millions of dollars-worth of drugs from military hospitals. This is not a country that any American should die for. How could any American leader have believed that such a country could ever become a functioning democracy or a reliable ally?

PRESIDENT HAMID KARZAI!

Karzai was the president of Afghanistan for over a decade, finally leaving office in September 2014. He was praised by two presidents during their state of the union addresses (Bush and Obama). He was the guy America installed to put Afghanistan on the road toward democracy. Yet Karzai vilified the United States at every opportunity and as usual the all-American suckers just took it.

He weakened our efforts against the Taliban by restricting our nighttime commando raids, airstrikes and drone attacks. His government released scores of prisoners with American blood on their hands. On October 8, 2013, Karzai said that the United States had inflicted needless suffering on Afghan citizens. He blamed the United States and its allies for the corruption which blankets his country, and said our development projects were ineffective.

Over the years, Admiral Mike Mullen, Chairman of the Joint Chiefs of Staff, made over 25 trips to Afghanistan often for the purpose of trying to persuade Karzai to be a more effective and less corrupt leader. Begging and more begging. And for what –

The privilege of pouring manpower and treasure into an ungrateful country.

General Eikenberry said that Karzai "continues to shun responsibility for any sovereign burden whether it be defense, governance or development...his record is one of inaction."

Karzai has called us "demons," he has said that the Taliban killing Afghan civilians is "in service to America." He has said that both America and the Taliban desire that Afghanistan remain unstable, and he has accused America of coveting Afghanistan's resources. Karzai has accused the United States and Pakistan of plotting with terrorists to divide his country. He has said that the Americans are – "trespassers and occupiers for their own purposes, for their own goals..." What self-respecting nation would tolerate these calumnies?

Our CIA, for more than a decade, financed a slush fund to pay off warlords, politicians and tribal leaders upon whom Karzai depended for support. Karzai admitted to receiving monthly deliveries of cash. He said something which may have hurt the most because it was truthful –

"The United States presence in Afghanistan has not brought security to us. It has caused more extremism."

The Obama administration desperately wanted Karzai to sign a bilateral security agreement which provided for a residual American force to remain in Afghanistan. We had to beg Karzai to allow our troops to continue to fight and die for his country – and we did beg but without success.

Karzai expressed happiness that America and other coalition troops were leaving the sacred soil of Afghanistan. "Our national sovereignty must be recognized and respected."

The United States plucked Karzai out of obscurity in December 2001 making him the leader of the post-Taliban government. A great track record – Maliki in Iraq, Karzai in Afghanistan, and Imran Khan in Pakistan.

Karzai refused to sign the Security Agreement in spite of the fact that he has said Afghanistan will not be able to support its own security forces financially for 15 to 20 years.

Give Karzai high marks for consistency. In his farewell speech he said – "America did not want peace for Afghanistan." The core of Karzai's fury toward the United States was the fact that we did not insist that Pakistan eliminate its terrorist havens. Karzai thanked other countries for helping Afghanistan but omitted any gratitude to America for our sacrifices over 13 years.

In August 2009, when Karzai was running for his second term, having first been elected in 2003, the Independent Electoral Commission discarded 1.3 million fraudulent ballots, nearly one fourth of all votes cast. Most of the tossed ballots were for Karzai but he won anyway after being forced into a runoff. In the parliamentary elections of September 2010 the Independent Electoral Commission invalidated well over one million votes. Elections yes – Democracy no.

Rampant fraud, corruption, and phony elections – our soldiers being killed by our Afghan allies – yet America is staying the course. That is a shameful policy.

ELECTIONS AFTER KARZAI

Karzai had served two 5-year terms. The Afghan Constitution prevented him from seeking a third term. Two major political figures competed in the 2014 presidential election - Abdullah Abdullah and Ashraf Ghani.

Ghani had spent many years in America. He was a professor at several universities and was a senior official at the World Bank for 15 years. He had served as finance minister under Karzai. Abdullah had been foreign minister in a Karzai cabinet.

The charges made against each other during the campaign were vicious. Each candidate claimed he had won. An audit confirmed that there had been massive fraud during the election.

Obama and Kerry came to the rescue, pushing for a deal where Ghani would become president and Abdullah would become the chief executive, a sort of vice president whose powers were ill-defined.

The deputy foreign minister said in October 2015 -

"Afghanistan is on a regressive path. The political arrangement between Abdullah and Ghani has become the opposite of everything it was designed to deliver."

By August 2016, Abdullah denounced Ghani as unfit to govern.

What did Ghani have to say about Karzai when he ran against him for the presidency in 2009?

"Over the past 5 years, Karzai has turned Afghanistan into one of the world's most failed and corrupt states."

"He has formed alliances with criminals."

"He has turned a blind eye to a multi-billion-dollar drug trade that has enabled the insurgency to flourish."

Karzai returned the compliment calling Ghani "a traitor." Yet America's leaders keep telling us that a normal, functioning democracy remained a realistic goal.

Parliamentary elections were held in October 2018. The voting had been delayed for 3 years. There were the usual charges and counter-charges. The fraud was so widespread in that election that ten election commissioners were convicted and sentenced to 5 years in prison. These were the supposed guardians of the process. Why can't our presidents understand that to praise elections and speak of democracy is to make a mockery of that word?

Another presidential election was held September 28, 2019 where Ghani was seeking a second 5-year term. His chief opponent was again Abdullah. Each claimed victory but it took until February 2020 to declare a winner. Ghani emerged as a very tainted winner. It was absurd to believe that Ghani, with only a financial background, could become an effective wartime leader.

THE UNFORGETTABLE PHOTOGRAPHS

On August 22, 2012, the New York Times published photographs of 1,000 dead, young Americans – white, black, Latino, Asian – men and women. They were photographs of the most recent 1,000 American deaths in Afghanistan – killed in the absolute prime of their lives – lives filled with promise – lives filled with plans, hopes and expectations. Killed by mortars, rocket-propelled grenades, gunfire and improvised explosive devices. Killed by suicide bombers.

The dead represented all of the services – Marines, soldiers, sailors, Air Force. There were four full pages of photographs which had to be small to accommodate all 1,000 – only headshots listing names and hometowns. Many of these victims came from small towns where they were taught patriotism, belief in their leaders, and love of country. Places like –

Boring, Oregon – Moreland, Georgia – Navarre, Florida – Ewa Beach, Hawaii – Lynch Station, Virginia – Atwater, Ohio – Cherokee, Iowa – Woodruff, South Carolina – Kuna, Idaho – Gaylord, Michigan – Wildwood, Illinois – South Sioux City, Nebraska.

In the campaigns of Obama and Romney, all they could talk about was the economy. Neither one questioned the decision to invade Afghanistan to get one man even though it led to the longest war in American history. There were no photographs of the 1,000 young Americans who were killed before this group, nor were there photographs of the thousands more wounded – many with multiple amputations, paralysis, and brain injuries.

The so-called beautiful people are not in Manhattan or Beverly Hills – those photographs represent the really beautiful people. Anyone who would spend five seconds looking at each picture would be haunted for a very long time. And one's anger would be immeasurable knowing that terrorists protected by our "ally," Pakistan, were responsible for many of those deaths.

This is what James Dobbins, the United States Special Envoy for Afghanistan and Pakistan had to say – "My view is the more the better – more time, more money, more troops, more people yields better results." What "better results" could he be possibly talking about? This up-beat crap must be unbearable to the survivors of those killed.

Obama could not be straight about America's failure in Afghanistan, so in mid-2014 as he announced the timetable of United States troop withdrawals, he adopted a new rationale – "We have to recognize that Afghanistan will not be a perfect place and it is not America's responsibility to make it one. The future of Afghanistan must be decided by Afghans." Had that been said by Bush, in 2001 the 1,000 would be alive.

This was a totally different tune to the one Obama sang when he first ran for president in 2008. Then he said – "as president I will make the fight against Al Qaeda and the Taliban the top priority that it should be. This is a war that we have to win."

Eight years and two terms later, Obama knew America had not won. The Taliban were stronger than ever, Al Qaeda still existed, and ISIS had become the most vicious terrorist organization of them all.

Although the Taliban ridiculed Karzai as a stooge propped up by the infidel Americans, his fervent desire was still to make peace with them, at times referring to them as "dear brothers" and their dead as "martyrs."

The Taliban made it clear that their reign of terror would continue. "The Mujahedeen of the Islamic Emirate will keep proceeding with their Jihad until it attains its goal."

Army Lt. General Daniel Bolger was a senior commander in both Iraq and Afghanistan.

After he retired, he said – flat out – what Americans hate to hear: we lost both wars. He says the "surge" in Afghanistan only delayed the inevitable. He was highly critical of the counterinsurgency strategy in both countries. General Bolger believed in the mission early on but says sadly – "I got it wrong... I argued to stay the course, to persist..."

As early as 2012, long before he became a candidate, Trump said –

"Why are we continuing to train these Afghans who
then shoot our soldiers in the back."

Much later he said – "We are building roads and schools for people that hate us. Time to come home." As President Trump shifted, he agreed to allow a residual force of several thousand.

In testimony before the Senate Armed Services Committee in June 2017, Defense Secretary James Mattis said we were – "not winning right now I believe the enemy is surging." Mattis is saying this sixteen years after America invaded.

Vice President Pence in December 2017 told our troops –

"We're here to stay until freedom wins, I believe
victory to be closer than ever before."

"Victory" was off the table, and Pence knew it.

Our military commander, later ambassador, Karl Eikenberry, said that everyone agrees that the war – "cannot be won militarily. We continue to fight simply because we are there. Our soldiers are volunteers permitting the American people and their elected representatives to be indifferent about the war." He uttered a very basic truth about the American attitude and its passivity for 20 years.

Susan Rice, Obama's national security advisor and former ambassador to the United Nations, said in an op-ed piece on March 15, 2018 that the war could not be won militarily. She said the annual cost to the United States of the war was $45 billion for 15,000 troops as opposed to the 140,000 U.S. and NATO troops at the height of the war. She said that the Taliban controlled or contested at least one third of the country. She went on –

"Our longest war will go on much longer (our presence) is essentially permanent."

A panel of former military and diplomatic leaders agreed with Rice concluding that –

"The United States-Afghanistan partnership should be recognized as generational in duration." A forever commitment. Unbelievable!

General Austin Miller assumed command of U.S. and coalition forces September 2, 2018 and said – "the world recognizes that we cannot fail." The crap talk goes on and on because the public never calls the liars to account.

Sorry to say, General Miller – but what the world recognizes is that after 18 plus years the United States has failed in its war against terror. Yet stubbornness, hubris and mythology prevent our "leaders" from admitting it.

Robert Gates, Secretary of Defense under both Bush and Obama, understood the root cause of America's failure in Afghanistan. He had been a true believer at the beginning. After leaving office he wrote a book, "Duty," in which he said –

"President Obama doesn't trust his commander, can't stand Karzai, doesn't believe in his own strategy, and doesn't consider the war to be his."

Gates had visited the battlefront multiple times. He spoke at length with our warriors and their commanders. No one understood the overall situation better than he. This was his conclusion – read it and weep –

> "Our lack of understanding of Afghanistan, its culture, its tribal and ethnic politics, its power brokers, and their relationships was profound. I came to realize that in Afghanistan, as in Iraq, having decided to replace the regime, when it came to – with what? – the American government had no idea what would follow. We had learned virtually nothing about the place in the 20 years since helping defeat the Soviets there. These experiences – these ghosts – led to my strong conviction that the idea of creating a strong, democratic (as we would define it), more or less honest and effective central government in Afghanistan to change the culture, to build the economy and transform agriculture, was a fantasy."

THE TALIBAN AGREE TO NEGOTIATE

Finally, the Taliban agreed to negotiate in late 2018. It had always been the position of the United States that the Taliban should negotiate directly with representatives from the government of Afghanistan. It has always been the position of the Taliban that they – "Do not recognize the stooge government" – the "puppet" government.

The United States caved, agreeing to negotiate directly with the Taliban without the participation of Afghanistan – proving the validity of the "stooge" assertion. That's exactly what happened decades earlier when our ally, the government of South Vietnam, was excluded from the Paris peace talks.

In September 2018 the United States appointed a seasoned diplomat to be our lead negotiator – Zalmay Khalilzad – a man who had been born in Afghanistan and served as America's Ambassador to that country.

There was round after round of talks. Khalilzad and our government naively believed it was possible that a power sharing deal could be reached. We still had no grasp of the Taliban mentality. The talks began in October 2018 – and a deal was finally reached on February 29, 2020.

President Trump said this to our troops Thanksgiving, 2019. "We're going to stay until we have a deal or we have total victory, and they want to make a deal very badly." No, it was America that wanted to make a deal very badly.

He knew that "victory" was off the table. It was Trump who wanted to make a deal before the November 2020 election – and he got it in February.

There were two main points to the agreement –

1. The most important point to the Taliban was the removal of all American

troops. The leader of the Haqqani network made that very clear – "The withdrawal of foreign forces has been our first and foremost demand." The United States agreed that 5,400 troops out of about 12,000 would leave within 135 days after the agreement was signed. Closing multiple American military bases would take months, as would the removal of weaponry, planes and vehicles. Our remaining troops would all be gone in about a year.

2. The Taliban would not allow Afghanistan to be used by terrorists to launch attacks, and they would not provide terrorists with a haven. No seasoned diplomat or politician could possibly believe that empty promise.

The United States participated in the talks in spite of the fact that the Taliban continued their killing sprees throughout the negotiations. Yes, thousands of attacks. The Taliban had refused to agree to a cease-fire. Our former Ambassador to Afghanistan, Ryan Crocker, told the bottom-line truth about the negotiations, saying they weren't –

"Anything other than a way out for us, that we can style as something less than losing the war."

Crocker knew that Khalilzad's dream was a fantasy – "that Afghans would sit together to negotiate an honorable and sustainable peace for a unified, sovereign Afghanistan."

The United States was doing something very concrete (removing our troops) in exchange for a promise that the Taliban could not fulfill, even had they been sincere. The Taliban had no control over Al Qaeda or ISIS; they could not prevent them from launching attacks.

The Taliban and Al Qaeda are allies. The Taliban and ISIS hate each other and compete with one another.

ISIS surfaced in Afghanistan in the year 2015 and has carried out horrible attacks. Their base was in Nangarhar province in the east. On April 13, 2017 an American commander with Trump's permission, authorized the most powerful conventional bomb in our arsenal to strike an ISIS cave and tunnel complex. It caused much destruction and many deaths but ISIS bounced back. Just like they bounced back after the United States killed their founder and leader-Baghdadi.

ISIS pays its members better than other terrorist organizations because it has perfected revenue streams through smuggling, taxes, the drug trade, and kidnapping.

In 2018, ISIS launched over 20 attacks in Kabul leaving hundreds dead or wounded. In August 2019, an ISIS suicide bomber struck a wedding in Kabul, killing about 80. A wedding attended by Muslims, including children. A United Nations Report of June 2021 reported that ISIS conducted 77 attacks during the first 4 months of 2021. ISIS members follow Sunni Islam, they hate Shiite Muslims regarding them as apostates even though they believe in Allah and revere the Prophet Mohammad. Most Shiites in Afghanistan come from the Hazara ethnic minority.

Where does such cruelty come from, this fanaticism? Most of it comes from indoctrination at religious schools beginning at a very young age. To kill fellow Muslims at a wedding or while engaged in prayer is incomprehensible to the western mind.

The Madrassas worldwide, which fuel the most radical, jihadist form of Islam, were funded generously by America's closest ally in the Arab world – Saudi Arabia.

Here are a few examples of the Taliban killing machine while the "peace" talks were ongoing.

On January 21, 2019, the Taliban struck the base of Afghanistan's intelligence agency, its Directorate of Security, killing about 50. These are the officials who should have the most up-to-date information on terrorist plans, yet they had no clue that the attack was coming.

On May 6, 2019, the Taliban killed 20 unarmed police who were waiting in line to receive their paychecks.

On May 15, 2019, the Taliban struck a key Afghan army base killing some 25 soldiers.

In a typical week of March 2019 the Taliban killed 120 soldiers, police and pro-government militia members. During this same month, nearly 300 Afghan soldiers surrendered to the Taliban.

Our people were in Doha talking to the Taliban – smiling, drinking coffee, and making small talk. No protests, no outrage at the charade of the negotiations.

The women of Afghanistan feared any so-called peace deal because they remember vividly how girls and women were always treated by the Taliban. One of the very few bright spots in the governance of Afghanistan since the American invasion had been the advancement of women.

A woman has served as Afghanistan's ambassador to the United States. They comprised nearly one-third of the national assembly. There were about 3.5 million girls in primary and secondary schools.

The constitution says that men and women have equal legal rights. Many women had become judges and lawyers.

One very bright example –

There is a high-quality maternity center in the Panjshir Valley which delivered 7,500 babies in 2018. And the staff is all female - 7 gynecologists, 39 midwives, 78 neonatal nurses. These dedicated women seek to reverse the fact that Afghanistan has one of the world's highest childhood mortality rates and one of the highest maternal mortality rates.

When the Taliban were in power, they did not allow girls to attend school; women were confined to their homes, unless escorted by a male relative. All this talent and creativity ruthlessly suppressed. The Taliban have not changed - attacks on schools tripled from 2017 to 2018 according to a UNICEF report of May 2019. According to that report more than a million children were unable to attend school.

Ambassador Crocker has said that -

"Acute misogyny in Afghanistan goes way beyond the Taliban." Yes, it is ingrained in a male-dominated culture. For a while after the Trump deal, the Taliban played the public relations game saying they would respect these female advances. Of course they reverted to form and reinstituted the previous harsh restrictions.

THE SCANDAL AND TRAGEDY OF CIVILIAN DEATHS

The United Nations reported that over 30,000 civilians have been killed in Afghanistan since 2009. A much larger number have sustained permanent injuries. The report said 2018 was the single worst year for civilian deaths since the agency started documenting deaths in the year 2009.

Civilians continued to be killed in 2019 – 18 years after our invasion. The United Nations reported that over 1,300 civilians were killed during the first half of 2019, and that more of these deaths were caused by the United States and government forces than were caused by the Taliban. A really great way to win hearts and minds. Americans are despised by the very people we had hoped to lead toward victory and democracy.

Hear this from Thomas Gibbons Neff, a Pentagon correspondent for the New York Times, who served as a marine in Afghanistan during 2008 and 2009. His article appeared in the Times on September 17, 2019.

"We didn't understand the Afghans. They mostly hated us for destroying their homes, accidentally killing them and telling them to respect a government in Kabul that they cared little about. The Afghan army was near useless then. When they weren't high on hashish, we were worried they were going to shoot us."

"We were fighting the Taliban to let Afghanistan build a democracy. Or something like that. That's how they presented it to us as they sent us in."

Another tragic mistake, of which there were hundreds. – A United States precision bomb struck a home because our pilots were told the Taliban were shooting from that location. Our bomb killed a mother and 11 children ranging in ages from 4 to 14, boys and girls. Afghanistan has become a land of widows, widowers and orphans, a land of cripples, bitterness and recriminations.

During the month of September 2019, United States aircraft dropped 948 munitions on terrorist targets, the most in any month during the last 5 years. Through August 31, 2019, our planes had dropped some 4,483 bombs. American aircraft dropped 7,362 bombs and missiles during the year 2018. These numbers are astounding and provide insight as to why we have killed thousands of civilians – women, children, entire families.

President Ghani, when interviewed on the CBS television program "60 Minutes," said –

"We will not be able to support our army for 6 months without U.S. support and U.S. capabilities." The Afghan forces depend on the United States for their salaries.

General Joseph Dunford, Jr., chairman of the joint chiefs of staff said in May 2019 –

"We will need to maintain a counterterrorism program as long as an insurgency continues in Afghanistan." Obviously, President Biden did not agree.

There was one sane voice – General Joseph Votel who had commanded our Central Command said on December 12, 2019 –

"Now is indeed the time to bring an end to our endless war."

General David Petraeus said that Trump should not make the same mistake that Obama made in Iraq – leading to "Iraq's collapse" after American troops left in 2011. He calls that collapse a "tragic experience" which led to the emergence and success of ISIS.

Army General Mark Milley, the new head of the joint chiefs of staff said in September 2019 that any premature withdrawal of forces would be a "strategic mistake." "Premature" – Is he kidding? We have been there 20 years.

Defense Secretary Mark Esper during his visit to Kabul on October 21, 2019 said that the United States –

"Will continue to pursue an aggressive military campaign against the Taliban and terrorist groups that continue to conduct violence against the people of Afghanistan."

General Petraeus has said there are as many as 20 terrorist organizations in the region. Terrorism knows no boundaries, plans and attacks can be launched from anywhere.

THE AFTERMATH OF ONE OF THE MOST HUMILIATING DAYS IN AMERICAN HISTORY

After the United States pulled out of Afghanistan, what became of those who helped us? About 120,000 Afghans fled to the airport hoping to leave on American aircraft. Yet thousands remained stuck in Afghanistan. The Taliban searched for those who had helped America as fighters, as interpreters, even those who had lowly service jobs.

There had been instances of Afghans clinging to the landing gear of our C17s as they were taking off. That's how desperate they were, these people knew what would happen to them if they remained.

Our State Department said in December 2021 that some 60,000 interpreters and other helpers who had applied for visas remained in Afghanistan. The need for so many interpreters (not all really qualified) is the background for many inevitable miscommunications which led to thousands of civilian deaths.

Thousands of Afghans are on American military bases because of bureaucratic red tape. There is uncertainty about whether they will ever be integrated into American society. Hundreds of CIA trained commandos were stuck in the desert of the United Arab Emirates. Those who left the airport on UAE planes did not go to the United States, they became stuck in refugee compounds in the Emirates.

Afghans who received special immigrant visas thought that could lead to permanent residence in America. Even they had to be vetted– a process which could take a long time.

On July 1, 2021, six weeks before the American defeat, we abandoned the Bagram airbase which had been the hub of our military efforts in Afghanistan. Thousands of our military members had been housed there; that was where we trained Afghan fighters. We simply walked away, leaving for the Taliban sophisticated weapons, vehicles, etc.

Why did so many Afghans join with America knowing that if the Taliban won their lives and the lives of their families would be in grave danger? The answer is because they said to each other – "how could the great America lose to a mere terrorist organization?" With over 140,000 American and NATO troops, how could they lose? With the most sophisticated planes and weaponry in the world, how could America lose to an organization that did not have the use of a single aircraft?

Valid questions. The answers are contained in this chapter. The hype began very early.

"Operation Enduring Freedom" was the label for our invasion. President Bush assured us that we were on the road to – "a victory for the forces of liberty." The fiction that we were doing well also began very early. Secretary of Defense Donald Rumsfeld said in 2003 –

"We clearly have moved from major combat activity to a period of stability and reconstruction activities."

During the 20-year fiasco, over 800,000 Americans served in Afghanistan. An astounding number. It is beyond tragic that young American volunteers were sent to fight, die, and sustain permanent injuries for such a country.

CHAPTER 2

PAKISTAN

To say that the relationship between the United States and our "ally" Pakistan in our war against terror is both sick and dysfunctional is an understatement. For years, terrorists in Afghanistan killed American soldiers, then crossed over the border into Pakistan where they were protected by the military and its all-powerful spy-intelligence service. Our government knew this yet continued to treat Pakistan as a worthy ally.

On September 22, 2011, Admiral Mike Mullen, America's number one military leader as Chairman of the Joint Chiefs of Staff, testified before the Senate Armed Services Committee –

"Proxies for the government of Pakistan are attacking Afghan troops and civilians as well as US soldiers. The Haqqani network (a branch of the Taliban) is in many ways a strategic arm of Pakistan's Inter-Services Intelligence Agency." No senator said – "Let's get the hell out of there." And no senator said – "stop giving Pakistan billions of dollars" – and no senator said – "this is not a country that young Americans should be risking their lives for."

General Karl Eikenberry was the top American commander in Afghanistan and later served as our ambassador there. He has said –

"Pakistan will remain the single greatest source of Afghanistan's instability so long as the border sanctuaries remain." Yes, the terrorists had sanctuaries in Pakistan.

A Pentagon report of December 2012 said –

"Pakistan's continued acceptance of sanctuaries for Afghanistan focused insurgents and its failure to interdict bombmaking materials continues to undermine the security of Afghanistan and poses a continuing threat to United States, coalition and Afghan forces."

President Clinton wrote a book four years after leaving office in which he said – "Pakistan supported the Taliban and by extension Al Qaedaand the Pakistan military was full of Taliban and Al Qaeda sympathizers." How can we continue to support such a country? And how can the American public remain passive in the face of such revelations? The passivity has continued for over 20 years.

Clinton knew this, so obviously President Bush and President Obama knew it during their combined 16 years in office. That didn't stop America from forking over billions of dollars every year for both military and economic assistance.

Zalmay Khalilzad has been America's ambassador to both Afghanistan and Iraq as well as our ambassador to the United Nations. Few people were in a better position to understand the region and its inhabitants. He was part of the Bush II administration and he tried to get our government to take a stand against Pakistan's treachery – but with no success.

Quoting Khalilzad – "Pakistan was playing a perfidious and dangerous double game and needed to be called on itthe resilience of the Taliban is primarily due to the military and intelligence services providing sanctuary and support."

Khalilzad explains Pakistan's motivation in supporting and sheltering the Taliban.

"Pakistan views the Taliban (and the Haqqani network) as an effective proxy to ensure Pakistan's dominance over Afghanistan and to limit Afghanistan's relations with India."

Husain Haqqani (it's a common name) was Pakistan's ambassador to the United States 2008 – 2011. He has confirmed that the Taliban received money, training and arms from Pakistan's Inter-Services Intelligence Directorate (ISI).

"The United States was effectively arming a country that was in turn arming insurgents who were killing American troops in Afghanistan." Read this statement again and again, and ask yourself how the American government could accept such a travesty under both Republican and Democratic administrations.

In spite of all this, the United States has designated Pakistan as a "major non-NATO ally."

Haqqani zeroes in on Pakistan's relationship to India.

"Competition with India remains the overriding consideration in Pakistan's foreign and domestic policies."

Haqqani became a professor of international relations at Boston University. He has written a book called – "Magnificent Delusions."

He says – "the relationship between the United States and Pakistan has never been good and embodies a history of failure. There is no reality to the so-called alliance and attempts to build a strategic partnership got nowhere." Obama thought or at least said that the "partnership" was wonderful.

The military has always ruled Pakistan, either directly or indirectly. It and the spy agency are the dominant institutions in Pakistan.

When the military became dissatisfied with the policies of a prime minister and his party, they would simply get rid of him or her and take over directly. The military controls an industrial conglomerate worth billions, including banking and real estate.

PAKISTAN'S INDIA OBSESSION

In order to understand Pakistan it is necessary to understand its enmity toward India. India was known as the crown jewel of the British Empire. Like all countries during the age of colonialism, India had an independence movement – one led by a unique figure, Mahatma Gandhi, who began agitating as early as the 1920s; he did not lead an army and he did not engage in terror. His credo was nonviolence and civic disobedience, and in many ways Martin Luther King, Jr., patterned his movement on Gandhian lines.

Although Winston Churchill was the man most responsible for saving Britain from defeat in World War II, when the war was won an election was held and the public dumped him in favor of Labor leader Clement Attlee. He recognized that the world had changed and the days of subject populations were numbered.

Considering India's patchwork of religions, ethnic groups and its caste system, it is amazing that for the most part Britain maintained order. Once it was certain that the British were leaving, Hindus and Muslims started killing each other in massive numbers. As but one example – trains would be stopped by either Hindus or Muslims, members of the other religion would be pulled off and hacked to death and this included women, children and the elderly; thousands of towns and villages were destroyed.

Pakistan does not want Afghanistan to succeed in the war against terror; Pakistan believes that instability in Afghanistan gives it leverage against India, and that the best way to achieve instability is to support terrorism. America is supporting a country which wants our war against terror to fail.

Over the years, India has given Afghanistan billions in aid and has helped train and equip its security forces. India has constructed a hydro-electric dam, built miles of highways, and has a strategic partnership agreement with Afghanistan. Pakistan hates that close relationship.

Although India tilted strongly toward the Soviet Union during the Cold War years, it now has a solid relationship with the United States which includes billions in bilateral trade. Pakistan is countering the India/Afghanistan relationship with a very close alliance of its own – with China.

Pakistan accuses Afghanistan and India of aiding separatists in the province of Baluchistan. Baluchistan has been agitating for independence for decades and Pakistan has found another use for "friendly" terrorists – the suppression of nationalist/separatist movements.

Pakistan and India both have huge arsenals of nuclear weapons, and if a nuclear war were ever to be fought the likeliest combatants would be these two. Our only interest in Pakistan should be to make sure that terrorists never get control of their nuclear weapons.

India, a majority Hindu nation, became independent on August 15, 1947, and Britain joined in their celebration. India's constitution mandates secularism. It did not want a repeat of the Hindu/Muslim bloodbath.

India's Muslims wanted their own country – not all Muslims but the political ones who followed the Muslim League and its leader Muhammad Ali Jinnah. Jinnah was not a religious fanatic – to the contrary, he was secular and pragmatic. Gandhi and India's first president, Nehru, wanted a unified India and were willing to accommodate the minority Muslims. Jinnah might have accepted a united India with full Muslim autonomy, but the emotions had been stoked and the fervor for a separate Muslim state would not be denied. Jinnah died on September 11, 1948 at which time he was the Governor General of Pakistan. His successor was assassinated – a common form of regime change in Pakistan, Afghanistan, and India.

Gandhi was a revered figure; he would visit Muslim villages preaching peace and brotherhood and an end to the killing. On January 12, 1948 Gandhi began another one of his many hunger strikes saying he would continue until the killing stopped. For six days he ate nothing, only sips of occasional water. On January 30, 1948 Gandhi was murdered by a young man, a Hindu, who was opposed to reconciliation with Muslims.

Nehru's daughter, Indira Gandhi (no relation to Mahatma) was a dominant political figure in India for decades, as was Benazir Bhutto in Pakistan. There are striking similarities between these two women. They both served multiple terms as their country's leaders, they were both removed from office, and both made remarkable comebacks. And they were both assassinated.

On October 31, 1984, Indira was assassinated by two of her Sikh bodyguards. She was never forgiven for unleashing an attack on the sacred Golden Temple which had been taken over by armed militants obsessed with the goal of Sikh independence. In the raid in June 1984, some 700 Sikhs were killed, plus about 70 Indian soldiers. Why did she insist on retaining her Sikh bodyguards?

Nepotism is as central to governance in India as it is in Pakistan. Indira's son, Rajiv, became prime minister and like his mother he was assassinated. Also, over an independence issue. He was murdered by Tamils who sought independence from Sri Lanka. His widow, Sonia, was born in Italy. She became the leader of the National Congress Party – the party of Gandhi and Nehru.

In my chapter on the false promises of both independence and democracy, I point out the universality of the desire for independence and the fact that movements to achieve it often continue for generations. Let's have a look at a new independent nation created in 1971 – Bangladesh which had previously been East Pakistan. Yes – a part of Pakistan which sought to secede. A war was fought between the two Pakistan's resulting in an unbelievable number of deaths – about three million. Most of the dead were Bengalis, the majority in East Pakistan who were battling against the Punjabis. Our leadership knew basically zero about the enmity between these two groups.

Sheik Rahman was the leader of the Bengali Awami League which was pushing for independence. Of course, he became president of the new nation. He was a dictator who was assassinated in a military coup in 1975. Sound familiar? Decades later his daughter became prime minister. Her main opponent was the widow of a former president. Political nepotism is simply part of the fabric of certain countries.

Bangladesh has suffered through dictatorships, coups, corruption, and a dysfunctional political and economic system. The garment industry was great for the factory owners not for the underpaid workers. In April 2013 a complex of garment factories collapsed, killing 1300. Walmart, the Gap, Armani, Ralph Lauren, and Hugo Boss all loved the cheap labor and Americans loved the relatively reasonable prices.

PAKISTANI CULTURE AND THEIR MENTALITY

On January 4, 2011, an elite police bodyguard pumped 27 bullets into the back of the Governor of Punjab, Pakistan's most populous province – obviously a trusted member of Salman Taseer's security detail. The killer's reason? Governor Taseer favored a change in Pakistan's blasphemy laws under which any person found guilty of insulting Islam or the Prophet Muhammed could be subject to the death penalty.

The other members of the security team stood idly by as the shots were fired; none of them shot the attacker. Taseer was widely respected, and in a normal country his murder would have aroused outrage. Instead, when the killer made his first court appearance he was showered with rose petals by the standing room only crowd, which included many prominent lawyers.

Five years later, the killer was executed. 100,000 Pakistanis attended his funeral. A mosque in Islamabad is named in his honor. Taseer's daughter, Aatish, has written – "the madness is not confined to radical mosques and madrassas, but is abroad among a population of nearly 200 million."

That is a very important point. Americans are sold the false narrative that the extremists are a few bad apples but that the great majority of Muslims are reasonable. Extremist views are widespread even among the educated and prosperous.

American politicians and diplomats always mouth platitudes about respecting the customs and traditions of other cultures even when they are horrified by them. There is a practice in Pakistan of trading women to settle disputes called "Baad." If someone has offended you in some way or turned down a marriage proposal or committed a minor slight such as not inviting you to a wedding, you can demand that the offending party give you his daughter to appease your anger. The daughter then becomes a member of a totally strange household, and in many instances the girls are mistreated physically, sexually, and psychologically.

Let's talk about "honor" killings where fathers murder their daughters, where brothers murder their sisters. It is a cultural crime to bring shame upon one's family. Often the "crime" is simply rejecting the man selected by the girl's family for marriage.

In June 2014 a couple were tied up and their throats cut with a scythe. By whom? The father of the girl. The girl's mother watched and supported her husband's action. The daughter, age 17, had secretly married a man whom the parents felt came from a less important tribe.

In July 2016 a brother killed his 26-year-old sister who had developed a following as a social media star presenting secular images. Her brother decided the death penalty was appropriate for the "shameful" pictures she had posted on Facebook.

In March 2019, Professor Khalid Hameed was stabbed to death in his office by a student who mistakenly believed that the Professor had insulted Islam. The Professor, a devout Muslim, was 6 months from retirement.

There are hundreds of honor killings in Afghanistan and Pakistan every year, nearly always inflicted by family members. Most are never reported, and criminal convictions are extremely rare. In many rape cases, it is the victim who is prosecuted for adultery. There are videos of crowds cheering as a suspected adulteress is executed. Many brides have been killed because there was a suspicion of a lack of virginity. Yes, by all means let's have some coffee and danish and reason together. Perhaps a lecture about due process, about the rule of law.

There were approximately 150 acid attacks in Pakistan in a single year by men angered at some affront to their manhood. Perhaps the most famous case of this outrage involved Fakhra Younas, who underwent over 30 surgeries in attempts to repair her mouth, nose and ears which had been melted by acid. Ms. Younas wrote about her ordeal; she made a heroic effort to adjust but ultimately could not – committing suicide at age 33. Her attacker had been acquitted by a judge years earlier.

POLITICS IN PAKISTAN

In 1973, Ali Bhutto, the father of Benazir Bhutto, became prime minister. In 1977, there were massive protests because of charges that Bhutto's party, the Pakistan People's Party, won the general election as the result of fraud. The unrest led to a military coup headed by General Zia-ul-Haq. It did not matter that it was Bhutto who had appointed Haq as army chief.

Bhutto was out. Not only out, but executed (hung in 1979), having been convicted of the murder of a political rival. Every political trial in Pakistan is suspect since when corruption is endemic it infects the legal system, the political system, and the marketplace. In Pakistan, the civilian leadership alternated for decades between the Bhutto clan and Nawaz Sharif of the Pakistan Muslim League. Benazir and Nawaz had a lot in common in that they both served as prime minister multiple times and were both thrown out of office on corruption charges. Both spent many years in exile.

Benazir's husband, Asif Zardari, earned the nickname of "Mr. 10 Percent" during his wife's terms as prime minister because he was alleged to take a cut from nearly every economic enterprise in the country. He actually spent years in prison.

Benazir returned from one of her multiple exiles on October 18, 2007. On that very day political opposition was expressed by two bombs that killed 150 people. She was favored to lead the country once again. On December 27, 2007, surrounded by a huge crowd of admirers, Benazir was killed along with 24 others – collateral damage to the killers. As is customary, no professional investigation was conducted and no one has ever been punished for her murder. Benazir's husband's criminal record did not prevent him from becoming Pakistan's leader in September 2008.

Who became the leader after Zardari? None other than Nawaz Sharif.

The United States was on the same page as Pakistan when we were both arming the Mujahideen against the Soviets in Afghanistan. Pakistan had been an ally of America during the Cold War and particularly so during the Eisenhower administration (1952-1960) when we showered them with aid. Pakistan joined two anti-communist alliances – the Southeast Asia Treaty Organization in 1954 and the Baghdad Pact in 1955.

The United States continued to have decent relations with Pakistan, until Pakistan began to pursue a nuclear program. This led to a cessation of aid and sanctions which became more severe after Pakistan engaged in underground testing in May 1998 (the very same time that India did likewise).

Obviously, the number one priority of a country which possesses nuclear weapons is to protect them from getting into the hands of terrorists. The main nuclear figure in Pakistan was a scientist named A. Q. Khan. He was the chief of the primary nuclear weapons laboratory and was usually referred to as the Father of Pakistan's nuclear program. Khan sold plans, designs and technology to three of the most dangerous and irresponsible countries on earth – Iran, North Korea, and Libya – and this went on for well over a decade. The likelihood is that Khan also provided Syria with plans to build the nuclear facility which Israel destroyed in 2007. Endemic corruption even infects brilliant scientists.

It is impossible that key figures in the military and intelligence establishments were unaware of Khan's activities.

In addition to sheltering terrorists who kill American troops, there are other reasons to despise Pakistani leadership.

On November 26, 2011, a serious mistake occurred when a U.S. helicopter attack killed 24 Pakistani soldiers. Poor communication led to this tragedy. Pakistan demanded an apology but all they got was an expression of regret. They were entitled to a full-throated apology.

Pakistan punished America by closing our supply lines into Afghanistan, and they were kept closed for 8 months. It was customary for about 5,000 NATO trucks per month to transport supplies to our troops. During the closure America had to find an alternative route and we did – through several central Asian republics. Pakistan saw this as an opportunity to gouge us, and they charged $5,000 per truck rather than the previous $250. Defense Secretary Panetta, testifying before Congress, said using the alternative routes added $100 million per month to our costs.

Did we say to Pakistan – "this is an outrage, our boys are dying to protect your people we've given you sophisticated weaponry, plus billions in military and economic aid – you will never get another dime from us unless you reopen the supply lines."? Of course we said nothing of the kind, as we said nothing of the kind about their terrorist havens.

Pakistan did not investigate those who aided Bin Laden for years, instead they investigated and punished those who supplied the United States with information about his location.

A Pakistani physician was convicted of treason, of acting against the state, and sentenced to 33 years in prison for assisting the United States in locating Bin Laden. The government arrested some 30 informants for providing the United States with tips.

A few days after our raid killed Bin Laden, the Chief of the Intelligence Service appeared before Parliament to denounce it. The reaction? Thunderous applause. America kills the world's arch terrorist and Pakistan is outraged.

Pakistan refused to allow American soldiers to be based on its territory, nor would it allow American and NATO forces to conduct commando raids – the single most effective method of disrupting attacks. Pakistan forced the United States to vacate Shamsi Air Base which was our prime base for launching drone attacks. Pakistan refused to allow U.S. Navy vessels to dock at its ports. They just love to humiliate us, and we take it.

In April 2011, Pakistan demanded that the U.S. withdraw hundreds of special-forces trainers, the best qualified people to train military and police. Pakistan has denied visas to Americans with expertise in operating sophisticated weaponry as well as large numbers of CIA officers.

PAKISTAN PROTECTS TERRORISTS BUT IT IS ALSO THE VICTIM OF TERROR

Some horrific examples –

Pakistan does not shelter the Pakistani Taliban which is an enemy of the government since their goal is to take over Pakistan. On December 16, 2014, the Pakistani Taliban perpetrated an atrocity which is beyond understanding.

They attacked the Army Public School in Peshawar killing some 150 children of military personnel, as well as teachers. Yes – children! And this cannot be repeated often enough – the killers and the victims are all Muslims. They all believe in Allah and the Prophet!

Thousands of Muslims have been murdered by their fellow Muslims while saying their prayers at mosques – mosques or shrines where devotees practiced a different strain of Islam-Sufi or Ahmadi. Christians have also been targeted in their churches.

Pro-government tribal leaders have been murdered by the Pakistani Taliban, who on one occasion killed over 80 cadets – young, paramilitary soldiers, who were scheduled to go home after enduring 6 months of hard training. On April 15, 2012, the Pakistani Taliban broke into a major prison, freeing 384. On another occasion, the Pakistani Taliban killed 17 government soldiers and released a video of their severed heads.

In August 2016, terrorists killed 70, mostly lawyers, at a hospital. The lawyers were paying tribute to a prominent lawyer who had recently been murdered.

Hundreds of relief workers have been killed – unarmed civilian do-gooders. One group of 10 consisted of a team of doctors, nurses, and technicians – several Americans who had left successful practices in order to serve humanity.

On April 22, 2018, a suicide bomber killed 57 Muslims who were lined up so they could register to vote. The victims included children on their way to school.

On January 30, 2023 the Pakistani Taliban (a suicide bomber) – struck a mosque in Peshawar, a mosque frequented mostly by police in an area surrounded by several government and military buildings. In an area considered to be very secure with multiple check points. Nearly 100 were killed in this attack, mostly police and relatives of police.

In addition to targeting police, the Pakistani Taliban were also striking military targets. This is the same military charged with the task of making sure that nuclear weapons do not get into the hands of terrorists. Pakistan blames the Taliban for this resurgence of terror. When Pakistan was successful in pushing the Pakistani Taliban out, they found a safe haven in Afghanistan. After 9/11 Al Qaeda was protected by the Afghan Taliban. Yes – a very hospitable group. The irony is that Pakistan protected the Afghan Taliban during the two decades that they were killing Americans. And now the Taliban who control Afghanistan are unleashing terrorists that attack Pakistan.

Islamic State Khorasan is also responsible for much terror in Pakistan. As part of Trump's deal with the Afghan Taliban they promised that once they were in power, they would not allow terrorist attacks on other countries. An empty promise.

Where have the terrorists been so indoctrinated that they can commit such horrific acts with a clear conscience? The answer is religious schools – madrasas. Pakistan has thousands of madrasas headed by clerics who are respected, even revered. Our wonderful friend, Saudi Arabia, for decades financed the most conservative madrasas – the ones which subscribed to the harshest forms of Islam and the need for Jihad. One madrasa in particular has been recognized as laying the foundation for the present leadership in Afghanistan – the Haqqani Seminary.

The New York Times has published an extraordinary photograph of hundreds of "students" studying at this seminary. It seemed to replicate exactly what an Orthodox Jewish yeshiva looks like in Jerusalem or America. All the Muslims were wearing white, their headgear was very similar to that worn by Jews. They are all sitting at desks with a pile of books in front of them.

The big difference is that in yeshivas there are no lectures about violence against any group. The gap between Orthodox and Reform Jews is every bit as wide as the gap between Sunni and Shiite Muslims, but they are not killing each other.

THE IMRAN KHAN ERA

Khan became an icon when, in 1992 as team captain, he led Pakistan to victory over England in the Cricket World Cup. He came from a wealthy family, was educated at Oxford University, and married a British heiress (they later divorced). He was a lady's man, totally secular. That all changed when he decided to go into politics and adopted a new-found religiosity. Appearing to be religious is always a smart political move in a Muslim country. He formed his own political party in 1996 and targeted the Sharif dynasty – his main charge being that they were corrupt to the core.

Khan led massive protests against Sharif's rule in 2014, and again in November 2016. He petitioned the supreme court to bring corruption charges against him, which it did.

The political turmoil was summed-up by Pakistan's former Ambassador to the United States, Husain Haqqani –

"Pakistan stays faithful to its 70-year tradition: No Prime Minister has ever been removed by the voters; only by Generals, Judges, bureaucrats, and assassins."

Although elected three times as Prime Minister, he never completed any full term. Pakistan held an election on July 25, 2018, and the winner was Imran Khan. He also did not complete his 5-year term.

A major theme during Khan's campaign was anti-corruption – He said, "Those people who have looted the country I promise they will be brought to justice." Soon after his victory, he revealed the extent of his anti-Americanism –

So, 17 years after our involvement in Afghanistan and Pakistan we get a Pakistani leader who hates America, sides with the Taliban, and has very friendly relations with China.

He has called the American war against terror "madness," a "deeply flawed and failed policy." He added that "Pakistan has suffered enough fighting America's war."

He has called the terrorist war against the United States in Afghanistan justified.

He has hailed the Taliban for waging a "holy war" against the United States.

When the Taliban won, Khan said they had – "broken the chains of slavery." None of these insults prevented Trump from inviting Khan to the White House in July 2019.

The worst charge that can be leveled against any government is that they are a puppet of America.

He has said that America "caused disaster in Pakistan."

Khan has made a point made by many others that the Taliban is – "driven by opposition to the United States' presence." It is considered a sin for foreigners to occupy holy Muslim soil.

Parliament got rid of Khan through a no confidence vote in April 2022. Also, in common with every other prime minister there were corruption allegations against him. So, who replaced Khan? Consistent with their tradition of nepotism, the new prime minister was the brother of Nawaz Sharif – Shehbaz Sharif.

Khan blames the military and the intelligence services for his removal from office. This is ironic because he had the military's backing where he won in 2018. He also claims that America is part of the conspiracy against him.

Khan was arrested on May 9, 2023 on corruption charges. What else? His followers protested in several cities. Mobs looted the official residence of an army commander. They pushed through the gates of the national army headquarters. In the past, attacking army installations would have been unthinkable because of the fear of consequences.

PAKISTAN'S ECONOMY

Although the economy of Pakistan has been on life support for many years, Khan made these absurd promises during his campaign.

He will create a social welfare state along with ten million new jobs. Pakistan will provide low-cost housing, with five million new homes.

When his opponents pointed out the impossibility of carrying out these pledges – Khan said he would "rather commit suicide" than go around the world begging for money. Yet that is precisely what Pakistan has done primarily through loans from the International Monetary Fund.

Pakistan has for decades survived on bailouts (handouts) from the International Monetary Fund, the World Bank etc. The following problems have persisted – budget deficits – a severe balance of payments problem – runaway inflation – poverty – unemployment, a huge trade deficit.

Pakistan's infrastructure is in awful shape. This includes their power grid. Power failures are common and often nationwide, causing millions to suffer in the dark.

In May 2019, Pakistan received yet another IMF pledge of $6 billion, and Khan did not commit suicide. The United States has historically been the largest contributor to the International Monetary Fund. The promise of billions from the IMF almost always came with conditions. Conditions which can cause rioting and the downfall of a government. Conditions such as the need to raise taxes and the need to slash subsidies. The IMF austerity conditions are designed to impose fiscal discipline but they often lead to higher food and utility bills.

Millions of Pakistanis suffer from hunger. Malnutrition is a huge problem. During Ramadan (April 2023), 22 were killed in a stampede when rushing to grab free food. It is a tradition for the population to feast at night after the month of day-long fasts.

And the country was hit with bad luck – Monsoon rains and floods which killed over 1700 and destroyed vast areas of farmland and crops.

Pakistan has significant oil and mineral wealth, as well as natural gas deposits. If they knew how to manage their economy and knew how to distribute wealth fairly, they would not need bailouts.

Tax collection in Pakistan is a misnomer because nearly everyone avoids paying taxes and prosecutions are rare, in spite of the fact that Pakistan has one of the lowest tax rates in the world. In February 2019, a financial watchdog – Financial Action Task Force – said that Pakistan was not doing enough to curb financing and money laundering for terrorists.

The IMF is not the only savior. Pakistan has received substantial loans from Saudi Arabia and the United Arab Emirates. The Saudi crown prince was in Pakistan in February 2019 and pledged $20 billion.

China has gotten its hooks into Pakistan big-time. It has loaned Pakistan $62 billion for huge infrastructure projects such as ports, roads and powerplants. China's ambitions are other-worldly – as part of their belt and road initiative they are lending upwards of a $1 trillion for a chain of infrastructure projects across over 50 countries.

This communist country has become the most aggressive capitalist entity in all the world.

China has not become Santa Claus – their financing terms and profit-sharing deals strongly favor them. The United States has accused China of debt-trap diplomacy. The government of Malaysia rejected a

$22 billion loan offer from China because it feared the consequences of incurring such massive debt.

The close relationship between China and a Muslim country is ironic since China discriminates harshly against its own Muslim population – the Uighurs.

A country that survives on financial bailouts is not a sovereign country. It is frightening that such a country possesses massive stores of nuclear weapons. More frightening is the prospect of terrorists gaining control of them.

President Obama met with then Prime Minister Sharif in October 2015 and said that he –

"Reaffirmed that a mutual commitment to democracy is a key pillar of the US Pakistani partnership."

Trump did not invent lying.

Obama knows that the military is the true power in Pakistan and he knows that Pakistan provided a haven for terrorists who killed Americans. No "democracy" and certainly no "partnership."

Trump's first Secretary of State, Rex Tillerson, continued the Obama nonsense in October 2017 saying –

> "Pakistan is important to the United States' security relationships and so important regionally to our joint goals of providing peace and security to the region."

"Joint goals"? Pakistan believes that an unstable Afghanistan is in their best interest.

This is what President Trump had to say about the American "partnership" with Pakistan–

> "Pakistan has given us nothing but lies and deceit. They take our money and do nothing for us. The United States has foolishly given Pakistan more than 33 billion dollars in aid."

It's statements like that which cause Trump's base to love him. No other politician could ever be that direct. You could agree or disagree with Trump, but you know where he stands.

Later on, Trump said something that Bush and Obama should have said but never did. That Pakistan knew for years where Bin Laden was living in their country but hid that fact from the United States.

Consider the leaders of our "allies." Karzai in Afghanistan – Maliki in Iraq – Khan in Pakistan. All have spit on America, and our "leaders" simply pull out the tissues and wipe off the spit.

Benazir Bhutto was murdered; her father, a former prime minister, was executed. Zardari spent years in prison, same with Sharif as well as other leaders. Who in their right mind would want to rule Pakistan? The lure of power trumps all other considerations for the politically addicted. Benazir's son became chairman of the family's Pakistan People's Party.

Benazir or any former prime minister could have become millionaires living in the United States. By making speeches, writing a book, receiving a high salary and prestige teaching at a university. Serving on corporate boards. Instead, they all return home. Money and adulation are no substitute for political power.

A Gallup poll was conducted in April 2023 to find out what ordinary Pakistanis thought about America. 72% thought of the United States as an enemy. Shocking! But it shouldn't be. We are seen as invaders who don't truly respect their culture or religion. So after billions of dollars and the sacrifices of young American lives, the thanks we get is the 72%.

Fundamentalism is on the rise in Pakistan. Khan actually favored making the blasphemy laws even stricter. Pakistan, like Iran, has refused to embrace ethnic differences and identities or religious pluralism.

THE PARLIAMENTARY ELECTION OF 2024

In my introduction, I discussed the imprisonment of Imran Khan by the military, and how he and his party were not permitted to participate in the parliamentary election of February 2024. However, many of his followers ran as independents and won. In spite of the severe economic problems, Khan remained very popular.

The election outcome came as a shock, since Khan's followers gained the most seats. Although not enough to form a majority. Somehow, a coalition would have to be established.

A coalition was established, and, of course, it excluded Khan's party. The coalition partners were the party of Nawaz Sharif, the Pakistan Muslim League. Joining that party in the coalition was the other political dynasty (the Bhutto clan), the Pakistan People's Party.

The co-chairman of the Pakistan People's Party is the husband of Benazir Bhutto (Zardari), who had become president after she was assassinated in 2007. In Pakistan, the office of the president is essentially ceremonial, the political power is in the hands of the prime minister. It is parliament, the national assembly, that appoints the prime minister.

A leader of the Pakistan People's Party is 35-year-old Bilawal Bhutto Zardari. His grandfather was prime minister, his mother was prime minister - one was executed, and the other was assassinated. In spite of that history, Bilawal has set his sights on becoming yet another prime minister.

On the day before the parliamentary election, 22 people were killed. Pakistan accuses Afghanistan of sheltering the Pakistani Taliban, who are close to the Taliban of Afghanistan, and to Al Qaeda as well.

Afghanistan accuses Pakistan of encouraging terrorist acts against it. I will not be surprised if a full-scale war breaks out between these two American "allies."

Khan has accused the United States of colluding with the military to kick him out of office. So the most popular politician in Pakistan remains strongly anti-American.

I worry about the strong possibility of terrorists capturing Pakistan's nuclear weapons. The Pakistani Taliban have been able to strike a supposedly secure air force base, as well as police installations. So who is guarding the nuclear weapons?

Pakistan has adopted an irrational policy which could lead to war with Afghanistan. They are expelling hundreds of thousands of Afghans, many of whom have lived in Pakistan for decades. Many thousands fled the Soviet invasion of Afghanistan decades earlier. Thousands have been born in Pakistan; it is the only home that they have known.

Over a half-million Afghans fled to Pakistan as a result of the Taliban takeover of their country. By and large, the Afghans have been loyal to their adopted country, yet they are all being expelled.

Forcible removal from one's home, a home filled with memories, births and family celebrations, is one of the most tragic events that can befall any family.

Resentments will persist for generations into the future – a future which will be devoid of democracy and any viable partnership with the United States.

CHAPTER 3

IRAQ

The United States invaded Iraq in March 2003 because President Bush (the son) told us that Saddam Hussein possessed weapons of mass destruction. We learned that was not true, yet we stayed and stayed and stayed.

A dictator had ruled Iraq for a quarter of a century. Under Saddam Hussein there were no suicide bombers, Sunni and Shiite Muslims were not killing each other by the thousands. The most vicious terrorist organization of them all (Islamic State – ISIS) did not exist. After our invasion a full-blown civil war broke out between Sunni and Shiite Muslims. Death squads proliferated on both sides. Let's go back to –

OUR FIRST INVASION OF IRAQ

On August 1, 1990 Arab Muslim Iraq invaded Arab Muslim Kuwait. 99% of Americans knew absolutely nothing about Kuwait – an oil rich, tiny, Arab country ruled by a royal dynasty. President Bush (the father) went to work trying to convince the public that the invasion of Kuwait was right up there with the attack on Pearl Harbor. All of a sudden, Americans were supposed to feel deeply about restoring the royals to their luxuries. Bush put together an international coalition of some 33 countries including Egypt, Syria and Saudi Arabia. It was a masterful job of lobbying and salesmanship.

The Gulf War was never about Kuwait. Just another lie told by an American President. Bush admitted this in a book he wrote with his national security advisor, Brent Scowcroft, called – "A World Transformed" (published six years after he left office).

President Bush – "I was worried that the Iraqis would indeed move into Saudi Arabia. With so many tanks heading south it seemed incontrovertible that Saddam had such plans. Our first objective is to keep Saddam out of Saudi Arabia. Our second is to protect the Saudis against retaliation ..."

President Bush told the Saudi king – "The security of Saudi Arabia is vital, basically fundamental to United States interests and really to the interests of the western world." Americans, Democrat and Republican, had a long history of sucking up to the Saudis, but no one reached the level of both Bushes.

After the tragedy of 9/11 – Bush (the son) arranged for the departure from the U.S. of all Saudi insiders so that they could not be interrogated about their knowledge of and possible involvement in 9/11.

The senior Bush still had to convince Congress that restoring the Royals of Kuwait was worth American lives.

Senator Daniel Patrick Moynihan of New York told a bottom-line truth when he said that liberating the royal family of Kuwait was not worth the life of a single American. With disdain he referred to "those Kuwaitis who have taken over the Sheraton Hotel in Taif (Saudi Arabia) and they are sitting there in their white robes and drinking coffee and urging us onto war ..."

Moynihan was chairman of the Senate subcommittee that monitored the Gulf; he was a former ambassador to the United Nations and to India and had been a valued advisor to several presidents on both domestic and international issues. President Mitterrand of France said he "would not risk the death of one single French soldier if war was exclusively in order to restore an absolutist system." There was never an issue about restoring democracy to Kuwait since Kuwait, like every other Arab country, had never experienced democracy.

The Kuwaiti model of governance was very similar to that of Saudi Arabia -- one based on bribery of its own citizens. The population of about 2 million pays basically no taxes. Social services are plentiful, including health care, housing, education, and generous subsidies. Foreigners constitute about 80% of the work force. The local insiders are tracking their investments, they are not into physical labor. Palestinians from Jordan and the West Bank made up the largest group of foreigners (nearly 400,000), many of them occupying well-paying managerial positions. Most of them applauded the Iraqi invasion, in spite of the fact that over the years Kuwait had given Arafat and the PLO billions.

Many members of Congress like Senator Moynihan refused to be swept up in the "liberate Kuwait" con. On October 30, 1990, President Bush received a letter signed by 81 Democratic members of Congress saying – "We are emphatically opposed to any offensive military action."

Among those in opposition – Senators Nunn, Mitchell, Kennedy, Glenn, Gephardt, Kerry and Biden. The pressure from the Administration was intense and unrelenting, and finally on January 12, 1991, the Senate and House voted to support the use of force. The Senate vote was particularly close (52-47), the smallest margin ever to vote for war. Congress did not pass a formal declaration of war, rather it took cover under resolutions passed by the United Nations. If not for Bush's aggressiveness, the United Nations would have talked a lot about Saddam's invasion, but it would not have intervened militarily.

In a stunning admission in "A World Transformed" President Bush said – "... in truth even had Congress not passed the resolutions I would have acted and ordered our troops into combat ... I felt the heavy weight of impeachment lifted from my shoulders ..." He would have risked impeachment for Saudi Arabia, not for Kuwait.

Bush's concern for Saudi Arabia is particularly galling in view of the fact that the Saudi brand of Islam, with its ultra-conservative clerics and religious schools, is the underpinning of political Islam and all the jihadist terrorist organizations. At a meeting President Bush had with Colin Powell and General Noman Schwarzkopf, the focus was on how quickly we could move our forces into the area.

Unbelievably, we had to beg the Saudis to accept our defense of them. From the Bush/Scowcroft book -

"We had F-15's and F-16's on standby and they could be deployed to defend Saudi Arabia. However, this would require that they be based there. So far, the Saudis had said no. To help persuade them to accept United States forces, we asked Ambassador Prince Bandar to come to the White House." How utterly humiliating.

Scowcroft asked Bandar – "why he appeared to have a problem with our generous offer. His answer really set me back. He explained that the Saudis were not at all sure they wanted to be defended by the United States. The United States, he said, did not exactly have a reputation in the region for reliability."

"He cited two examples to make his point. In 1979, when the Shah was forced to flee Iran, the United States offered a squadron of F-15's to Saudi Arabia as a gesture of support and of warning to the Iranian radicals. The Saudis had immediately accepted. Then, as the aircraft were on their way, Washington announced that they were unarmed."

"The second example he described was the United States intervention in Lebanon in 1982-84. We sent the Marines into Beirut with great fanfare. Our Marines were there risking their lives to protect Arafat's PLO. Shortly after the terrorist attack on the Marine barracks (which killed 241 young Marines) the United States quietly loaded the Marines back on their ships and slipped away. Why should the king not be concerned that if the going got tough, the United States would behave in the same manner once again?"

The United States never avenged the deaths of our Marines, killed in their sleep.

(Scowcroft speaking) - "I could give him a pledge that if the troops were offered and accepted, we would stand with them to the end. Bandar said these assurances transformed the situation."

Saudi Arabia has spent billions of dollars to purchase the most modern and sophisticated military equipment; they are a prized client of American defense contractors. They have had decades to train pilots and build a formidable military machine, yet in President Bush's mind it was the responsibility of Americans to risk their lives in defense of the kingdom.

Although Iraq invaded Kuwait August 1, 1990 the slow-moving United Nations gave Saddam until January 15, 1991 to leave. Saddam, having zero interest in preserving human life, ignored the ultimatum. America began bombing Iraqi targets on January 16; the bombing continued for 42 days – basically unopposed.

We destroyed a good part of Iraq's civilian infrastructure including electrical power systems, sewage treatment systems, irrigation systems, bridges, railroads and communication links of every type. Ordinary Iraqis had good reason to despise America.

Bombing is never pinpoint at precise targets, so it was 100% certain that Iraqi civilians would be killed. Hussein knew American troops would attack, and he had to know that his army would be defeated. Yet he never sought to make a deal or to simply leave Kuwait. Americans trying to figure out an Arab mentality is a lost cause. Central to that mentality is to never appear weak.

President Bush was unable to persuade Jordan to join the coalition in spite of the fact that for decades America had a close relationship with King Hussein. The King (no relation) was Saddam Hussein's biggest apologist who did everything in his power to discourage American military action.

King Hussein had a face-to-face visit with Bush on August 16, 1990, but the president could not budge him. The king, like his namesake, had a stubborn, irrational streak. In 1967 when Nasser of Egypt kept threatening Israel (the Six-Day War), the Israelis were unable to persuade Hussein not to join Nasser's folly. By not listening, Hussein lost control of the West Bank and East Jerusalem.

President Bush in "A World Transformed" – referring to King Hussein - "He was loudly opposed to allowing foreign forces on Arab soil ... he was berating us in speeches ... it appeared that Jordanian bankers were laundering money for Iraq, helping it evade financial sanctions, and that Amman was acting as a conduit for the delivery of Iraqi oil ... Hussein refuses to admit that (the other Hussein), is a madman." Throughout the Arab World and including all the terrorist organizations there is almost total agreement on being opposed to "foreign forces on Arab soil."

Yet several Arab states welcomed a temporary presence of American troops to force Iraq out of Kuwait. They knew that if Saddam acquired Kuwait's oil, he would become the dominant figure in the region.

<u>We did not begin the ground war until February 24, 1991 – and four days later the war was over. Yes, the four-day war!! We sent a half-million troops to the Arabian desert to fight a four-day war – and to protect two of the most undemocratic regimes on earth.</u>

President Bush was certain, but totally wrong, that Saddam would fall from power after such a humiliating defeat. Bush said in his diary that with Saddam in decline "there will be dancing in the streets, and they will say that he was brutal and a bully and they will rejoice when he is gone ... I am confident of that." You have to give President Bush credit for including this naïve and totally wrong opinion in his book.

The high I.Q. policy makers in the Kennedy Administration believed the Cuban people would rise up to topple Castro after the Bay of Pigs invasion. A half-century later, the Castro brothers were still in charge. The Bay of Pigs fiasco conferred heroic status on Fidel and was a major ingredient of his longevity. What Americans can never seem to grasp is that many dictators are idolized by their own people. Castro and Nasser are but two examples of many. They would have won democratic elections in landslides.

President Bush did not have the right to be naïve. His resume was far more impressive than many of our presidents. For example – Reagan, Carter, Clinton and Bush (the son) had all been governors having zero experience dealing with foreign affairs or terrorism. Kennedy, Nixon and Ford had served in Congress, as had Bush (the father) but Bush had these added qualifications – He had been Director of the CIA, Ambassador to the United Nations, Chief of the U.S. Liaison Office with China (before full diplomatic relations); plus having served 2 terms as Vice President under Reagan.

With this resume, as an incumbent president, he was defeated by a former Governor of Arkansas who had never served in the military, had zero foreign policy credentials, and was a serial violator of his marriage vows. President Bush had served his country well in combat during World War II. Like Jimmy Carter, Bush became a one-term president – a rebuke that his son could never accept and which explains in part our invasion of Iraq in 2003. He had to redeem his father who had allowed Saddam to remain in power for 12 more years after the 1991 Gulf War. One of the worst presidential decisions ever.

On the day the ground war ended (February 28, 1991) President Bush spoke to his diary again – "He's got to go...obviously when his troops straggle home with no armor, beaten up, 50,000 and maybe more dead, the people of Iraq will know. Their brothers and their sons never to return."

Bush continues– "Almost every leader in the coalition had told me that in defeat Saddam would not be able to keep his hold on power." Just how wrong can supposed experts be?

It was inconceivable to the Shiites and Kurds of Iraq that America would allow Saddam Hussein to remain in power. It should also have been inconceivable to any normal American. It was likewise inconceivable to them that if they rose up to take Hussein down, that America would refuse to help, particularly since President Bush had strongly encouraged them to do just that. Yet, that's precisely what happened! They rebelled, and America sat on the sidelines.

After having been killed and oppressed for decades, the Shiites and Kurds did rise up in an attempt to overthrow Saddam. The pathetic rationalization of both Bush and Scowcroft as to why America refused to help – because that would be – "well beyond the bounds of the United Nations' resolutions guiding us" – our mission was to "restore Kuwait's leaders."

Pointing to the United Nations was a fiction created to camouflage both a policy failure and a failure of will. The coalition was a fiction; invasion was an American decision and it was America's war. We did not need a coalition of some 30 nations to help us fight a four-day war.

Not only did we leave Hussein in power, we left him all powerful. General Schwarzkopf allowed Saddam to retain helicopter gunships which he used very effectively to crush the Shiite and Kurd uprisings within three weeks. Most units of his elite Republican Guards remained intact, and they stayed loyal to Saddam.

Surprise, surprise. Bush and Scowcroft – the most elite part of Saddam's military remained loyal, so did the rest of his military. You were "confident" that after suffering a humiliating defeat he would be deposed. You were wrong because you had zero understanding of the dynamics of Iraqi society. Thousands of Shiites and Kurds lost their lives – leaving relatives with a justified hatred toward America.

Iraq had requested permission to take possession of the helicopters. General Schwarzkopf, who was without instructions, granted the request. Without instructions? Bad enough that we did not aid the rebellion, we also provided the "madman" with the means to demolish it.

How could America retain any vestige of self-respect after allowing Saddam to remain in power? He took 163 Americans hostage. The Iranians took American hostages in 1979, and Saddam took American hostages in 1990. Had we learned nothing in those eleven years?

Finally, on December 9, 1990, after four months of captivity and humiliation the American hostages were released. On December 13, President Bush met with a group of them at the White House and wrote – "As I listened to them, and saw how little media coverage was given to their experiences, I was angered feeling that America didn't seem to care." During the Iranian hostage crisis which lasted over a year the media coverage was intense and was a major factor in Jimmy Carter's crushing loss to Ronald Reagan.

Why was our embassy in Kuwait kept open? When Iran got rid of the Shah, we knew that the new regime hated America, yet we kept embassy personnel there as sitting ducks. For about a month before the invasion of Kuwait, Iraq had amassed 120,000 troops on their border. Yet President Bush was surprised that Saddam invaded and he was surprised that Americans were taken hostage.

President Bush and Scowcroft were well aware of Hussein's grievances against Kuwait. From their book -

"Tension between the two countries had been high for weeks, with a confrontation in OPEC over oil production and prices." And yet President Bush wrote – "I find it hard to believe that Saddam would invade." Yet another striking admission of being totally wrong, and unbelievably naïve.

According to "A World Transformed," at the time of the invasion there were some 3,800 American civilians and 130 embassy staff members in Kuwait. There were 500 Americans and 42 embassy personnel in Baghdad. John Sununu, President Bush's Chief of Staff, asked – "Is there any plan for protecting our embassy in Iraq?"

The answer that he got from none other than Colin Powell was a stunner – "No!" That wasn't the right question. The right question should have been – "what is our plan for getting all embassy personnel out of both Iraq and Kuwait and fast?"

Bush had immediate access to every Arab leader, to every scholar of the Middle East, and he certainly had access to Israeli Intelligence. There was no point whatsoever in keeping our embassy in Kuwait staffed; it was pure stubbornness and hubris; the whole idea of embassies being important as a cog in our national security apparatus is a fiction. Most ambassadorships are political plums given to wealthy contributors who lack expertise about the countries to which they have been assigned. For the most part embassies serve a ceremonial and public relations function.

Embassies are the most convenient target for those who hate us. Our embassies have been attacked again and again, and often in countries which are our supposed allies. Every time there is an anti-American protest or demonstration the focus of the crowd's anger becomes the luxurious American Embassy. Need I mention Benghazi in Libya? It made absolutely no sense for America to maintain an embassy there. Especially so with the anniversary of 9/11 approaching – the very date of the Libyan attack. The attack in Benghazi occurred more than 20 years after Saddam took Americans hostage – an attack that killed our Ambassador plus three other brave and patriotic Americans.

President Bush in "A World Transformed"-

"In mid-August I became deeply concerned about the safety of U.S. Citizens in Kuwait... my constant worry was that we would be presented with a hostage situation along the lines of the 1979 Tehran embassy crisis. My fears were soon confirmed. Bob Gates called on August 17 and told me the speaker of the Iraqi Parliament said they were going to detain foreigners, they would place them in various facilities near oil dumps or chemical plants – whatever – clearly putting them there so the facilities could not be bombed. Blatant hostage-holding. Another blatant disregard of international law by a cruel and ruthless dictator." Did Bush believe for a minute that Hussein gave a damn about "international law"?

"I cannot tolerate nor will I another Tehran. I am determined in that. It may cost American lives but we cannot sacrifice American principle and American leadership. Nothing angered me more than the cowardly use of human shields ... there would be no compromise, no bargaining for hostages, no tradeoffs. It galled me when people played into Saddam's hands by trying to negotiate for the hostages."

The only reason Americans were in a position to be taken hostage was Bush's failure of foresight and stubbornness, coupled with his throwback belief that, image wise, keeping embassies open was a matter of national pride. Bush was told on August 17, 1990 that Iraq was going to take hostages, yet he did nothing. Hard to believe.

Had Hussein done nothing more than imprison American hostages, that would have mandated his removal. But he did much more -

On February 25, 1991 (the second day of the ground war), one of Saddam's Scud missiles killed 28 Americans. They died for Kuwait and Saudi Arabia. How do their loved ones live with that?

Iraq pumped millions of tons of crude oil from Kuwaiti storage tanks into the Gulf and set hundreds of oil wells on fire, thus creating the worst deliberate manmade environmental catastrophe in the history of the planet.

Saddam had many months to ravage Kuwait. He invaded August 1, 1990 and our 42-day bombing campaign did not begin until January 16, 1991. While in Kuwait the brave Iraqi forces murdered, tortured, mutilated and executed their fellow Arabs, both Sunni and Shiite. They killed Arab babies in their incubators. They engaged in horrific, gratuitous cruelty – and we left Iraq with this monster in charge for 12 more years.

Our Air Force bombed a bunker in Baghdad thinking it was a military installation. Instead it was being used by the cynical mass murderer as a shelter for civilians. Several hundred Iraqis were burned to death – yet another reason for Iraqis to hate America.

After our victory in the four-day ground war, President Bush spoke to the nation (February 27, 1991) saying – "Kuwait is liberated...Kuwait is once more in the hands of the Kuwaitis, in control of their own destiny." Just another presidential lie to which the American public reacted passively, as usual.

The truth was that Kuwait was once more in the hands of the royal family. Of course, President Bush did not discuss our real objective (protecting Saudi Arabia), nor did he explain why we were leaving Saddam in power with his Republican Guard solidly behind him. And he certainly did not explain why we were mere spectators while helicopter gunships were crushing the Shiite and Kurd rebellions.

The one country that President Bush definitely did not want to be a part of his coalition was the one democratic country in the Middle East – Israel. President Bush, salesman in chief, got Israel to agree not to retaliate even if Iraq hit it with missiles. An amazing concession since retaliation is a core component of Israel's defense mentality.

Saddam struck with Scud missiles into Tel Aviv and Haifa. Israel dispensed degrading gas masks to its citizens. Bush was willing to humiliate one of America's closest allies.

OUR INVASION OF IRAQ IN 2003

America invaded Iraq for the second time because Bush's son told us Saddam possessed weapons of mass destruction.

The mentally ill leader became America's accessory in promoting that fiction. He was greatly feared and respected if others believed that he possessed such weapons. All Saddam had to do to avoid the American invasion and his own capture and execution, and the violent deaths of his two sons, was to allow inspectors from the United Nations to search for the non-existent weapons. In the years after the Gulf War, Saddam did the opposite, constantly hassling UN inspectors and refusing them access, deliberately creating the impression that he had something to hide.

The pre-invasion hype hinted at a collaboration between Osama Bin Laden, al Qaeda and the Iraqi regime. No such linkage was ever established. Nor was a linkage ever discovered between Iraq and the tragedy of 9/11. In his State of the Union address, President Bush spoke ominously of Iraq obtaining uranium ore in Africa. Congress bought the propaganda and authorized the invasion by an overwhelming bipartisan majority.

And of course, the public just went along, having great faith in what their "leaders" were telling them. The media jumped on the patriotic bandwagon, almost never asking probing questions about so-called weapons of mass destruction.

David Kay was a nuclear arms expert, an official with the International Atomic Energy Agency. He spent over a year in Iraq. His unambiguous conclusion: there were no weapons of mass destruction in Iraq.

Iraq would have possessed nuclear weapons if not for the fact that Israel, on June 7, 1981, destroyed the Osirak nuclear reactor. Israel didn't go to the United Nations asking for permission or resolutions or coalitions– they simply did what they had to do to protect their citizens. They could not allow an unpredictable madman to acquire nuclear weapons. That should have been the American attitude toward Iran and North Korea.

The condemnation of this unilateral act by Israel was universal, including from the United States. The pundits, the editorial writers, the talking heads on television all joined the chorus – and no one ever apologized to Israel. If you want to know about the existence of weapons of mass destruction in the Middle East, call the Israelis, who way back in 1981 knew the precise location of Iraq's nuclear reactor. Had Iraq possessed such weapons, that would have been a grave threat to Israel, not to the United States. When Israel learned of Syria's nuclear plans in 2007, they obliterated that site. Iraq did not retaliate against Israel in 1981, nor did Syria in 2007. They sought to disguise rather than advertise their humiliation.

The phrase – "Weapons of mass destruction" constituted a political scare tactic, a propaganda tool which achieved the goal of broad public and congressional support.

No one said – Are you telling us that Iraq has an atomic bomb, a nuclear weapon? Is our intelligence so porous that Iraq could have developed such a weapon without America having a clue? Are you telling us naïve and passive patsies that Iraq has a weapon which could reach the United States?

Operation Iraqi Freedom began March 20, 2003. Remember that the United States was heavily involved in Afghanistan by this time. We entered Baghdad in early April, and on May 1 President Bush announced that "major combat operations have ended." He was only wrong by 19 plus years.

Just how delusional can an Arab leader be? Saddam Hussein had months of notice that the United States was going to invade. Obviously, the American military was going to be victorious in 2003 as it was in 1991.

When the Arab Spring began in Tunisia, the long-time president left the country. When Batista saw that Castro was going to be successful, he left Cuba. When Idi Amin realized that his time was up, he left Uganda for Saudi Arabia. That's what dictators do. But the arrogant, delusional and egotistical Hussein hung around; he didn't even have a hiding place. It took our troops months to find him but eventually we did in December 2003. He was cowering in an ill-equipped spider hole in a rural area. Yes, a man who had his pick of multiple palaces.

Hussein was imprisoned, tried, and hung on December 30, 2006. He turned out to be the role model for Qadaffi of Libya. After 42 years in power, Qadaffi did not have an escape plan either. He was caught crawling through a sewer, beaten, and killed.

American-led inspection teams found no stockpiles of banned weapons nor any trace of continuing programs to produce them. Before the invasion the Swedish diplomat and former foreign minister, Hans Blix, led the United Nations' effort to find traces of such weapons. He, as well as others, said the United States went to war before the inspections were completed. He concluded that the American arguments for going to war were "absurd."

What I find to be amazing is the fact that when the public learned there were no weapons of mass destruction in Iraq there was no outcry, no protests, and no consequences. It was this same passivity which allowed Americans to tolerate a 20-year war in Afghanistan.

President Bush revered his father; he was crushed by the fact that Bill Clinton denied his father a second term. He understood that leaving Saddam Hussein in power for 12 more years was a permanent stain on his father's legacy.

Once the United States captured Saddam and learned that Iraq did not possess weapons of mass destruction, we should have simply left. But by this time Bush had another agenda – nation building and democracy promotion.

There was no debate about what would follow the capture of Hussein – the public had no idea that we would be involved for 20 plus years. That young Americans would be dying for a political fantasy. No one in Congress had the guts to say that Iraq was never going to become a democracy.

MUSLIMS KILLING EACH OTHER AND AMERICANS

The insurgency began almost immediately in Anbar Province. Muslims hated the foreign invaders and wanted us out. The fighting was fierce and lasted several months. We prevailed but the sacrifice was great. Some 1300 American soldiers and Marines, all brave and patriotic volunteers, were killed. The "victory" in 2004 did not end the insurgency.

Several years later, the terrorists, who are very patient, regained control of Anbar. How must that make the loved ones of the 1300 feel?

The wanton, indiscriminate killing was led by Al-Qaeda in Mesopotamia headed by Abu Mussab Al Zarqawi who was finally killed by an American airstrike in June 2006. After his death the slaughter continued. That's the horror of terrorism – there is never a shortage of replacements; there is never a shortage of suicide bombers.

The terrorist goal was the creation of chaos and a civil war between Sunnis and Shiites. The terrorists succeeded, with the seminal event being the bombing by Al Qaeda of a major Shiite mosque in Samarra – the golden-domed Askariya Shrine – in February 2006 where a revered Imam is buried. The Shiites retaliated and destroyed dozens of Sunni mosques, murdering many clerics.

The Army of Abdul Aziz Al Hakim, leader of the Supreme Council for the Islamic Revolution in Iraq, fought a war against the Mahdi Army of Moktada Al Sadr in 2006. Rivalries between these two Shiite dynasties went back decades. Both had received training and equipment from Iran's Revolutionary Guards. Iran is a Shiite Muslim country but not an Arab country. It is beyond ironic as to how much power Shiite Iran has gained over Sunni Arab countries.

Iraq also is a Shiite majority country, about 60% of the population. In spite of that, the Sunnis comprising about 20% were always in charge and, of course, Hussein was Sunni. Kurds comprised the other 20%.

Yes, religious leaders had their own armies. The worst years of the civil war were between 2005-2007. The United Nations reported that in 2006 over 34,000 Iraqi civilians were killed, mostly by their fellow Muslims.

SOME RANDOM ACTS OF TERROR

In February 2007, a female suicide bomber killed 40 students (mostly Shiite) at the elite Baghdad University. Yes, a female. Brainwashing begins almost at infancy.

Also in 2007, in the City of Sinjar, several trucks driven by suicide bombers killed 500. Hard to believe – 500 victims in a single operation.

The main target were Yazidis, a sect whose beliefs and practices combined elements of Islam with doctrines of ancient Persian religions.

On November 3, 2010, during mass at Our Lady of Salvation Catholic Church, an attack killed 68. Two days later, in 13 separate attacks against Christians, the death toll was 76.

There was once a vibrant gay culture in Baghdad. Both Sunni and Shiite death squads killed many gays and lesbians. In 2005, Grand Ayatollah Ali Al Sistani (the most revered Shiite figure in Iraq) issued a decree that gay men and women – "should be killed in the worst, most severe way of killing." Israel allows gay pride marches in Jerusalem, yet many gays are anti-Israel and pro-Arab.

All American combat troops were supposedly gone (as of December 2011). Iraq had experienced several elections; it had a parliament and a prime minister – yet the killing continued. How were the terrorists doing in 2012? – NINE YEARS AFTER OUR INVASION.

Within a week after our troops left, there were over a dozen attacks killing more than 60. And remember whenever there is a statistic for deaths, the number of wounded is usually two or three times greater and many of the injuries are permanently disabling.

On January 5, 2012, a series of bombings killed 69, mostly in Shiite areas.

On March 20, 2012, a string of suicide attacks and car bombings killed 43 in a half-dozen cities. The terrorists were so numerous and so disciplined that they could coordinate attacks on a given day in totally different locations far apart from one another.

There were 320 Iraqi victims of terror in April 2012. In a single week in June 2012 the terrorists managed to kill over 150 of their fellow Muslims. According to United Nations statistics more Iraqis died from attacks in the first six months of 2012 than in the first half of 2011 – 2,101 as against 1,832.

On July 23, 2012, Al Qaeda hit Shiite targets plus a military base killing 100. There were 40 separate attacks throughout the country on that date. On August 16, 2012 there was another wave of coordinated attacks killing over 100, including dozens of women and children at an amusement park – (these were Muslim women and children). The murderous rampage included Baghdad and five other provinces. I selected the year 2012 at random. The massacres and atrocities continued for years afterward. 95% of American troops were gone yet Muslims were killing Muslims in these astounding numbers.

As American combat troops had gone by the end of December 2011, President Obama made an incredulous observation – "We're leaving behind a sovereign, stable and self-reliant Iraq, with a representative government." Trump did not invent presidential lying.

The truth was that we were leaving behind a slaughterhouse, a killing field with a corrupt, undemocratic government. In spite of this, Obama easily won re-election over Mitt Romney in 2012. Iraq was barely discussed during the campaign. President Bush (the son) had said during his tenure.

"The establishment of a free Iraq at the heart of the Middle East will be a watershed event in the global democratic revolution."

It is hard to imagine a more absurd, untrue statement. Again, no consequences from a passive public obsessed with their iPhones and with how the stock market was doing.

IRAQ – AN INVENTED STATE

Iraq was a screwed-up state from its inception. It was invented by the British, the victor in World War I, when they combined three provinces of the disintegrated Ottoman Empire – Baghdad, Mosul, and Basra. The British installed an Arab King (Faisal) who had been their ally during the war. The government, such as it was, was overthrown several times in the years leading up to World War II. During that war, Iraq favored the Nazis. The leader of the Palestinians, the Mufti of Jerusalem, was a zealous supporter of Hitler. Britain occupied Iraq during the war and for a time thereafter.

Political instability returned to Iraq after the war. No change of government was ever peaceful. In a military coup in 1958, the king, the grandson of the original, along with his entire family, were murdered. Regime changes in the Arab world!

There were military coups in 1963 and 1968. Leaders of the various overthrows did not last long. In 1968, Saddam's cousin, Ahmed Hasan Al-Bakr, became president. He appointed Saddam as the head of the security agencies. Saddam was on his way to ultimate power, and by 1979 he had acquired it. For the first time, Iraq achieved stability under this ruthless dictator.

ELECTIONS, YES – DEMOCRACY, NO

On March 7, 2010, there was a national election for members of parliament. Prime Minister Nuri Kamal Al Maliki lost to a coalition headed by a former prime minister, Ayad Allawi -- 91 seats to 89. Neither group had enough seats to form a government. Allawi, a Shiite like Maliki, headed a unique coalition made up of Sunnis and secular Shiites who were attracted to his nationalist, secular program. Allawi had once belonged to the Baath party, he became an opponent of Hussein and worked for our CIA. With American support, he became Iraq's interim prime minister.

Allawi and Maliki negotiated for months in 2010 as to who would be prime minister, but they got nowhere. Then along came a savior – a Shiite cleric, a religious leader – Moktada Al Sadr -- whose 40-seat win allowed him to become a kingmaker. He was able to control several ministries. In 2008 Sadr and his Mahdi army were becoming a threat to the central government, so Maliki, with America's help, defeated Mahdi. In spite of that history, Sadr backed Maliki in 2010.

Sadr hated America every bit as much as the Ayatollah Khomeini had hated America. Sadr's militia had killed hundreds of American soldiers in two separate prolonged battles during 2004. When there was a discussion about American troops remaining after the December 2011 deadline, Sadr said that if they stayed, he would mobilize his army to kill more Americans. This is the guy who gains 40 seats in a "democratic" election – demonstrating clearly how a large segment of the Iraqi population felt about America. This is the guy who commissioned Shiite death squads against Sunnis during their civil war. This is the guy who is a major player in America's pipe dream for Iraqi democracy.

Sadr's followers demonstrate against the American invasion every April 9th – the anniversary of the fall of Baghdad in 2003. Bad enough to be the parent or spouse or child or sibling of a soldier killed in Iraq, but to have a loved one return in a casket whose death was inflicted by Sadr's army would have to be unbearable.

Sadr is revered by his followers in Sadr City, a Shiite slum in Baghdad, because his father, a genuine Ayatollah, was revered. His father was killed by the Hussein regime, America got rid of Hussein and made it possible for the first time in Iraqi history for the Shiites to gain political dominance. One would have thought that on that basis Sadr would have been strongly pro-American.

It took nearly eight months to form a government after the parliamentary elections. In November 2010 Maliki and Allawi, with prodding from the United States, reached a power sharing agreement which promptly fell apart. Power sharing and national unity are part of the American mythology concerning the Arab world.

Maliki remained prime minister. The two agencies in charge of security (Interior and Defense) were without permanent leaders for close to two years. Allawi and Maliki could not agree on the appointments, so Maliki appointed himself to head both. Maliki was very adept at consolidating power and appointing his Shiite supporters to key posts. The former Sunni insiders had become distant outsiders.

The first national vote in Iraqi history had taken place in 2005, and America's leaders gushed that democracy was on the horizon. There were multiple elections in 2005, including a positive vote on a constitution. A combination of Shiite religious parties was the victor in the December 2005 election gaining 128 seats compared to 44 for Sunni candidates. Most Sunnis boycotted this election believing the vote was rigged in favor of the Shiite candidates. Boycotting elections, elected officials boycotting parliament, stalemates, and paralysis became everyday staples of Iraqi political life.

The victorious United Iraqi Alliance fell apart after the 2005 election. The government was paralyzed for several months since the factions could not agree on a prime minister. Finally in May 2006 Maliki emerged as the leader. By this time the civil war was in full flower.

Maliki remained as prime minister and sought a third term in 2014. Arab strongmen do not retire. But by 2014, both America and the Iraqi establishment had soured on Maliki's method of governance – a method which favored Shiite cronies irrespective of competence. That's how Saddam governed, and it is traditional. Give power to those from your tribe, your sect, your hometown.

By September 2014, Iraq had a new prime minister, a Shiite named Haider al Abadi. Abadi seemed sincere and competent; Obama backed him strongly but the government was as ineffective as ever. During the summer of 2015, there were massive protests against corruption and nepotism. During the spring of 2016, Parliament faced walkouts and sit-ins during anti-government protests.

Now I turn to the most significant protests of all which began in October 2019. These were anti-Iran protests.

MOKTADA AL-SADR REINVENTS HIMSELF

Like many American politicians, Sadr reinvented himself. He became a "nationalist," presenting himself as a unifier. He strongly opposed the power of the Iran-backed militias. He wanted to disband the militias and turn their weapons over to the national army. Would he be willing to do that with his own Mahdi Army? He was opposed to Iran's influence even though he had spent years studying in Iran hoping to become an Ayatollah. When his army was killing Americans, Iran supplied it with weapons.

Parliamentary elections were held in October 2021. To America's amazement, Sadr's bloc came in first, winning the most seats – 73! Sadr wanted to stamp out corruption, and wanted to end the sectarian system where the prime minister had to be Shiite, the President Kurd, and the Speaker of the Parliament Sunni. He wanted a cabinet of technocrats rather than one devoted to sectarian alliances. Some of his proposed reforms were actually quite positive. Sadr remained adamant about wanting American troops to leave.

In spite of coming in first Sadr, was unable to form a governing coalition. The Iran-backed parties were strongly opposed to him. The alliance of parties that came in second were pro-Iran and anti-American.

During the summer of 2022, Sadr's followers occupied the parliamentary grounds for over a month, preventing the parliament from functioning. By the end of August, Sadr was so disgusted he talked of retiring from politics.

A new government was not formed until October 2022 – a full year after the election. That is the history of Iraqi elections. Because of bickering and violence and the unwillingness to compromise, it often took months to agree on a prime minister and a governing coalition.

Mohammed Sudani became prime minister at the end of October 2022. The Iranians were happy with him; he had been a member of Maliki's Dawa party. Parties controlled by Iran dominated several ministries.

So after the sacrifices and bravery of the protestors, Iraq going into 2023 remained a country in which Iran was still in charge. And after America's 20 years of sacrifices and bravery our "ally" was controlled by our arch enemy.

Millions had begun to realize that they were actually governed by Iran and the Iranian-backed Shiite militias. Shiites were demonstrating against a Shiite government and the Shiite nation of Iran.

Unheard of – the protesters torched the Iranian consulates in the holy Shiite cities of Karbala and Najaf. Several million Iranian pilgrims worship in Najaf every year. The protestors did the same to Iran's consulate in Basra. They torched the headquarters of the Badr organization, a political party with its own militia closely allied with Iran, and destroyed portraits of Iran's supreme leader – Ayatollah Khamenei.

The protestors demanded the resignation of the entire government. Coupled with that political earthquake, there were the usual demands to end corruption, provide jobs and basic services such as reliable electricity and clean water. The bravery of the protestors was remarkable. They were representative of the broad spectrum of Iraqi society –

educated, urban, rural, poor, and middle class. These were countrywide demonstrations.

The head of the Quds force of the Islamic Revolutionary Guard Corps, General Qassim Soleimani, was called upon to deal with the protests. According to the United Nations Special Envoy to Iraq, over 500 protestors were killed, over 19,000 wounded during the first 5 months of protests. The killing was done by the Iranian-backed militias. Yes, Shiite Muslims killing Shiite Muslims. The militias are the most powerful military and political force in Iraq.

The leaders of the militias, comprising about 125,000 members, are untouchable. The Iraqi government pays their salaries and our government rationalizes this lunacy. Several Iraqi military bases are controlled by the Iranian militias. Protest leaders are hunted down, and activists are murdered. To a certain extent, the militias have become part of the Iraqi military and security forces, but they take their orders from Iran. In a normal country that would be intolerable.

Prime Minister Abadi had this to say about the militias – "No one can control them. It is a very dangerous cocktail of militias and mafia."

I repeat –it is extraordinary how much power non-Arab Iran has acquired in Arab countries. Not only Iraq but also Syria, Lebanon through Hezbollah, and Yemen.

While the protests were continuing, Iran's No. 1 militia, Kataib Hezbollah, was firing rockets at Iraqi bases where American troops were housed. On December 27, 2019, one of their rockets killed an American contractor and wounded several other Americans. Trump retaliated, killing some 25 members of Kataib Hezbollah.

The continuing rocket attacks and the protests influenced Trump to order a drone strike that killed Soleimani at the airport in Baghdad on January 3, 2020. Killed alongside him was the deputy leader of the Popular Mobilization Forces – the umbrella organization for all the Shiite militias.

The protestors who had directed their anger at Iran switched to attacking America. This made no sense since Soleimani was a hated figure in Iraq, being responsible for many deaths.

There was a January 5, 2020 parliamentary vote to expel all American troops. Sadr was totally in favor of this move. If America left, ISIS would gain control of the country, as they came close to doing in 2014 when they conquered Mosul. It was the dominance of ISIS which brought back American troops. Secretary of State Pompeo said that our troops were not leaving, that – "We are going to continue the mission against ISIS."

Believe it or not, some Americans demonstrated against the killing of Soleimani – a man who had the blood of hundreds of young American soldiers on his hands, a man whose life was devoted to attacking Americans, a man who led and reveled in chants of – "Death to America."

No American demonstrations against two disastrous 20-year wars in Iraq and Afghanistan, sacrificing the lives of so many Americans for unobtainable goals; but yes, demonstrations against the killing of a mass murderer, beloved in a country whose leadership despises America.

Iran directly lobbed missiles at Iraqi bases housing Americans in response to the killing of Soleimani. He was so revered that during his funeral Khamenei was seen to be crying.

PRIME MINISTER ABADI VISITS OBAMA

Abadi met with President Obama in April 2015, with Obama calling him "a strong partner." While in the United States, Abadi had meetings with the World Bank, the Export-Import Bank of the United States, and the International Monetary Fund. Iraq still needed handouts in addition to America's billions.

In February 2018, there was a fundraising conference in Kuwait attended by some 40 foreign ministers including our then Secretary of State Rex Tillerson. The Iraqi government said that it would take $88 billion to rebuild their country.

Amazingly (to me), our military was strongly in favor of continuing to send billions to Iraq. A group of 151 retired senior military commanders including former chiefs of the Army, Navy, Marines, Special Operations, and Air Force sent a letter to congressional leaders saying that cuts to aid programs would threaten the gains made against ISIS. This level of groupthink at this high level of supposed expertise is scary.

As America made a 20-year-plus commitment to dysfunctional, corrupt and unappreciative Afghanistan, we have done the same for dysfunctional, corrupt and unappreciative Iraq.

By early 2012, the United States had spent approximately $60 billion on reconstruction, and we were voluntarily committing ourselves to spend many billions more in the years to come. And remember – this self-imposed commitment all began because the American people were told that Iraq had weapons of mass destruction.

We have built and continue to build schools, hospitals, roads, bridges, police stations, and water purification plants. In July 2011, the Inspector General appointed by Congress to oversee reconstruction said that corruption was continuing unabated.

When our troops left Iraqi cities, the people celebrated that as a day of liberation. The Obama administration was willing to allow a contingent of troops to remain in Iraq after the deadline for withdrawal if they would be granted immunity from Iraqi law – the usual arrangement when foreign troops are needed to protect the host country. Iraq refused!

In spite of America's billions, electricity remains heavily rationed. It is an everyday occurrence for millions of Iraqis that when they turn on a light switch or an air conditioner – nothing happens. Sometimes the wait is hours, at other times it may be for days. 40% of the population lacks access to safe drinking water.

Maliki said in April 2009 - "Today we face a new wave of subversion, sedition and suspicion." Yet in spite of that reality and the poor quality of Iraqi security forces Maliki, infected with the Arab strongman virus of pride and arrogance, encouraged all American troops to leave at the end of 2011.

WHY DID AMERICA FAIL SO MISERABLY IN IRAQ?

Perhaps the worst mistake in our Iraqi misadventure was made in 2003 with the decision to disband the Iraqi military. The timing of this decision and the lack of thought and debate about it is astonishing. It appeared to have been made by L. Paul Bremer III – a man that Americans knew nothing about.

Bremer had retired from the State Department after 23 years. He had been our ambassador to the Netherlands. After Bremer's retirement he became managing director at Kissinger Associates (global consulting). Yes, that Kissinger! Bremer became the senior civilian official in Iraq as head of the Coalition Provisional Authority in 2003 and 2004. Retired Lieutenant General Jay Garner had briefly been our first administrator in Iraq. The public had no understanding of why Garner or Bremer had been selected or why they left.

The United States invaded Iraq on March 20, 2003; Baghdad was conquered April 9; President Bush announced on May 1 that America was basically victorious. By May 23, the decision was made to disband the army, putting over 300,000 angry soldiers on the street with no jobs, with nothing to do, and possessing few marketable skills other than knowing how to kill. Well, the Sunni commanders found something to do. Many joined Al Qaeda; later many joined ISIS.

President Bush gave his full support to Bremer's decision. Secretary of State Colin Powell (a former chairman of the Joint Chiefs of Staff) says he was never asked for his advice. Right – the man who spent his life in the military, an expert on armies and warfare was not asked for his input. National Security Advisor Condoleezza Rice was taken by surprise by the decision, but knowing it had the backing of Bush she did not seek to reverse it. No, Secretaries Powell and Rice there is a time for obedience and there is a time to tell any President that he is making a crazy decision, one that will cost American lives.

Lieutenant General David McKiernan, field commander of the coalition troops, was out of the loop as well, and disagreed with the decision. Making matters even worse was the fact that in the pre-invasion discussions, a tentative plan relied on the Iraqi military to help secure and protect the country and to play a major role in reconstruction. Bremer was very firm in saying that the decision was not his alone. "The decision was thoroughly considered by top officials in the American government."

Was our understanding of the Muslim Arab Iraqi psyche so poor that no one predicted a Sunni insurgency after the fall of Saddam and the emergence of a Shiite power structure?

This is not Monday-morning quarterbacking – rather it is the exercise of common sense when attempting to predict actions in an Arab nation. The Sunni minority had controlled Iraq since the founding of the state after World War I. For all of Saddam's reign, the Shiites had been discriminated against; when the Shiites arose in 1991 to overthrow him, he crushed them. Did it not occur to the American policymakers that the Shiites would seek revenge? Or that the Sunnis, who were always on top, would not quietly adjust to being on the bottom?

Bremer made a startling admission – "we did not have a plan to provide the most basic function of any government – security to the population."

We disbanded the most cohesive component of Iraqi society. An army where Shiites and Sunnis fought side by side. Shiite Iraqis fought for Iraq against Shiite Iran during their disastrous eight-year war in the 1980s. For decades in many neighborhoods, Sunnis, Shiites and Christians lived together peacefully. In another awful decision by the Bush administration, Baath Party members were eliminated from all positions of power.

They were kicked out of the government ministries which ran the nuts and bolts of the country's infrastructure. Many Baathists were simply civil servants, technocrats and administrators. Many Iraqis joined the Baath party even though they may have hated Saddam Hussein. It was difficult to achieve success in any field absent such membership. By late June 2004, Bremer was gone from Iraq and the Coalition Provisional Authority ceased to exist.

On August 21, 2022, Bremer wrote an article which appeared in the Wall Street Journal. Nearly 20 years later, he does not deal with the terrible decisions relating to the Iraqi Army and the Baath Party. Rather, he spouts the same crap that got us involved in a 20-year war in the first place.

"Iraqi forces have the ability to secure their nation's borders, domestic peace and democratic institutions."

The Iraqi forces were defeated by ISIS which took over a third of their country.

Bremer doubles down on the fantasy of Iraq becoming a democratic country –

"Iraq is on course to becoming a self-reliant democratic state. The Taliban triumph in Afghanistan makes the victory of democracy in Iraq all the more important."

20 years is not enough for Bremer – He says that our troops must stay indefinitely. Madness!

A CATALOGUE OF AMERICAN MISJUDGMENTS

1. The foundation for all the other failures was the fact that Iraq did not possess weapons of mass destruction.
2. Our failure to get rid of Saddam Hussein after our military victory in the first Gulf War in February 1991.
3. Bringing a half-million Americans to the Middle East to fight a four-day ground war.
4. Leaving our embassies open and staffed so Saddam could imprison 163 American hostages 11 years after Iran humiliated us by imprisoning over 50 Americans for 444 days.
5. Failure to assist the Shiites and Kurds when they revolted to overthrow Hussein in March 1991. Allowing Iraq to retain helicopter gunships so that Saddam could more easily crush the rebellion.
6. Believing the myth that by continuing to spend billions of dollars we could create a democracy in a country which had never experienced democracy.
7. Once we got rid of Saddam (12 years too late) and verified that there were no weapons of mass destruction, America should have left Iraq.
8. Backing prime minister Maliki and not insisting that he have a unity government that was inclusive and fair to the Sunnis.

Lt. General Daniel Bolger was a senior commander in both Iraq and Afghanistan. After his retirement Bolger was able to say – "The surge in Iraq did not win anything. It bought time."

In 2007, America and its allies had some 165,000 troops in Iraq at 500 bases and outposts. That number is astounding – we were fighting factions of terrorists which did not have an air force or a navy or weapons of mass destruction – and we were unable to defeat them.

Between 2003 and 2010 America spent between $750 billion and $1.1 trillion on our own military, on Iraq's military and on civilian infrastructure. In spite of these sacrifices Iraqi gratitude was in very short supply. Obama's Ambassador to Iraq, James Jeffrey, said in May 2016 – "United States influence (in Iraq) is not very big. It hasn't been big for a long time."

A United Nations report detailed the fact that between January 2014 through October 2015 the Iraqi people had suffered 19,000 deaths plus 40,000 wounded (many of whom died later) with nearly three million civilians being displaced from their homes.

By the summer of 2016 some 4,500 brave American military volunteers had been killed in Iraq. 32,000 more had been wounded. Overall about 150,000 Iraqis had lost their lives, mostly civilians. None of these tragedies would have occurred but for the fiction of weapons of mass destruction plus the myth of a democracy-spreading agenda.

Maliki went to Washington to meet President Obama on November 1, 2013. Yes, the same Maliki who had kicked America out in 2011, the same Maliki who is Iran's best friend, the same Maliki who mistreated the Sunnis causing thousands of them to join ISIS. In spite of all this, he has been praised by President Obama as "the elected leader of a sovereign, self-reliant and democratic Iraq." I repeat – Trump did not invent presidential lying.

Of course, Maliki came to the White House with a shopping list. He wanted F-16 fighter jets, helicopter gunships, missiles, reconnaissance drones, and American intelligence. Iraq hired a Washington, D.C. lobbying firm (the Podesta Group) to rewrite history. Maliki wrote an article which appeared in the New York Times on October 30, 2013 saying –

"Al Qaeda in Iraq and its affiliates are conducting a ruthless terror campaign... – Iraq doesn't have a single fighter jet ... no Air Force or air defenses to speak of."

Yet he kicked America out over the immunity issue.

And then there is a very "nice, nice" statement – the kind of language the administration uses to camouflage defeat – Maliki said –

"Iraq is on the road to security, democracy and prosperity. While we still have a long way to go, we want to walk that road together with the United States." Sadly, Iraq was on the road to none of those things.

ISLAMIC STATE (ISIS) AND THEIR DREAM OF AN ISLAMIC CALIPHATE

ISIS took control of Mosul, Iraq's second largest city, with a population of 1.3 million, in June 2014. They gained control over Ramadi, Sinjar, Tikrit – overall about one third of the country. How could that happen considering that the Iraqi security forces numbered about 330,000? In the battle for Mosul, the Iraqi army simply melted away, refusing to engage the enemy. Many of the retreats were led by the commanders, the supposed leaders.

The Iraqi military does have some elite components, counter terrorist commandos, special forces, who are willing to fight and are effective, but they represent a small minority.

Yes, the Iraqi Army upon which the United States lavished multiple billions of dollars and thousands of hours advising, training and equipping, simply melted away. ISIS became the government in Mosul providing many of the services usually provided by civilian municipal workers.

Many ordinary Iraqis turned to ISIS because in many ways they were more efficient than the government.

It was at one of the most famous mosques in all of Iraq, the Al Nuri Grand Mosque, where Abu Bakr Al Baghdadi declared himself to be the caliph of a new Islamic Empire stretching across Iraq and Syria. The city of Raqqa was ISIS headquarters in Syria.

The declaration of an Islamic Caliphate was a great recruitment tool because that was the goal of all the terrorist organizations. Thousands of foreigners, many from western European countries, rushed to join ISIS and were willing to die for that mirage. And they were even more willing to kill.

To the American-backed government of Iraq, losing Mosul was a profound humiliation. There were endless meetings over many months as to how to retake the city. In an attempt to get things moving, Vice President Biden, Secretary of State Kerry and Defense Secretary Carter visited Iraq in April 2016. When ISIS began making its inroads, the United States military had been invited back and Obama complied, although with a limited number of troops.

Finally, the United States and the Iraqi government agreed on a strategy, and the operation began on October 17, 2016. A huge force was amassed of some 100,000 troops – the Iraqi Army, the Iraqi police, multiple Shiite militias, Kurdish fighters and, of course, heavy involvement by the Americans – mainly special operations forces. Remember that Obama had promised that America's combat role ended at the end of 2011. Ironically, the Iran-backed militias were our allies in the effort to defeat ISIS. And they were effective.

Considering that ISIS had about 5,000 fighters in Mosul in October 2016, the war should have been over quickly. It wasn't – getting ISIS out of Mosul took several months resulting in hundreds of allied deaths. Our forces were also able to remove ISIS from the other cities it had conquered. Consider the weaponry that each side possessed.

ISIS doesn't have a single fighter jet or a single destroyer. What it did have were factories for car bombs and truck bombs, roadside bombs and suicide vests. Skilled snipers – landmines – booby traps – improvised explosive devices – rockets and mortars. They have drones capable of unleashing bombs, plus a rocket-propelled grenade system. ISIS had a network of tunnels which enabled them to hide and dodge many bombs, missiles and drones. The best weaponry that ISIS had was American made – stolen from Iraqi military bases.

On the other side of the ledger – there was a coalition of over 30 countries against ISIS. The American side had rockets, armed drones, hellfire missiles, Apache attack helicopters, tanks, armor-plated bulldozers and Humvees. Our Apache helicopters are able to sight targets miles away with sensors, and hit them with guided missiles. American airstrikes were hitting ISIS targets using F-15, F-16 fighter jets and B52s.

The United States has given the Iraqi military F-16s as well as attack helicopters. We have trained their pilots, we have supplied them with armored Humvees, tanks, howitzers, artillery, armored bulldozers and mine clearing equipment. Yet ISIS had been able to take over one third of the country.

The destruction America caused to the once proud city of Mosul was enormous. Mosul had a distinguished university; it had a top of the line, 5-star international hotel. It had five magnificent bridges which linked the eastern and western parts of the city across the Tigris River. American airstrikes destroyed all the bridges.

The inevitable American miscalculation caused tragedy on March 17, 2017, when our airstrike collapsed a building in west Mosul causing hundreds of civilian deaths.

Both our Defense Department and State Department utilized the services of thousands of contractors to perform duties which in years past had been performed by military personnel. The American public was for the most part ignorant of both the numbers and duties of this shadow army, and would have been amazed that the defense department at one time had some 55,000 contractors on its payroll.

This army was not regulated or overseen carefully. It does not have a chain of command or an adherence to discipline, as does the regular army. Many of the members were previously in the Special Operations Forces, and they are both brave and competent. Other members are soldiers of fortune, men looking for adventure and the relatively lucrative compensation. These private contractors protect our diplomats, they work alongside CIA operatives in counter terrorism operations, they guard military bases, transport ammunition, fuel, and food.

Blackwater was the most powerful of the security contractors; it had at one time a $1 billion contract with the U.S. government. An incident occurred in Baghdad in 2007 when Blackwater guards using machine guns and grenades fired upon unarmed Iraqi civilians. It is unclear why one or more of the guards perceived that they were in danger; they were not. Ten women, two men and two children were killed.

Add to this another tragic chapter when United States Marines for no valid reason killed 24 Iraqi civilians at Haditha. Then there was American abuse of prisoners at Abu Ghraib Prison which received front page publicity for months. And we wonder why Iraqis were happy to see us leave!

It is to be remembered that when American troops (not all) left Iraq in 2011 and left Afghanistan (not all) in 2014, the vast majority of both populations were happy to see us leave.

Nearly a million residents of Mosul had been displaced, forced to leave their homes, to be housed in one of 68 refugee camps. Several thousand Iraqi civilians had died in the nearly 10-month battle to oust ISIS. Defense Secretary Mattis said in July 2017 that 1,200 Iraqi forces had been killed, plus 6,000 wounded.

The terrorists can easily blend into local populations to regroup. They have plenty of sleeper cells which they can count on. The director of the National Counterterrorism Center said in May 2017 – "The global reach of ISIS is largely intact."

ISIS has confirmed the truth of that statement by carrying out attacks in many other countries. The Combatting Terrorism Center at West Point issued a statement about the extraordinary reach of ISIS. That ISIS had carried out nearly 1,500 separate attacks in 16 cities across Iraq and Syria after those countries had succeeded in displacing ISIS from vast territories that it had once controlled.

How is it possible to recruit thousands to murder unarmed men, women and children – fellow Arab Muslims? In November 2018, there came a joint report of the United Nations mission to Iraq and the office of The High Commissioner for Human Rights which said that in areas once controlled by ISIS, there were discovered over 200 mass graves holding as many as 12,000 human beings including many children. I can't repeat often enough that ISIS did not exist on 9/11! That's what Bush and Obama's War Against Terror wrought.

On June 20, 2017, ISIS murdered over 1,000 Shiite Air Force cadets. In 2014, ISIS killed 1,700 Shiite recruits at an Iraqi air base. Also in 2014, ISIS killed thousands of Yazidis in the city of Sinjar. In July 2016, one of their truck bombs killed over 320 civilians in Baghdad.

Just contemplate those numbers. How could Iraq's defenses be so porous as to allow so many young military hopefuls to be slaughtered? The answer is the same in both Iraq and Afghanistan – the terrorists infiltrate and have sympathizers in the military and security services, and they are tipped off about holes in the security apparatus.

Our ambassador to Iraq, James Jeffrey, 2010-2012, said –

"Under Iran's influence, Syria and Iraq so oppressed their Sunni populations that they turned to ISIS."

Yes, our guy Maliki, who was in control for 8 years, was in large measure responsible for the rise of ISIS! Politically, even as late as 2023, Maliki remained a major power broker.

In my chapter on Afghanistan, I point out how active ISIS had been in that country, killing thousands. And how active they continued to be even after we killed their leader – Baghdadi.

THE KURDS

Guilt-ridden over our refusal to assist the Kurds in their attempt to overthrow Saddam in 1991, America established a no-fly zone over a Kurdish region in northern Iraq. This protection allowed the Kurds to flourish. Saddam had spewed forth poisonous gas on the city of Halabja in 1988, causing horrifically painful deaths to some 5,000 civilians – men, women and children. There was something called the Anfal campaign during the 1980s which killed well over 50,000 Kurds. Knowing this, the United States allowed Saddam to dominate for 12 more years.

Spread out over Iraq, Iran, Syria, and Turkey, over 30 million Kurds are still pining away for independence or at least meaningful autonomy. The Kurdish Regional Government in Iraq is the closest thing the Kurds have ever had to independence. Kurdistan is a de facto state with all the normal indicia of statehood – a president, a prime minister, parliament, judiciary, and civil service. America has a military base in the capital of Erbil.

The Kurds were successful in capturing from ISIS many villages on the outskirts of Mosul which allowed roads to open up so that Iraqi counter-terrorism forces could enter the city. The Kurds are great fighters. Absent the contribution of the Kurds, it is doubtful that ISIS would have been defeated in Mosul. The Kurds were able to control many areas that had not been part of their autonomous region.

In Syria, the Kurds were likewise America's strongest ally in defeating ISIS. One of the worst things that Trump ever did was to abandon the Kurds leaving them to be attacked by Turkey. Turkey and its leader, Erdogan, were always opposed to a Kurdish independence movement.

It is to be noted that the Kurds were on America's side in 1991 during the Gulf War and in 2003 when we invaded Iraq for the second time. While it is true that some Kurds the (PKK) have engaged in terror (primarily against Turkey) they have never engaged in terror against the United States or Western targets. Yet the United States has never advocated for Kurdish independence – the opposite of our attitude toward the Palestinians – which demonstrates the power of lobbying, public relations, media bias, and terrorism.

The issue which brought to a head the conflict between the Iraqi government and the Iraqi Kurds was the decision by Kurdish President Masoud Barzani to hold a referendum on independence September 25, 2017. Every nation that expressed an opinion was opposed to the idea of holding a referendum (with the exception of Israel). America was strongly opposed; our state department called the referendum "provocative and destabilizing." A hell of a way to treat a faithful ally. Particularly in view of the fact that America almost always favors independence movements.

The referendum was approved by over 90% of the voters. Independence referendums almost always pass overwhelmingly. But the victory turned out to be hollow. Iraq mobilized troops to retake those areas which the Kurds had annexed to their semi-autonomous region. The

Arabs who had fought alongside the Kurds did not want them to retain possession of the newly acquired cities and towns.

The government, with the help of Iranian militias, got back the oil-rich and critical city of Kirkuk, which the Kurds had acquired by conquering ISIS there. The Kurds defeated ISIS after ISIS had defeated the Iraqi Army in Kirkuk. The loss of that city deprived Kurdistan of nearly 70% of its oil revenues – a crushing economic blow.

President Barzani resigned after over a decade in power on October 29, 2017.

There had been other unresolved disputes between the Iraqi government and the Kurdish government. How would oil revenues be shared? What would be the legal status of oil deals that the Kurdish government had signed independently with oil companies?

There are two major political parties in the Kurdish region, and there is a strong rivalry between them. There was actually a brief civil war where Kurds were killing Kurds. The Kurdistan Democratic Party was the party of Barzani. The Patriotic Union of Kurdistan (PUK) was opposed to holding the referendum on pragmatic grounds.

Although the Sunni Kurds and Shiite militias fought on the same side to defeat ISIS, that did not stop them from killing each other during a brief encounter in April 2016. That is the tragedy of the Middle East: factions that are willing to resort to violence to prevail. Leaders whose stubbornness and arrogance prevents them from agreeing to reasonable compromises. I do not expect that tradition of governance to radically change anytime soon – maybe never!

CHAPTER 4

IRAN – AND HOW AMERICA HAS DEALT WITH THIS STATE SPONSOR OF TERRORISM

On October 7, 2023, when Hamas murdered 1200 defenseless Israelis, when they beheaded and burned babies and raped women, they also killed some Americans and took some Americans hostage. Amazingly, the Biden administration and the American people were not outraged. This is what President Biden should have said to Iran – "Your proxy, Hamas, has killed Americans and taken Americans hostage. If the Americans are not freed in 48 hours we will attack Iran with massive force. We will destroy your capacity to produce a nuclear bomb."

"We possess an array of nuclear weapons; nothing is off the table. We never avenged your murder of 241 sleeping American marines in Lebanon, as we never avenged your kidnapping of American hostages that you held captive for over 400 days. American civilians who never did your country any harm. And don't bother telling us the lie that Hamas is independent and will not follow your instructions."

Yes, let the world know that if you kill Americans or take Americans hostage there will be actual consequences instead of meaningless threats.

I am well aware that all the policymakers, the pundits and the editorial writers will severely criticize my recommendation to attack Iran. They will accuse me of oversimplification, they will wring their hands about escalation and a wider war.

No, I am not guilty of oversimplification. It is they who are guilty of overcomplication.

Iran's Revolutionary Guard Corps Quds Force is spread throughout the region, training, providing intelligence, and equipping Hamas and its other proxies with drones, rockets, and missiles. Its other proxies include Hezbollah in Lebanon, the Houthis in Yemen, and its militias in Iraq.

I am convinced that if the United States did attack Iran, the regime would collapse. Not immediately but over time. There are millions of secular Iranians who hate the regime, there are millions of Iranian women who hate the mandatory requirement of having to wear the hijab – the garment which covers them from head to toe.

The best evidence for this dissatisfaction is the parliamentary elections that were held on March 1, 2024. Millions boycotted the election. The former president, Mohammad Khatami, the founder of the Reform Movement, refused to vote.

Only 41% of eligible voters cast ballots in spite of the regime stressing the importance of voting. That was the lowest turnout since their Islamic Revolution 45 years ago. In the capital, Tehran, the turnout was only 25%.

Reformists were banned from running for office. These were mass disqualifications by the twelve-member Guardian Council that has the responsibility of vetting candidates. All the winners were approved by the regime, all ultra-conservatives.

There have been periodic protests against the regime, always ruthlessly suppressed. The supreme leader is the supreme power. Ayatollah Khamenei has held that position for 36 years.

There were huge protests in Iran 2022 and 2023 over the death of a young woman while in police custody – Mahsa Amini. Her crime – wearing her hijab incorrectly. Perhaps her elbow was visible. A United Nations fact finding commission concluded that 551 Iranians were killed by the security forces, including many women and children. Killed during peaceful protests. I guarantee you that relatives of the 551 would love to see an American invasion.

Iran's most serious internal enemy is ISIS, which in January 2024 unleashed a suicide bomber who killed over 100 Iranians. Muslims killing Muslims. Terror begets more terror.

The earlier protests never brought about real change. When so-called "reformists" led the government, real improvement did not occur. There are reformers in the trade unions and in various student associations. Many reformers actually seek engagement with the West. They do not see the United States as "The Great Satan."

They are not happy with the 88-member Assembly of Experts that will select the next Supreme Leader – another arch conservative.

Other reasons for unhappiness with the status quo: a declining standard of living, poor economic growth, unemployment, corruption, mismanagement of the economy and nepotism. An American invasion would energize the dissenters.

THE OBAMA/KERRY DEAL

After many months of Secretary of State John Kerry negotiating for a deal and begging, President Obama hailed the final pact as a great foreign policy achievement. The public seemed to agree.

Iran got something very concrete from us – the release of $100 billion in frozen assets and our abandonment of most sanctions. What we got in return was an empty promise, which was a lie: that Iran would not seek to develop a nuclear bomb.

Trump called it the worst deal ever, and as president he abandoned it. He reinstated many sanctions. Iran had developed, along with allies, a sanctions evasion network which included secret subsidiaries.

Iran blocked inspections of military sites. They were enhancing their uranium enrichment program at their underground Fordow nuclear site. Why underground? To hide from the naïve Americans that they were violating the terms of the deal.

The deal placed no restrictions on Iran's ability to develop ballistic missiles. General Kenneth McKenzie who had been the head of U.S. Central Command said –

"They have over 3,000 ballistic missiles of various types. Their missiles have significantly greater range and enhanced accuracy."

They are precision guided and would be capable of carrying nuclear war heads. Great job Obama and Kerry. These are the same missiles used by the Iranian militias in Iraq to attack American soldiers.

Hard to believe but Biden was worse. He begged and begged to get Iran to reinstate the Obama deal. But arrogant Iran kept saying – "NO!" They refused to even discuss missiles, drones or their proxies. In November 2023, our State Department reissued a sanctions waiver that gave Iran access to over $10 billion. This is the country that blew up 241 young, healthy, brave Marines. This is the country that even we recognize as the world's largest state sponsor of terrorism.

Our nation cannot allow a regime like Iran to possess nuclear weapons. They would be perfectly capable of using them. We dawdled with North Korea for decades, and now they have a huge arsenal of such weapons. Their leader would be perfectly capable of unleashing them, and some already can reach our shores.

I am convinced that Iran may actually possess the bomb or could bring it to fruition in a couple of months. Blinken repeats the usual assurance –

"The United States does not seek conflict with Iran."

So Iran knows, as they march toward their ultimate goal, that America will do nothing to stop them.

A significant footnote. The Obama/Kerry deal was not presented as a treaty which would require Senate ratification. The agreement got a different label, which enabled it to bypass Congress. Clever lawyers worked that out and nobody in Congress made a fuss.

As Biden was pleading with Iran, their militias in Iraq were attacking American bases both in Iraq and Syria. During the several months preceding February 2024, there had been over 165 attacks by Iran-backed militias against our troops. Attacks using rockets, missiles, drones and mortars. When we responded and struck the militias, Iraq complained that we were violating their precious sovereignty.

The only reason that Iraq has any semblance of sovereignty is because we defeated ISIS which had taken over one third of their country. If our residual force of about 2,500 were to leave Iraq, ISIS would likely make a comeback.

When President Obama pulled out over 95% of our combat troops at the end of 2011 he said –

"We're leaving behind a sovereign, stable, self-reliant Iraq."

He could not possibly have believed that!

Iran, its militias, and the political parties linked to it dominate Iraq. Iraq which engaged in long months of protests (unsuccessful) against Iranian control is anything but sovereign.

Prime Minister Abadi said –

"No one can control Iran's militias. It is a very dangerous cocktail of militias and mafia."

Long-time former Prime Minister Maliki said in April 2009 –

"Today we face a new wave of subversion, sedition, and suspicion."

A finance minister, Ali Allawi, resigned with this going away blast –

"Vast undergrounds of networks of senior officials, corrupt businessmen and politicians that dominate entire sectors of the economy and siphon off billions of dollars from the public purse."

No Mr. Obama – this is not a "sovereign, stable, self-reliant" country.

Our twenty- plus-year misadventure in Iraq has resulted in control by our arch enemy – Iran.

On January 28, 2024, a Kataib Hezbollah drone hit a remote military outpost in Jordan, killing three and wounding over forty, many with traumatic brain injuries. Two of those killed were young female soldiers. A proud strike by one of Iran's most prominent militias.

Way less than 1% of Americans had any idea that we have troops in Jordan. They, like our troops in Iraq and Syria, are there to fight ISIS. Yes ISIS, which did not exist on 9/11.

So a quarter of a century after 9/11, we are still engaged in Bush's "Global War Against Terrorism." A war that he thought would bring democracy to Iraq and Afghanistan.

Another Iranian proxy, the Houthis of Yemen, have for months fired missiles, drones and rockets at ships traversing the Red Sea – navy vessels and commercial shipping. Hundreds of ships avoid the Suez Canal causing them to go an extra 4,000 miles around southern Africa. The canal lies at the northwest end of the Red Sea.

The United States has attacked Houthi targets numerous times but they persist. Iran is behind all these disasters, and America continues to guarantee their security.

CHAPTER 5

THE PHENOMENON OF DONALD TRUMP

THE 2016 PRESIDENTIAL ELECTION

How would any American answer this question? "Do you think that a 70-year-old man could be elected president even though he had never held any political office, had never served in the military, was married three times with two of his wives being foreigners – and had a reputation of being a braggart, a business schemer and a serial adulterer? And how about a candidate who insulted all his opponents and refused to release his tax returns?" The answer would be "no way!"

Hillary Clinton often held the title of the most admired woman in America. She was a very involved first lady to a two-term president, she had been a United States Senator from New York, she was Secretary of State for four years. Her name recognition was universal. How does this woman lose to Trump? Well she lost to Obama eight years earlier, a man unknown to the public-at-large until he gave a very well received speech at the Democratic Convention which nominated John Kerry for president.

Yes, somehow, she lost to a community organizer from Chicago, a first term senator, a glib quick-witted speaker who had a very meager record of accomplishments and zero experience in foreign affairs.

Obama gave Hillary the consolation prize of Secretary of State. In that position Hillary used a private e-mail server which violated State Department rules. That's all Trump needed to crown her with the tag – "Crooked Hillary" – and to energize his crowds to scream – "Lock Her Up." Absent that terrible decision she would have become president.

How could she leave herself vulnerable to an FBI investigation? The server issue was an everyday staple in the media, as were the thousands of emails she deleted. She talked a good game about transparency but what she really valued was secrecy.

She had to endure months of agony waiting for the FBI investigation to be concluded.

Hillary said – "I never sent or received anything that was marked classified." FBI director, James Comey, called her a liar without directly calling her a liar. He cited over 100 classified emails, 36 of which were marked as top secret.

The use of her private server (actually she used multiple private servers) was exposed in March 2015. On July 10, 2015, the FBI opened a formal investigation after receiving a referral from two inspector generals who asserted that – "hundreds of potentially classified emails" – were discovered on her personal server. Comey did not conclude his investigation until July 5, 2016. So for a year, the server issue was front and center. Comey said that Mrs. Clinton was – "extremely careless in her handling of very sensitive highly classified information."

Comey was not recommending criminal charges. Why was Comey in charge of the investigation rather than his boss – Attorney General Loretta Lynch? She was very close to the Clintons and would have protected Hillary. She most certainly would not have conducted a one-year investigation.

She was out of the picture because she and Bill Clinton did something incredibly stupid. As fate would have it, they were at the same airport at the same time but on different flights. When Bill heard that Loretta was there, being one of the all-time schmoozers, he decided to pay her a social call. This was the self-inflicted wound which Bill added to his wife's self-inflicted wound.

Because of inevitable suspicion about the meeting, Lynch recused herself from the investigation and left the final verdict to her subordinate, Comey. She did not have to recuse herself. The criticism would have faded with her and Bill insisting they never discussed anything political, that it was merely a quick social call.

Hillary despises Comey and attributes her defeat in large part to him. Even worse than his "extremely careless" conclusion is what Comey did on October 28, 2016 (days before the election). Comey told Congress that the FBI had new evidence to review and that the investigation was being reopened.

What was the new evidence? A trove of emails on the server of Hillary's closest aide and vice chair of her campaign, Huma Abedin, who happened to be married to Anthony Wiener. Wiener had sent pictures of his crotch to underage girls – a stunt which landed him in prison. Wiener had served in Congress; he was young and many thought he had a bright political future in front of him. A couple of days before the election (Hillary vs. Trump), Comey said the new emails did not change his initial judgment. The irony of all this is that Comey was a Trump-hater, yet his investigation was gold for the Trump campaign. In addition to the private server problem, Hillary had another huge problem – Senator Bernie Sanders, her primary opponent.

She could not focus on Trump because she was battling Sanders in primary after primary. He actually beat her in 21 states including Michigan, Minnesota, Wisconsin, Indiana, Colorado and West Virginia. Sanders an elderly Jewish socialist from a sparsely populated state (Vermont), became very popular with college students. He drew large, enthusiastic crowds who loved his pitch against Wall Street, the super-wealthy, and the tax cheats who hid their wealth in offshore shell companies.

Sanders made one of the dumbest comments in the history of presidential debates when he said that he was sick and tired of hearing about Hillary's private email server. He thought that taking the high road would make him look presidential. Trump took the low road and won.

Sanders should have pounded relentlessly on the email scandal and the myriad conflicts of the Clinton Foundation. Both of those vulnerabilities showed the true character of Hillary – devious, secretive, and greedy. Their foundation, without question, did some very good things, but it was a hotbed of conflicts. Nearly every country and major company in the world had given money to the foundation. During Hillary's tenure as Secretary of State, foreign governments were donating to the foundation.

Sanders should have pounded even harder on Hillary's Wall Street speeches, particularly since his major theme was that the superrich controlled both the economy and politics. Some of the things Sanders should have said directly to Hillary during their debates – "You received $675,000 for three speeches you made to Goldman Sachs. I've heard of Wall Street lawyers charging $1,000 per hour, you got over $200,000 per hour. The Goldman Sachs people know a hell of a lot more about finances and the economy than you will ever know – you were not being paid for your expertise, they paid you for access and to do their bidding. These obscene payments are legal bribes pure and simple."

"And it is outrageous that you have refused to release the transcripts of your speeches. I'm sure you made it very clear to Goldman Sachs and other investment banks and private equity firms that they would have a friend in the White House. Trump refuses to release his tax returns and you refuse to release the contents of your speeches."

Sanders could have talked about the $11 million she was paid in 2014 and the first quarter of 2015 for 51 speeches mainly to investment banks, hedge funds and other heavyweights in the world of finance. Hillary's husband gave 104 speeches for which he was paid $25 million in the 16 months before the start of her campaign. Between the two of them, they took home approximately $125 million since leaving the White House in 2000. Why do they need all that money and adulation? How boring it would have to be to give the same basic speech over and over again. But applause is intoxicating to people who at bottom are very shallow.

They will talk to any group if the price is right. Examples – Hillary in a Las Vegas casino in April 2014 spoke to the Institute of Scrap Recycling Industries for a fee of $200,000. Bill was paid $260,000 speaking to the Fragrance Foundation, a trade group for the perfume industry. The former president received $700,000 for some speeches in Nigeria. Beyond embarrassing to a normal electorate.

Had Sanders won the nomination, he would have lost to Trump who would have tagged him as being an anti-capitalist socialist who spent his honeymoon in the Soviet Union. Trump would have eventually called him a "communist." Bernie's constant screaming and preaching would grow very tiresome.

In spite of all the speeches, interviews, and advertising, the public was basically in the dark about the views of the candidates on basic issues. A vivid reminder of the shallowness of our political system. This is what Robert Gates, Secretary of Defense, under both Bush and Obama, had to say on this subject.

He pointed out that – neither candidate has expressed any views on how they would deal with Putin. Neither candidate has set forth any new ideas about how to deal with the Middle East; the public knows basically zero about their views on Iran, North Korea, etc.

Gates took a dim view of Trump's experience on the Apprentice, his buildings, and golf courses. "On national security I believe Mr. Trump is beyond repair. He is unfit to be commander-in-chief." President Obama said the same thing about Trump as he was traveling on Air Force One from one location to another campaigning vigorously for Hillary. He knew that if Trump won, his precious legacy would be trashed. How did his experience as a community organizer qualify him to be commander-in-chief?

This is what Hillary should have pounded away at during every debate with Trump.

"Since 1952 every candidate for president has released his tax returns. Of course, you don't care about precedent because you are an egomaniac who thinks rules don't apply to you."

"I know why you will not release your returns. You are very proud of your cleverness in avoiding taxes. You live like a billionaire yet there have been years when you paid zero in taxes."

That would have hit home with the millions of Americans who have their taxes automatically withdrawn from their paychecks. "It is fine with you that firefighters, police, paramedics, construction workers pay their taxes because your strategies are unavailable to them – and you dare to present yourself as a friend of the working class."

In the last two weeks of August 2016, Hillary took in $50 million at 22 fundraisers. She was spending all of her time with the richest 1% of Americans. Construction workers, retail workers, clerks, cashiers, nurses' aides, were not attending these fundraisers.

It is impossible for any politician to pitch for money at hundreds of fundraisers and remain normal. The whole process is beyond phony – gushing over every cliché uttered by a candidate, nonstop smiling, fawning over ever insipid comment. At a single event in New York ten millionaires, perhaps billionaires, paid $250,000 to meet Hillary and have their picture taken with the next president of the United States. Beyond sick and beyond shallow!

President Obama made one of the most honest comments of his entire presidency about the corrupting nature of fundraisers – "I know that as a consequence of my fundraising I become more like the wealthy donors I meet." He proved that after he left office.

He and his wife signed multi-million-dollar book deals; in a deal with Netflix they will rake in about $50 million to produce films and documentaries. Magically, they have become producers. As the Clintons loved and admired the Hollywood crowd, so too do the Obamas.

There is a revealing footnote to Obama's political career. He did very well for himself against opponents who ran poor campaigns (John McCain and Mitt Romney) but he did horribly for his fellow Democrats. During Obama's eight years in office, over one thousand elected Democratic officials lost their jobs to Republicans. Democrats were decimated in state legislatures, and they lost many governorships. Yet both Obamas remain beloved.

THE 2020 ELECTION

As Trump watched the Democratic debates, he saw that Biden was ineffective. The public agreed. When the voting began in the primaries, Biden was embarrassed - he came in fourth in the Iowa caucuses and fifth in the New Hampshire primary. He had been a disaster in his earlier runs for the presidency when he was young and vigorous.

When Biden ran in 1987, he was engulfed in a plagiarism scandal and dropped out before the first contest. In 2007 he dropped out after getting about 1% of the vote in the Iowa caucuses. Yet his dream of becoming president remained intact. Nothing is as addictive as the quest for political power.

How did Biden get his party's nomination after his poor showing in the debates and in the early primaries? The answer is Jim Clyburn, the powerful Black representative from South Carolina. His strong endorsement allowed Biden to win South Carolina behind a huge Black vote.

Bernie Sanders had to be stopped because Clyburn and the Democratic establishment realized that this abrasive Jewish socialist had no chance of winning a national election. Sanders had a strong base of followers, but it was not large enough to bring victory in a national election.

Biden's choice for his running mate was a shocker. He selected Kamala Harris who had insulted him during a primary debate about his early stand on school busing. That exchange was her one shining moment during the debates – what seemed like a rehearsed attack. Biden's response was flat; he appeared rattled. Harris did not compete in a single primary; her poll numbers were awful. The possibility of a President Harris was a frightening prospect to many.

Several vice presidents have become president – Theodore Roosevelt, Harry Truman, Lyndon Johnson, Richard Nixon. Considering Biden's age, his choice was particularly important.

Biden had served six terms in the United States Senate. When he was 29, he ran against a Republican incumbent from Delaware and won. He kept winning in subsequent elections. Shortly after his initial victory,

Biden suffered a terrible tragedy. His wife and 13-month-old daughter were killed in an automobile accident; his two sons were severely injured but survived. One of them was named Hunter.

In the Senate, where longevity is the key to power, Biden served as Chairman of the Committee on Foreign Relations and Chairman of the Judiciary Committee. His profile was substantially raised in that position as the Clarence Thomas—Anita Hill drama unfolded.

Biden had five straight deferments from the draft during the Vietnam War. Trump could hardly make that an issue because he, like Clinton, never served in the military.

There is a famous quote from Robert Gates who served as defense secretary under both Republican and Democratic presidents – Bush and Obama. Gates said Biden had been -

"Wrong on nearly every major foreign policy and national security issue over the past four decades."

A couple of examples of Biden's poor judgment - he was against the plan to kill Bin Laden when after ten years we finally learned of his location in Pakistan.

He voted in favor of our invasion of Iraq, accepting without asking a single penetrating question as to whether Saddam Hussain really possessed weapons of mass destruction.

HAD TRUMP HANDLED THE PANDEMIC IN A NORMAL WAY, HE WOULD HAVE BEEN REELECTED

But he did not handle it in a normal way.

His predictions were absurd, saying that we might be returning to normal quickly. He always downplayed the magnitude of the pandemic even as deaths were piling up in every state. He kept referring to the scourge as "low risk," comparing it to a run-of-the-mill flu outbreak.

He never formulated a unified, national policy. Trump ridiculed the use of masks and never set a good example for social distancing.

The point that had to be stressed again and again by any normal politician was that the primary goal had to be the prevention of death. He actually could have become a sympathetic figure facing a monumental crisis which he did not cause.

He could have said –

"Yes, my fellow Americans, there are measures which can be taken to reduce the harm from this awful plague. Believe me, I will ease or even eliminate the restrictions as soon as possible consistent with safety. When this pandemic abates, we will do everything within our power to get you back to where you were at the start of 2020 when our economy was flourishing."

He held almost daily briefings that were often characterized by hostile questions leading to defensive and confused responses.

Trump could have pointed to the great scientific achievement during his administration – the development of vaccines that were effective. Operation Warp Speed was a sprint to a successful vaccine in less than a year. It can take a decade for a pharmaceutical company to develop a vaccine that conquers a disease.

Governor Cuomo of New York handled the pandemic in a normal way. His daily press briefings were praised as being informative and re-assuring. The media loved him, even Republicans praised him. There was serious talk of him becoming a future president.

Had Trump followed the Cuomo script he would have been re-elected in a landslide in 2020 against Biden. I will get to Cuomo's downfall later.

THE KILLER POLLS

Every poll at every stage of the campaign showed that Biden was ahead, often by wide margins. Karl Rove a seasoned Republican strategist who engineered Bush's two victories said on the day before the election that Trump had not led in any of 80 national polls that had been taken since Labor Day.

As he didn't believe the election results, Trump also didn't believe the polls. Could a rational person believe that 80 polls could all be wrong? He had to change his behavior but his ego intervened.

Trump had the opportunity to broaden his appeal at the virtual Republican Convention that was held between August 24 and August

27, 2020. Instead, it became very close to being a family love-in. Melania spoke for 25 minutes, Ivanka for 18, Eric and Donald, Jr. about 10 minutes each - Tiffany about 7, and Lara Trump 7½.

Mitch McConnell the Senate majority leader got 2½ minutes and Kevin McCarthy the number one Republican in the House got 3. The convention demonstrated that the old Republican establishment had abandoned Trump - no Bush appeared, no Baker, no Cheney, no Dole. The Republican icon, Reagan, was almost never mentioned.

The convention provided an opportunity for Trump to soften his image to win back suburban voters, particularly women. He could have admitted to mistakes. Instead, speakers acted as though his handling of the pandemic had been superb.

Something extraordinary happened in both 2016 and 2020. In 2016, 50 senior Republican national security officials warned that Trump -

"Would be the most reckless president in American history."

In 2020 the number jumped to 70. That group took out full page ads which said that they were all voting for Biden because Trump has -

"Divided our nation" -

"Is dangerously unfit to serve another term" -

"He has aligned himself with dictators" -

"He has engaged in corrupt behavior that renders him unfit to serve as president" -

"It is imperative that we stop Trump's assault on our nation's values and institutions."

Seventy solid Americans including generals, a former head of the CIA, a former director of National Intelligence, Colin Powell (former Secretary of State and former Chair of the Joint Chiefs of Staff), were all opposed to Trump. These are people you would expect Trump's base to admire and respect. How could Trump have not been worried? How could he not understand that he had to modify his behavior? Anyone else would be totally demoralized that so many highly respected people could have such a low opinion of him.

The loyalty of Trump's base is a mystery. The vast majority of his followers have nothing in common with him. Few of them have ever lived in the kind of luxury in which Trump has always been immersed - Trump Tower in Manhattan and the estate in Palm Beach. Yes, they have nothing in common with this quintessential, elite New York real estate tycoon. They pay their taxes yet are not angry at their idol for avoiding paying his. That would be a puzzle for a platoon of psychologists.

TRUMP ANNOUNCES THAT HE WILL RUN FOR PRESIDENT AGAIN IN 2024

In his speech he was silent about the reality of multiple desertions. His daughter, Ivanka, and her husband, Jared, said they would not be involved in his upcoming campaign. No two people were closer to him during his presidency.

The New York Post was for years the strongest and most consistent media backer of Trump. They were also by far the strongest attacker of Biden and his son Hunter. The Post pounded away at Hunter's laptop in multiple front-page stories which strongly implied that both were corrupt.

The Post did more than an about face, they became viciously anti-Trump. When he announced for the presidency in November 2022 the paper ridiculed him by a one-liner at the very bottom of Page 1 -

"Florida man makes announcement."

On another front page, The Post did even worse, showing Trump as Humpty Dumpty –"About to have a great fall."

As Trump was abandoned by the New York Post and the Wall Street Journal, he was also abandoned by the icon of the conservative movement -the National Review -which said -

"Republicans: Trump is your problem. Wake up."

But that's why Trump's base loves him - he is admired as a fighter, as someone who refuses to quit or surrender or apologize. In the history of American politics, no candidate for the presidency has had to absorb the insults leveled at Trump.

Trump made his announcement at Mar-a-Lago to an audience of about 500. No broadcast network carried his speech.

All the pundits would be wrong again as they were in 2016 saying that Hillary would crush Trump. Now they are saying Biden would defeat Trump easily since Trump's base was not broad enough to win a national election. They would point to the fact that Trump-endorsed candidates did poorly in the 2022 midterms.

Assuming that Biden is the candidate, this is how Trump could beat him. Show an ad over and over again displaying all of Biden's verbal stumbles. Stopping in mid-sentence and appearing confused - forgetting the names of people that he's known for 40 years - being unable to string together a coherent paragraph. Even stumbling when reading from a teleprompter.

But this is the killer example of why he could not be trusted to have his finger on the nuclear button. He could forget that he gave an order, or he might not remember an order he gave. Biden was in the middle of a speech when he looked out at the audience and said --

"Where's Jackie"?

That Jackie had been a respected member of Congress. Biden knew her well - she had been killed in a tragic automobile accident a few months before. Flags were at half-mast. At great length, politicians talked about her passing. Somehow Biden forgot that she had died.

Trump would look very sincerely into the camera after that ad and say -

"I know a lot of you don't like me but I am competent. The simple truth is the man that you have been watching does not have the capacity to remain as president. He does not have the capacity to deal with critical issues, and that will be totally obvious to foreign leaders."

Trump believes that the millions of Democrats who were opposed to Biden seeking another term would vote for him even if they were holding their noses while doing so. Trump would be supremely confident of crushing Biden in a debate if Biden were to agree to one.

Trump would remind America of how Biden presided over the worst debacle in American history. How America left Afghanistan having been beaten by a terrorist organization – the Taliban. Biden pulled out all our troops – 100%. He did not leave a residual force to protect the Afghans who were on America's side.

He would remind America that Biden said that we could leave because – "I trust the capacity of the Afghan military which is better trained, better equipped and more competent than the Taliban in terms of conducting war."

As the Taliban marched toward their victory in August 2021, the Afghan military did not contest them at all. All the Trump people would need to do would be to show repeatedly the chaos, death, and humiliation at the airport as thousands of Afghans tried to flee the conquerors.

How many people would vote against Biden if he kept Kamala Harris on the ticket?

TRUMP AND THE MEDIA THAT HATE HIM

Yes, "hate" is the right word. On November 1, 2020, less than a week before the election, the New York Times did something extraordinary. The paper devoted an entire section to explain why it would be a tragedy to reelect Donald Trump. Fifteen of their writers competed as to which one would win the insult contest.

From the front page of the Anti-Trump Section –

"WHAT HAVE WE LOST?" What follows is a mere sampling –

Trump "nurtures hate" –

He is a – "lying, grifting, shady, carnival conductor" –

He is – "a demagogic tyrant worshiper" –

He has caused – "moral injury" –

"How could we have been so blind?"

"Trump has normalized selfishness" –

"The whole world has gotten darker" –

During Trump's term as President I don't think a single day passed without a negative reference to him in the Times. Often there were several insults on a single day.

The Times has three intelligent opinion writers – Paul Krugman, Bret Stephens and Thomas Friedman. Krugman is a Nobel Prize winning economist, Stephens a highly respected conservative, and Friedman, the author of several successful books mainly about the Middle East.

They have used harsher language against Trump than they have ever used against Putin.

Stephens called Trump–

"A lawless, immoral, terrifying president."

"A malignant, narcissist, fraudster, bully, demagogue – a thug who engages in non-stop mendacity."

The mountain of insults caused Trump's base to become even more devoted. Millions were motivated to protect him from the attacks of the elite. Didn't all the high-IQ people at the Times understand that when they insult him, they are calling the millions who voted for him –

Stupid! How could those millions be taken in by this monumental fraud? And don't they understand how these over-the-top insults create irreparable divisiveness? Yes, in spite of their preaching about the need to bring Americans "together." No president or aspiring president has ever been subjected to such unrelenting abuse.

One can be strongly anti-Trump and also strongly against the anti-Trump media. We get it – these outlets despise Trump. They think he is unfit to be president. Their Trump obsession says more about themselves than it does about Trump. There are many who will vote for Trump just to watch those on the left cringe.

Rachel Maddow of MSNBC, obviously bright and competent, would giggle and smirk with every piece of news that made Trump look bad. The guy who followed her show, Lawrence O'Donnell, was worse – he took great pleasure in asserting, over and over again, that Trump was one of the worst human beings on the planet. His insults were searing; for a time he pushed the idea that Trump was abnormal, deranged and should be removed from office as mentally unfit. He urged Trump's removal under the 25th amendment.

Trump thrives on enemies – that is a central feature of his personality. His lodestar is loyalty – you are either with him or against him. He is able to brush off the insults as coming from "losers," coming from those who are jealous of how high he has risen and the adoring crowds who back him.

America has never experienced an unfiltered president like Trump – all the other presidents would go through layers of briefings and revisions before they spoke to the public. America knew exactly what Trump was thinking at any given point in time through his rants on social media. He would answer questions from reporters as he was walking to board Air Force One. It was that openness and spontaneity which endeared him to millions.

An affection and loyalty that the haters could never understand. It was their frustration with that loyalty which caused them to overreact with their over-the-top attempts to destroy him.

WHAT HATRED OF TRUMP LEADS TO – SPECIAL COUNSEL MUELLER

On May 9, 2017, President Trump fired FBI director James Comey. Comey despised Trump but he got his revenge days later when Robert Mueller was appointed as special counsel to investigate whether the president colluded with Russia to help him win in 2016.

Comey and Mueller were very close. Mueller had been the director of the FBI for 12 years and, as far as the public knew, his leadership was solid. He left that position with an overall excellent reputation.

Throughout the Mueller investigation (nearly two years), night after night after night, the Trump-hating media simply assumed that there was collusion. The most persistent advocates of that line were Rachel Maddow, Lawrence O'Donnell and Chris Matthews of MSNBC and Anderson Cooper and Chris Cuomo (the governor's brother) on CNN. And almost always giggling and smirking. Maddow is the champion of the gigglers.

These talking heads would have guests and panels nearly every night all chiming in on the same monotonous theme – that Trump was guilty of collusion. I do not exaggerate – during this timeframe the word "collusion" was uttered thousands of times by hosts and their guests.

When President Clinton was impeached, his nemesis was Kenneth Starr a former federal judge and solicitor general. Starr's designation was "Independent Counsel" but the law creating that office expired after the Clinton impeachment (he was not convicted by the Senate). That's why Mueller's label was that of "Special Counsel," an office with less power than the Independent Counsel had.

Mueller hired some 59 lawyers and investigators. They interviewed several hundred individuals and issued hundreds of subpoenas. They never got to interview President Trump who did provide written answers. As to be expected, his answers were vague. They never subpoenaed Trump and they never got his tax returns.

Finally, on March 22, 2019 (22 months after his appointment), Mueller issued his 488-page report. It was not released to the public until April 18.

THE BOMBSHELL! FROM THE REPORT – "The investigation did not establish that members of the Trump campaign conspired or coordinated with the Russian government in its election interference activities."

The lead FBI investigator, Peter Strzok, who was strongly anti-Trump, to his credit concluded – "We are unaware of any Trump advisors engaging in conversations with Russian intelligence officers."

Did Rachel or Lawrence or Chris or Anderson apologize? Did any of their hundreds of guests apologize? Not a chance. The media pivoted to their new obsession – OBSTRUCTION!

Attorney General William Barr issued a four-page summary of the Mueller report on March 24, 2019. Barr concluded that Trump had not obstructed justice since with a finding of no collusion there was no underlying crime to obstruct. It is to be recalled that the senior President Bush had years earlier selected Barr as his Attorney General.

Mueller provided some ammunition to the anti-Trumpers.

– "If we had confidence that the president clearly did not commit obstruction of justice, we would so statewe were unable to reach that judgment. Accordingly while this report does not conclude that the President committed a crime, it also does not exonerate him. The Constitution requires a process other than the criminal justice system to formally accuse a sitting President of wrong doing."

That "process" obviously refers to impeachment.

Democrats in Congress wanted Mueller to testify and elaborate on his report. Mueller did not wish to do so. He made this very clear when he spoke publicly for the first time on May 29, 2019 –

"Any testimony from this office would not go beyond our report the report is my testimony. I would not provide information beyond that which is already public in any appearance before Congress. Now I hope and expect this to be the only time that I will speak to you in this manner."

Mueller could not withstand the pressure so he did appear before Congress.

The egomaniacs in Congress knew coverage would be intense and they could strut their stuff before a huge audience. Mueller was very uncomfortable in that setting and he showed it.

FISA – THE FOREIGN INTELLIGENCE SURVEILLANCE COURT
ANOTHER CONSEQUENCE OF TRUMP HATRED

The FISA Court was mentioned hundreds, perhaps thousands, of times by the talking heads on television and by the print media during Trump's presidency. Probably less than 1% of Americans had ever heard of this court or had any idea of its function. The Chief Justice of the United States Supreme Court has the discretion to select any federal judge to head this court.

The rulings of the FISA judge are secret. The Court decides whom the government may wiretap. It is only the government that appears before this court. The purpose of the court is to protect America from spies, from any foreign entity seeking to do us harm. Congress created the court in 1978 and expanded its powers following 9/11.

In the lead up to the 2016 election between Clinton and Trump, the Clinton campaign hired a research firm, Fusion GPS, to dig up dirt on Trump. Digging up dirt on an opponent is the name of the game in American politics. That and raising money. Politicians search an opponent's prior votes, statements, inconsistencies – anything that they can use to criticize or demean. But the holy grail of opposition research is to unearth a secret scandal in your opponent's background. Something like a bribe or a sexual relationship outside of marriage or undisclosed abuse or mental problems.

Trump's call to the President of the Ukraine to dig up dirt on Biden was well within the tradition of political "dirty tricks." Oftentimes, a single slip-up can doom a presidential campaign. For example – Mitt Romney's father, who had been Governor of Pennsylvania, said he had been brainwashed about Vietnam. Senator Muskie was crying when defending his wife against a negative article in a newspaper in an early primary state. Gary Hart was caught having a fling with a model. That was the end for all of them. Kennedy and Johnson had multiple affairs, but the mainstream media back then considered that subject to be off limits.

Fusion hired a British guy with an intelligence and investigative background, Christopher Steele, to come up with anything negative on Trump. The infamous Steele dossier was the product, and if true, it was dynamite. The problem for the Democrats was that it wasn't true. The dossier contained gossip and rumors and hearsay as well as unnamed sources.

Knowing that, FBI Director Comey used the dossier in his application to the FISA Court to obtain a warrant to wiretap a low-level Trump advisor – Carter Page. The FISA Court, historically, is a rubber-stamp for FBI or CIA applications. Comey got his wiretaps approved.

The FBI had spent days interviewing the primary source for the information contained in the Steele dossier. They had serious doubts about the reliability of the source. That didn't stop Comey. He used the dossier as the basis for four wiretaps on Page. The court was not told about the FBI's doubts.

The wiretaps on Page turned out to be a huge embarrassment to both the FBI and the Justice Department. Both institutions always took pride in their reputations for never being motivated by political considerations. When it came to Trump, they could not disguise their desire to get rid of him.

The Justice Department has an inspector general who was able to review the situation and tell the public at least part of the truth. He found that there were serious errors and omissions by the FBI in their wiretap applications.

The whole idea of wiretapping Page was bizarre. He was not a member of Trump's inner circle, and even a superficial search of his background would have shot down the possibility of his being a Russian agent.

Since the anti-Trump partisans could not bring down their main target, they went after his associates. Such as three-star General Michael Flynn, who had served 33 years in the military.

They destroyed Paul Manafort, who had served as Trump's campaign manager for a time. Manafort had also worked on the campaigns of Reagan, Dole, and Ford.

Congress will rarely pass up an opportunity to showboat. The Senate Intelligence Committee spent nearly 3 years covering the same ground as Mueller's two-year investigation. The Committee Report. consisting of thousands of pages, was issued in August 2020 – a year- and-a-half after Mueller's Report.

Their report concluded that Russia tried to influence the 2016 election in Trump's favor. They came up with the startling revelation that Putin wanted Trump to win, but they did not conclude that the Trump campaign engaged in a coordinated conspiracy with Russia.

The Senate Report stated the obvious – that Carter Page played an insignificant role in the Trump campaign. It is beyond embarrassing that our government would have used the discredited Steele dossier as a basis for wiretapping an insignificant figure in the whole episode. The substance of the wiretaps was of zero value. Well, not zero, for they showed the lengths our government would go to bring down a political figure who they despised.

CHAPTER 6

JANUARY 6, 2021 – HOW COULD WE HAVE BEEN UNPREPARED FOR THE ATTACK AT THE CAPITOL?

The January 6, 2021 attack on our nation's capital could not have been more predictable. This point is not hindsight – all one had to do was focus, to pay attention.

During the whole of the Trump presidency, Democratic politicians and most of the media, were repeating thousands of times that Trump's followers were dangerous, and that many were armed and belonged to extremist groups.

The vast majority of Americans believed that Biden won the election fair and square. Thousands of Trump followers (perhaps millions) believed what he had been telling them every day for 2 months – that the election had been stolen.

If a person truly believes that a presidential election has been stolen – the normal reaction would be furious anger, which usually leads to violence. These were the people who were traveling to Washington to hear Trump speak on January 6. Obviously, Trump would seek to inflame them.

January 6 was the day Congress was set to certify the results – making it official that Biden won. So obviously, Congress would become the target.

All anyone had to do was spend 5 minutes reviewing what had happened in the state of Michigan and that person would have realized that the National Guard had to be present on January 6.

On April 30, 2020, dozens of heavily armed militia members convened in the State House in Lansing. Why? To protest the Governor's stay-at-home order in response to the pandemic. They came with assault rifles; in Michigan, it is legal to openly carry firearms in public.

This happened 8 full months before the Trump speech. Arrests were made in October, days before the election. It was fresh in everyone's minds. There had been social media posts between the amateurish conspirators about the kidnapping or maybe killing some of the Governor's security people. A similar mentality was present in some of those coming to hear the speech. Do you think Pelosi, Schumer, the FBI and the Department of Homeland Security had enough notice that January 6 was going to be wild?

The Democrats and their media allies were able to point to the plot to kidnap the Governor as evidence of the "crazies" who loved Trump. What would they be capable of after hearing a "Fire and Brimstone" speech from their idol?

It is inconceivable to me that neither Pelosi, nor Schumer, nor any other member of Congress would have said the obvious – something like this –

"That Trump is great at agitating a crowd of his followers, that they were agitated already believing that the election was stolen. Violence is a likelihood, so we must have the National Guard fully prepared to deal with a very dangerous situation."

The House of Representatives and the Senate each have a Sergeant at Arms responsible for the security of the Capitol.

Also available for protection –

The Capitol Police Force, which has an intelligence division –

The FBI, which has a domestic terrorism operations section.

Director Christopher Wray and everyone else knew of extensive social media efforts to block certification, online posts about bringing weapons to the rally.

The Washington D.C. Metropolitan Police --

The Capitol Police Board which was somehow involved in giving permission to request the Guard – Permission? Hard to believe!

The Washington D.C. National Guard –

The Federal Department of Homeland Security, which has a branch of intelligence and analysis. This department was created on 9/11 to identify threats and coordinate responses. On January 5, the Department said that they had – "nothing significant to report."

Sharing intelligence is crucial. To our government's credit, it created Fusion Centers in every state to improve intelligence sharing between local, state and federal law enforcement and emergency response agencies. On January 4, the head of the Fusion Centers convened a national call to discuss information they were gathering about the Trump rally. This was a very smart thing to do. But there was no intelligent follow-up.

Testifying before Congress the official who oversees the DC Fusion Center said –

"THE ISSUE HERE WAS NOT LACK OF INFORMATION, THE ISSUE WAS THE INABILITY OR THE UNWILLINGNESS TO ACT ON THE INTELLIGENCE."

The available intelligence confirmed that a siege was planned and that the radical groups were coordinating with each other. Yes – What the hell is the matter with us?

What happened after the speech and after it became obvious that the crowd was marching toward the Capitol?

At 1:09 p.m., Steven Sund, Chief of the Capitol Police, frantically called the House Sergeant at Arms telling him that the National Guard was needed. He did this at about the same time that Trump ended his speech.

Sergeant Paul Irving asked Speaker Pelosi's chief of staff for permission to call for the National Guard. According to Sund, he heard from Irving an hour after his call telling him that Pelosi had approved his request for the National Guard. Why didn't Sund simply call for the Guard himself? Everyone is a technocrat obsessed with procedure.

There are some complex statutory and regulatory requirements for calling out the National Guard. The situation called for the exercise of common sense rather than adhering to bureaucratic rules.

Sund called Major General William Walker, the Commander of the D.C. National Guard.

There was an issue as to who had to give the final authorization to activate the Guard. Was it the Secretary of the Army or the acting Defense Secretary, Christopher Miller? In a January 4 memo from Miller, he made it clear that the D.C. National Guard was to do nothing without his – "personal authorization."

Miller's thinking was off the wall. He thought that the presence of the Guard would cause Americans to believe that "a military coup" was about to occur. He told Congress that a military presence was warranted – "only as the absolute last resort." And I guess the fools in Congress bought that line.

General Walker said that days before January 6, the Pentagon had removed his authority to quickly deploy his troops. Was that another terrible decision by Miller? Common sense out the window.

Sund had called another general in addition to General Walker, asking him to get approval from the Army Secretary. That general's response shocked Sund – saying that he would not like the "visuals" of the National Guard dealing with civilians and that he would recommend to the army secretary that the Guard not be activated. Hard to believe! Generals thinking like hack politicians!

In General Walker's attempts to obtain approval, he testified before Congress that –

"The word I kept hearing was the optics of it." How it would look –moronic political considerations.

Sund said that in his initial call to the Sergeant at Arms to get Guard approval, Sergeant Irving mentioned – "optics." Irving denied using that term. A clear emergency situation existed; immediate action was required, not silly debates.

Acting Defense Secretary Miller approved General Walker's urgent request to activate the D.C. National Guard at 3:04 p.m. Miller was "acting" because President Trump had fired his previous defense secretary shortly before he had to vacate the White House. I wonder who recommended Miller to him.

The Pentagon did not actually authorize General Walker to send troops to the Capitol until 5:08 p.m. What was going on at the Pentagon between 3:00 p.m. and 5:00 p.m.? Were they debating "optics"? Hours wasted from the time of Sund's original call. Hours wasted responding to General Walker's urgent request.

The National Guard troops did not arrive at the Capitol until 5:40 p.m. By that time, the rioters were out of the building. Within 24 hours, Chief Sund and both Sergeants at Arms had resigned. Nobody laid a glove on Schumer or Pelosi. Believe me, if either one had called the Pentagon and screamed, the National Guard would have been on the scene in a flash. And remember, after the Vice President, Pelosi would be next in line to become president.

What could Trump have been thinking? How could he not have understood that Pence had no power to stop the certification of the Electoral College vote. He had no power to rule on disputes. He was limited to opening the envelopes and reading out the results.

Trump had tweeted at 3:13 p.m. –

"I am asking for everyone to remain peaceful. No violence. Respect the law..."

By this time the Capitol had already been breached. His tweet at 6:01 p.m. came after Biden had been declared the winner.

"These are the things and events that happen when a sacred landslide electoral victory is stripped away from great patriots who have been badly and unfairly treated for so long. Go home with love and in peace. Remember this day forever."

The media were not criticizing members of Congress for their lack of foresight. Their whole focus was on the impeachment circus. A great diversion from an analysis of the lack of preparedness.

THE GREAT DIVERSION

Congress conducted multiple investigations relating to January 6, but, of course, they did not investigate themselves. They did not investigate why Pelosi and Schumer and the membership of both Houses did not prepare for the attack. Congress ignored multiple clues that violence would occur on January 6.

There had been a rally against the election results attended by thousands on December 12, 2021.

On December 19, Trump tweeted –

'Big protest in DC on January 6. Be there, will be wild."

On December 21, the intelligence arm of the Capitol Police issued a report tracking comments made on the "thedonald.win" account. Comments such as –

"Confronting members of Congress and carrying firearms during the protest."

"Bring guns, it's now or never."

Social media posts such as –

"Storm the capital" –

"Don't be surprised if we take the Capitol Building."

"If there ever was a time for there to be a second civil war, it's now."

In a Stephen Bannon podcast of January 5, he said – "All hell is going to break loose tomorrow."

I guess the members of Congress were attending so many fundraisers that they were too busy to notice.

The Proud Boys and the Oath Keepers would, of course, be there on January 6. Both groups had reputations for violence.

A year after the attack, a former Senate Sergeant at Arms (1985-88), Ernest Garcia, in an article in the Wall Street Journal, told the truth about congressional malfeasances. This former United States Marine Colonel said –

"Congress is ultimately responsible for the Capitol's security. They need to examine their own culpability." YES!

He pointed out that in June 2021 the Senate Homeland Security and Rules Committee issued a report criticizing the Capitol Police as well as the Senate and House Sergeants at Arms. Schumer, a member of that committee, called for the firing of the Senate Sergeant at Arms. Not a word in the report about Congress' oversight responsibility.

The Inspector General of the Capitol Police said that the Department of Homeland Security had warned the police on December 21 about comments appearing on pro-Trump websites that advocated attacking Congress. Although the Capitol Police have a civil disturbance unit which is charged with containing crowds and responding to protests, it was missing in action on January 6.

By June 2022 there had been over 700 arrests. Over 160 of the poor suckers who believed Trump have pled guilty. Eleven Oath Keepers were charged with the serious crime of sedition. Hundreds will spend years in prison while Trump is in Palm Beach or playing golf while raising money and making speeches.

To me, the absolute worst thing that happened on January 6 was the killing of an UNARMED woman by a Capitol Police officer. I refer to Ashli Babbitt, age 35, who served 12 years in the Air Force and Air National Guard. She was trying to enter the Capitol through a broken window when a poorly trained cop shot and killed her. His pathetic explanation was that she did not obey his command. Hundreds of people were already in the building, many had entered through broken windows. What was he accomplishing by keeping her out? Of course he was charged with nothing.

The major investigation and the one which received massive media attention was the House Select Committee, which was still investigating over a year-and-a-half after the attack. The staff of over 40 interviewed hundreds and examined thousands of documents. The staff included several former federal prosecutors and two former U.S. Attorneys.

This was absurd overkill – anything to divert attention from the House and Senate politicians. What the hell was there to investigate?

There was a direct line from the claim of a stolen election and Trump's speech to the attack on the Capitol.

The same Inspector General, after reviewing the lapses in law enforcement on January 6, made the astounding number of 103 recommendations for improvement. Astounding indeed – 103 screw-up areas.

The committee and its most vocal member, Liz Cheney, wanted to see Trump in prison. They were out for blood. January 6 had become the main Democratic election strategy for the November 2022 midterms. Not a single pro-Trump Republican was on the committee.

In a December 29, 2001 article in the New York Times, Professor Laurence Tribe along with two former U.S. Attorneys pressured Attorney General, Merrick Garland, to conduct an investigation focusing on Trump. Tribe had been a law professor at Harvard for decades.

"We implore the attorney general to bring charges. Not doing so would amount to appeasement. Those who plot to end democracy, to overthrow the government must be held accountable. It would be a grave mistake not to go after Trump."

Garland was certainly on board. He was bitter over the fact that the Republicans denied him a hearing after Obama nominated him to be a Justice on the United States Supreme Court.

CHAPTER 7

ROBERT CARO ON THE EXERCISE OF POLITICAL POWER IN A DEMOCRACY

Robert Caro has written books about two individuals which explain how power brokers function in a democracy – Lyndon Johnson at the national level and Robert Moses at the municipal urban level.

His book, "The Power Broker," about Robert Moses, was published in 1974. In 1976 he started working on the first of five volumes about Johnson, and in 2023 he was still immersed in the final volume of the Johnson series. Caro's researching, interviewing and writing have been prodigious and superlative.

He has said –

"Really my books are an examination of what power does to people."

Robert Moses held power for 44 years, from 1924 to 1968, during the tenures of five New York City mayors and six governors. Although he was never elected to any office, he was more powerful than mayors and governors.

Moses had absolute discretion over the awarding of contracts by the city and state in every field of public works. Any person or business that ever sought a contract with the city or state had to deal with Moses.

He built bridges, parks, parkways and expressways. Seven great bridges have been built to link the boroughs together – he built all of them. He was responsible for building 15 expressways, plus the Westside Highway. In New York City and its suburbs, he built a total of 627 miles of expressways and highways. Just to name a few of his infrastructure projects–

The Triborough Bridge –
The Henry Hudson Bridge –
The Verrazano Bridge –
The Cross Bronx Expressway –
The Brooklyn Queens Expressway –
The Staten Island Expressway –
The Long Island Expressway –
The Van Wyck Expressway –
Harlem River Drive –

There was a huge price to be paid for all these massive projects. One horrible example of many – to build the Cross Bronx Expressway, Moses had demolished 54 apartment buildings. Think of the raw power one has to have to cause that much destruction – buildings where people had lived for generations and brought up their families. The thousands of tenants without lobbyists or financial or political clout were no match for Moses' power and vision.

Moses' genius was his ability to visualize a neighborhood and somehow see in great detail how it could be replaced with an expressway. Lacking the technical knowledge of an engineer or architect he could see the contours, curves and direction of a highway extending for many miles.

In his desire to remake a modern metropolis he evicted a half-million people from their homes – mainly poor, Black, and Hispanic. That's why Caro sizes Moses up as "an utterly ruthless person."

And yet he did some wonderful things. As parks commissioner for nearly 30 years he was responsible for building over 600 playgrounds. His Long Island parkways enabled poor city dwellers to go there and enjoy the beaches. He controlled the New York City Housing Authority which under his tenure built over 1,000 apartment buildings housing a half-million people. He both built and he destroyed.

The man was a phenomenon and a contradiction. He headed 12 government entities at both the state and city levels. As the chairman of various public authorities he had unbridled power. Power unmatched by any other municipal figure in the history of not only New York but in the entire United States.

The Caro book is an account of how a single individual, unelected to anything, was able to amass such power and retain it for so long. The general public, even the politicians, had no appreciation of the role of public authorities in the life of the city. Moses studied them, shrewdly realizing that they could become the vehicles which would propel him to unrivaled power.

When Nelson Rockefeller became governor in 1968, Moses' career ended; although still vigorous and ambitious he never built anything again. Rockefeller was himself a builder and he would not tolerate Moses' power.

CARO ON JOHNSON

Caro considered President Johnson to be a "political genius" because of his ability to pass groundbreaking legislation as the majority leader of the Senate. And yet as a human being he sized Johnson up as – "ruthless and cruel."

Caro knew better than anyone that both Moses and Johnson were rotten human beings in many ways. Yes, they got things done and served as superb models for Caro's demonstration of the uses of political power and the impact of that power on millions of lives.

If I was interviewing Caro I would ask him this question – I understand that you regard Moses and Johnson as men of great accomplishment – but how do you deal with the fact that you have dedicated your working life to writing about two men who were devious, hypocritical, selfish, obsessive and mean?

Johnson was Majority Leader of the United States Senate for a mere 6 years. Caro regards the Senate as a dysfunctional mess, both before and after Johnson's tenure, making his accomplishments all the more remarkable. Before Johnson, no civil rights bill had been passed in 89 years. President Kennedy introduced a civil rights bill in June 1963 but it went nowhere.

These were the monumental pieces of legislation passed into law during Johnson's presidency –

The Civil Rights Act of 1964 – Johnson had done a lot for civil rights as senate majority leader.

The Voting Rights Act –

Medicare –

Medicaid –

Head Start –

A liberal immigration bill –

Some 70 different education bills –

Many war-on-poverty bills.

Caro is not reluctant to expose Johnson's scars. He was a liar, a hypocrite, a cheat, and a serial adulterer. As the press ignored Kennedy's affairs, they also ignored Johnson's.

Yet he was a do-gooder devoted to social justice. Caro established that Johnson stole the election that put him in the Senate in the first place defeating an opponent who was morally superior to him in every way.

Johnson came to Congress in 1937. Between 1937 and 1957, he voted against every civil rights bill that was introduced, including anti-lynching bills. The Southern racists in the House and Senate were convinced he was one of them. Think of the lies he had to tell to convince them of that. Part of Johnson's drive and ambition came from the fact that he attended Southwest Texas State Teachers College, unlike the presidents who attended Harvard and Yale.

As Senate majority leader, it could be argued that Johnson was the second most powerful person in our government. As Vice President, he had no real power. He hated being Vice President. Johnson was not part of President Kennedy's inner circle. Johnson being on the ticket probably was the deciding factor in Kennedy's razor thin victory over Nixon in 1960.

JOHNSON AND VIETNAM

Johnson may have been brilliant in getting his legislative programs through Congress, but when it came to Vietnam, he failed miserably.

War? Our constitution is very clear, giving Congress the sole power to declare war. That never happened! Instead, Congress passed something called the Gulf of Tonkin Resolution which authorized the use of military force.

Johnson said the Gulf of Tonkin Resolution was – "Like grandma's nightshirt, it covered everything." Johnson loved the power the Resolution gave him.

Congress did not insist upon its sole authority to declare war. Although Americans were fighting and dying in Vietnam from 1965 to 1973, our citizens never made the lack of a declaration of war an issue. The vote in Congress was shameful.

The Resolution passed the House unanimously after only about 40 minutes of debate. In the Senate, there were two senators who voted against it – Wayne Morse, Democrat of Oregon, and Ernest Gruening, Democrat of Alaska. Senator Gruening objected to – "sending our American boys into combat in a war in which we have no business, which is not our war, and to which we have been mistakenly drawn, which has steadily been escalated." Sage advice which was ignored.

Senator Morse said the Resolution would be – "a historic mistake." And was he ever right.

One of the many things Johnson had said –

"Communist domination of Southeast Asia could bring a third world war closer to reality."

When Johnson was vice president, he said that if we lost South Vietnam, we would have to – "surrender the Pacific." That was nonsense. President Kennedy had sent about 16,000 troops to Vietnam to act as advisors and trainers, they were not to engage in combat.

Kennedy said – "For us to withdraw it would mean a collapse not only of Vietnam, but Southeast Asia. So we are going to stay there."

Those statements were part and parcel of – "THE DOMINO THEORY" – that if South Vietnam fell to the communists, other countries in the region would likewise fall like dominoes. That was the discredited theory that got Americans to support the "war" which became America's war.

Communism was not a monolithic entity totally dominated by the Soviet Union.

There had been rivalries within that world. Think of the murderous purges of fellow Communists by Stalin, his hatred for Trotsky, the antipathy that he and Mao had for one another. Mao and Khrushchev were bitter enemies as well.

When Tito of Yugoslavia left the Soviet realm, he suffered no consequences. He and his country remained communist, but it was a nationalist brand. Vietnam in 1978 invaded communist Cambodia to defeat the genocidal regime of the Khmer Rouge.

And remember the Nixon and Kissinger visits to Communist China in 1972. Toasts, compliments, smiles, and dinners between capitalists and communists.

"Made in China" labels were everywhere and no American refused to wear a garment because it came from China.

Americans were suckered to believe that South Vietnam was a worthy, upstanding ally. South Vietnam was corrupt and repressive. In no way did it resemble a democracy. It was also an unstable country; there had been several coups. But it was enough for us that they were strongly anti-communist. We had historically supported ruthless dictators simply because they were anti-communist. All foreign countries had to do was stress their love of capitalism and their hatred for communism and they would get bundles of aid from America.

70 to 90% of Vietnams population was Buddhist, yet its president, Ngo Dinh Diem, was Catholic. So were all the insiders who ran the country. The Diem regime, instead of promoting religious freedom, severely discriminated against the Buddhists.

That policy led to massive protests and eventually to civil war. By June 1963, Buddhist monks were burning themselves to death. Madame Nhu, the wife of Diem's powerful brother, referred to the immolation of the monks as a "barbeque show" saying that she would provide the matches. Nice lady!

In a stunning decision, the United States backed not only a coup against Diem, but his murder in November 1963. That was a decision approved by President Kennedy who later that very same month was himself assassinated.

By mid-1965, General Nguyen Cao Ky and General Nguyen Van Thieu took charge as prime minister and president respectively. The Buddhist uprising was over, but our ally was hardly unified.

Robert McNamara was our defense secretary under both Kennedy and Johnson. In June 1967 he commissioned what became known as the "Pentagon Papers" which were to be classified, kept totally secret from the public. The study contained, in great detail, the history of our involvement in Vietnam. It provided a forum where our political and military leaders could give their honest assessments of how the war was going.

An analyst at the Defense Department named Daniel Ellsberg, thinking that the American people should know the truth, leaked the Pentagon Papers.

The United States Supreme Court upheld the right to publish, and the New York Times did so on June 13, 1971. So too did the Washington Post. In spite of the publication, the war continued and American deaths continued.

Anyone reading the Pentagon Papers would understand that the United States and South Vietnam were not going to achieve victory. But our generals and politicians continued to parrot optimistic assessments. There was a lot of talk about "body counts," that we were killing more of them than they were killing us, which was true. We were not talking about the thousands of civilians we killed with our incessant bombing. We dropped more bombs on Vietnam than we did on Germany during all of World War II.

A full-fledged anti-war movement had taken hold in America. There were parades and demonstrations – thousands of young men were burning their draft cards. The leadership in North Vietnam saw all of this and knew that all they had to do was remain patient until America caved.

As early as October 1969, there had been a nationwide day of protests and a march on Washington. In April 1971, there was a protest which attracted 250,000 people.

When Nixon was elected President in 1968, he could have brought our troops home, but he too had to prove that he was a tough guy. He repeated many times that North Vietnam could not defeat or humiliate the United States. He was wrong! Similar to what Biden said about the Taliban decades later.

Nixon and Kissinger knew from the Pentagon Papers and from their military leaders that the North was going to defeat the South. Yet they continued the war where young Americans were dying, day after day.

Eventually Nixon told the American people he had a plan that would end the war. "A just peace through a negotiated settlement."

He had a plan alright – a plan to disguise defeat. He had said this knowing that our ambassador to Vietnam, Henry Cabot Lodge, made it clear that – "Hanoi has refused even to discuss our proposals." Lodge had written a letter to the North's leader, Ho Chi Minh, who – "flatly rejected my initiative." Of course – the North knew they were going to win.

Nixon said that – "In the previous administration we Americanized the war, in this administration we are Vietnamizing the search for peace. The primary mission of our troops is to enable the South Vietnamese forces to assume the full responsibility for the security of South Vietnam." He began a timetable of removing troops at intervals.

We were unable to defeat the North when we had a half-million American troops there. That's how gullible Nixon and Kissinger believed the American public to be.

Kissinger negotiated an accord with the North Vietnamese after many months of wrangling in Paris. By January 1973, our military involvement was over. The South continued to fight on but their defeat was inevitable. Our long-term ally was not a party to these negotiations. Decades later, that's exactly what happened in Afghanistan when Trump negotiated with the Taliban without the participation of the Afghan government.

On June 4, 1973, the United States Senate put an end to the U.S. funding of the South Vietnamese forces. Kissinger called that an act of betrayal. By April 30, 1975, the North had achieved total victory. Their flag flew over the presidential palace in Saigon. The South had surrendered.

Lyndon Johnson had crushed Barry Goldwater in the presidential election of 1964. By 1968 the political landscape had changed. Prominent Democrats had become leaders of the anti-war movement strongly opposed to Johnson's policies. Protestors stressed the numbers of civilians our bombing raids killed. Johnson had to listen to shouts of –

"Hey, Hey, LBJ, how many kids did you kill today?"

In a primary contest against Johnson in New Hampshire, Senator Eugene McCarthy of Minnesota received 42% of the vote – a shock to an incumbent Democratic President. A few days after that result Robert Kennedy announced that he would compete in primaries.

Johnson had had enough – on March 31, 1968 he announced that he would not seek reelection. A testament to the limits of political genius. A couple of weeks before that decision Johnson had said – "We shall and we are going to win." Yes – a macho Texan to the very end.

Nixon played the same card – "I will not be the first President to lose a war." Right – just keep sending thousands more American 19-year-olds to die in an unwinnable war.

The American people were never told this simple truth – that a unified Vietnam under Communist rule was not a threat to the United States. That was proven after the North won.

In June 1968, Robert Kennedy defeated McCarthy in the California primary 46% to 42%. A few minutes after celebrating his victory he was murdered at age 42 by an Arab as he was taking a short cut through the hotels kitchen.

THE AGENT ORANGE CATASTROPHE

North Vietnamese soldiers were able to hide in very dense rainforests along with their equipment. In order for our B52s to be able to expose targets, the vegetation had to be cleared. To accomplish that, we sprayed millions of gallons of a toxic chemical contaminant containing dioxin – Agent Orange.

The bombing went on for years and was extended into both Laos and Cambodia. We destroyed millions of acres of forests and thousands of acres of cropland.

The defoliant campaign caused birth defects, malformed babies with missing eyes, club feet, cleft lips. Adults and children suffered from multiple cancers, spinal abnormalities, heart defects, etc.

Thousands of our soldiers developed debilitating, chronic illnesses. For years our government stonewalled their claims. Finally, in 1991, the Agent Orange Act was passed providing for some (not nearly enough) compensation. It wasn't until the year 2000 when we admitted the incredible harm we caused to the local population. Yes – people we were trying to save from communism.

All these tragedies were caused by a propaganda fueled belief in "the domino theory." North Vietnam won and there was no avalanche of dominoes.

Communist China and Communist Vietnam have both become aggressively capitalistic. Vietnam has sought good relations with the United States as a counterweight to the growing power of China.

By 2018, annual trade and goods between the United States and Vietnam was over $60 billion. My Fruit of the Loom underwear was made in Vietnam. I never noticed until I focused while writing this section. Communist Vietnam wants to sell stuff to America.

On September 10, 2023, President Biden was at the Presidential Palace in Hanoi having a very friendly visit with Vietnam leader Nguyen Phu Trong. The visit was a success. Trong said the relationship between the two countries had been "elevated to a new height."

A comprehensive strategic partnership now exists between our two countries which is pretty much the same relationship that Vietnam had with China and Russia. Vietnam's foreign policy is based on pragmatism.

Annual trade between our countries more than doubled during the past 5 years. Apple and Nike have expanded their production bases in Vietnam. Intel has a plant in Ho Chi Minh City.

When countries focus on doing good for their citizens, the labels of communist and capitalist can become relatively meaningless.

Vietnam does not sponsor terrorism or proxy militias to act against the United States. Compare that record with Iran, a fiercely anti-communist country. Beware of labels!

SOME CLOSING THOUGHTS –

In 1963 we had about 16,000 non-combat troops in Vietnam. By 1968 we had over a half-million troops there. General Westmoreland would periodically ask Johnson for 50,000 more troops, saying in effect the additions would turn the tide in our favor. Johnson always complied.

It is beyond tragic that over 55,000 young, brave, and patriotic Americans died in Vietnam. Between soldiers and civilians, the North lost nearly a million. The South lost over 180,000 in the armed forces, plus 50,000 civilians.

Yes, 55,000 dead Americans plus well over 200,000 wounded. Horrendous injuries including paralysis, missing limbs, blindness, burns, disfigurements. Many veterans would need care for decades; thousands would grow old on disability.

Adding insult to injury, the American people did not greet the returning soldiers warmly. The overall attitude was that our war was a terrible mistake. Millions were ashamed that they had supported it, they wanted to put it behind them. The Vietnam War Memorial in Washington, D.C., recognizing the sacrifices of our young men and women, was not installed until 1982.

It seems as though America has amnesia. Had we remembered Vietnam we never would have embraced 20-year wars in Afghanistan and Iraq. Had we remembered the aftermath of the Korean War and the Chinese Civil War we would have recalled that Chiang Kai-shek in Taiwan and Syngman Rhee in South Korea were dictators who had killed many thousands of their own protestors. How could we have not understood that if South Vietnam had won its government would have been a dictatorship?

Johnson said in 1963 – "We are not about to send American boys nine or ten thousand miles away from home to do what Asian boys ought to be doing for themselves." From that lie to 55,000 dead Americans.

Beware of jumping on dishonest political bandwagons!!

CHAPTER 8

HOW STORMY DANIELS BECAME FAMOUS – HOW MICHAEL AVENATTI BECAME INFAMOUS –

On April 4, 2023, a Manhattan grand jury indicted Trump on 34 felony counts of falsifying business records. This was the first criminal indictment of a former President in United States history.

The claim was that the records were falsified to disguise reimbursements to Trump's "fixer," Michael Cohen, as legal fees. The $130,000 payment was made to Stormy Daniels to buy her silence about having sex with Trump. The payment was made on October 27, 2016 – days before the Presidential election which Trump won.

How did this one-time fling become a burning issue that captivated millions? It was investigated for years by law enforcement agencies – federal and state. What a pathetic waste of time, energy and resources.

Trump denied that it ever happened. Stormy said it happened only once and it was entirely consensual. She said Trump promised that she would appear on his highly rated television program – "The Apprentice." That never happened.

The media saw the issue as a ratings bonanza. Who was telling the truth?

Anyone with an ounce of common sense would have believed Stormy and anyone with an ounce of common sense would not have cared. Once Trump's payment was revealed it was obvious that his denial was a lie. I think Trump was crazy to pay her anything. Had he in a forthright way admitted to the one-night stand and apologized to his wife, I don't think that would have hurt his electoral chances at all. He would have cornered the adultery vote.

The media debased itself with its coverage of this saga.

CNN and MSNBC were the worst offenders. Stormy's lawyer, Michael Avenatti, often appeared several times a day on both networks. In a span of about 5 months, he appeared over 300 times on network and cable television. If he had had to pay for all that airtime, it would have come to several hundred million dollars. When Avenatti announced that he was considering a run for the presidency, the hosts did not dismiss that idea as the lunacy it was.

Anderson Cooper of CNN is a bright guy and a competent interviewer and analyst. How could he have given this man so much free airtime? The answer for Cooper and all the others is that their hatred of Trump trumped their respect for journalistic ethics. In addition to his own program, Cooper interviewed Stormy on CBS' highly rated "60 Minutes."

The anti-Trump media referred to the encounter as an "affair." No, idiots – an affair implies a relationship, not a one-shot deal devoid of meaning. And they referred to her as an "actress." No, idiots –

There is no acting involved, there is no plot. People do not watch pornography for a story line.

Avenatti acted as though he was representing a legitimate film star, and the interviewing lap dogs went along. I think that in the view of most Americans, a woman who allows her sex acts with strangers to be filmed has a lower status than a prostitute. Anyone with an ounce of judgment would have sized-up Avenatti as a self-promoting faker, as an ambitious phony.

Lawyers saw him as a publicity seeker looking to enhance his name recognition and bolster his law practice. Few realized that he was a criminal, and a dumb one at that.

He tried to blackmail Nike saying that he had evidence of corruption in how the company promoted various athletes. On February 13, 2020, a federal jury in Manhattan found him guilty of trying to extort $20 million from Nike.

Avenatti even stole from Stormy. She was to receive nearly $1 million from a publisher for a tell-all book that she and a ghostwriter would produce. Avenatti forged a letter directing Stormy's literary agent to send him $300,000. In federal court in New York, a jury found him guilty of stealing his client's money. Another sterling example of shallowness – that a publisher would pay that kind of money to a porn "star" for some titillating crap.

Avenatti topped himself by doing something truly evil. He lied about settlements he had procured for several permanently injured clients and stole millions from them. He had not told them that he had settled their cases. A California federal court sentenced him to 14 years in prison for these thefts.

This is the guy our media invited into millions of homes, night after night. They lavished him with praise for telling the truth.

Thousands of men have paid hush money to keep affairs secret from their wives, children, and business associates. And they have engaged in subterfuges to hide the payoffs. How many of them have been charged with crimes? Close to zero. One can despise Trump yet acknowledge the targeted absurdity of the felony charges by a district attorney determined to enhance his status by satisfying the lust of his Trump-hating constituents. Biden won Manhattan in a huge landslide over Trump in the 2020 Presidential election. It would be almost impossible to select a jury in Manhattan that would be neutral toward Trump.

Americans know next to zero about how the grand jury system works. There is a longstanding lawyer joke told, mainly by defense attorneys, that any competent prosecutor could manipulate a grand jury into indicting a ham sandwich.

There is some truth to the joke. It is a totally one-sided process. The grand jurors hear only what the prosecutor wants them to hear. Grand jury proceedings are secret, which adds to their feelings of importance.

Who was the star witness before the Trump grand jury, the man who spent multiple hours before them over several days? The answer is Michael Cohen.

Cohen had idolized Trump. He admired how Trump avoided paying taxes and how he constantly outsmarted the "losers." Cohen proudly announced that he would take a bullet for Trump. But Cohen turned on Trump, testifying before Congress and in other venues that Trump was dishonest to the core.

In August 2018, Cohen pled guilty in federal court to several criminal charges including non-stop lying. He was sentenced to 3 years in prison, but served only 13 months. He got himself a lucrative book deal and his own podcast.

Federal prosecutors had investigated all the Stormy Daniels' circumstances, and they declined to prosecute. The Federal Election Commission took no action against Trump.

Cyrus Vance Jr. was the district attorney in Manhattan for over a decade before Alvin Bragg took office in January 2022. Vance investigated all the Stormy Daniels' circumstances and did not indict Trump. Bragg reviewed all of the Vance material and conducted his own review and decided not to indict.

BUT BRAGG CHANGED HIS MIND! OR HAD IT CHANGED!

He caved to the Trump haters in the New York political world and in the media.

In New York, the falsification of business records is a mere misdemeanor for which there would be no grand jury and no felony inditement. Bragg had no interest in charging Trump with a mere misdemeanor, so he concocted a theory to charge Trump with a felony.

Now let's have a look at the craziest case of all – a case which demonstrates the hatred that New Yorkers have for Trump.

A New York Magazine writer, Jean Carroll, claims that Trump raped her in a dressing room of Bergdorf Goodman, a luxury department store in Manhattan, in the mid-1990s. If a woman in Bergdorf screamed "rape" she would quickly be surrounded by a crowd, including security. She did not scream, she did not leave the store hysterical, she did not call the police. There were no witnesses. She never reported the "crime" and never sought a medical examination.

In 2019 she wrote a book claiming that Trump raped her. That's well over 20 years after the supposed assault. Trump denies it ever happened; he says he never met her. She sued him for defamation in a civil case because Trump insulted her and her allegations.

A Manhattan jury was selected, and Trump refused to appear. His deposition was introduced in which he denies ever meeting her. In the deposition he is shown a photograph in which a much younger Jean Carroll appears. Trump misidentifies her as one of his ex-wives. Bizarre!

The jury returns a verdict in her favor for over $60 million – mostly for punitive damages designed to punish.

Ms. Carroll is a sophisticated New Yorker. She has never given a convincing answer to this question – WHY DID YOU WAIT 25 YEARS TO WRITE A BOOK ABOUT "THE RAPE"?

The book came out while Trump was President. A book charging a sitting President with rape will get a lot of attention. You don't have to be very sophisticated to know that Trump will call her a liar. She will be able to sue him for defamation in a city that despises him.

She says she wrote the book so that she could get her life back. Please!

Donald Trump has a lot of enemies. But in a very real sense – he is his own worst enemy. Like not appearing at the trial to look her in the eye and deny that it ever happened. And look at the jurors and say the same thing plus – "you may not like me but I would have to be a lunatic to pull my pants down at Bergdorf Goodman."

"And your dislike for me would have to triumph over your common sense to believe that she didn't scream, she didn't report the imaginary rape and kept quiet for over 20 years."

Yet another self-inflicted wound – calling her "a nut" and not showing up at the trial. I have an entire chapter dealing with intelligent, sophisticated people who make very stupid decisions.

CHAPTER 9

OTHER HIGHLY INTELLIGENT AND ACCOMPLISHED PEOPLE MAKING INCREDIBLY DUMB DECISIONS

Chris Christie is a sterling example. Christie was the two-term governor of New Jersey; he was re-elected in a landslide in 2013. He was considered by many to be the favorite to win the Republican nomination for President in 2016. Unlike Trump he had a political and governing track record.

Christie's downfall was yet another classic example of a self-inflicted wound. He was nursing a grudge against the mayor of Fort Lee who had refused to endorse him in 2013. He obviously did not need his endorsement. That's the get-even mentality of so many politicians.

A notorious email surfaced from Christie's deputy chief of staff, Bridget Kelly, on August 13, 2013 – "time for some traffic problems in Fort Lee." Three lanes of traffic were closed for 5 days, the phony excuse being that a traffic study was being conducted. Traffic came to a near standstill, the innocent residents of Fort Lee, as well as thousands of other users were being punished. The shutdown began on the first day of the school year – school buses, ambulances, people going to work or to medical appointments were all delayed, angry and frustrated. It was beyond stupid, petty and mean.

There would be an outcry by scores of angry people, an investigation would be called for, and the residents would come to understand that the traffic study story was a lie.

There was an investigation, one of the insiders confessed and pled guilty. There were criminal convictions but no charges were brought against Christie.

Did Christie know about the bridge plan? Of course, he did. Christie was a hands-on, detail-oriented governor, and his subordinates were fearful of his temper. On their own they never would have undertaken such an action. It amazes me that no one in Christie's inner circle told him the obvious – that the closure of the bridge was a crazy idea, that it would hurt people who voted for him and that the truth would become known. And more fundamentally, who gave a damn about the Mayor of Fort Lee? Enjoy your victory and forget about him.

That would have been a normal response, but in the political world there is very little that is normal, straitforward or honest. During the 2016 Republican debates, Trump ridiculed Christie for pretending that he did not know about the bridge plan. Christie, a former prosecutor, actually did well during the debates but he was unable to overcome the scandal.

THE GENERALS

Americans are very impressed with generals, as they should be. Several military leaders have become Presidents – Washington, Jackson, Grant, Eisenhower.

Americans assume, and rightly so, that to become a general one must be highly intelligent and certainly a person possessing excellent judgment. Generals are responsible for thousands of young lives.

General David Petraeus had reached such a high level that he commanded all coalition forces in Iraq (2007-08) and all coalition forces in

Afghanistan (2010-11). Upon his retirement he was appointed Director of the Central Intelligence Agency (2011-12) by President Obama. He was being encouraged by many to run for president, and his resume would have made him a formidable candidate.

But Petraeus screwed up big time. A married woman with children wanted to do a book about him. As such they would necessarily be spending a lot of time together. Her work would not be objective; she was in awe of him.

A zillion articles had been written about Petraeus; members of Congress complimented him non-stop – he did not need a book. Most generals have gigantic egos – think of Douglas MacArthur, the World War II hero who was fired by President Truman during the Korean War because he was insubordinate. Truman was decisive, as demonstrated by his decision to unleash atomic bombs on Japanese cities. It should have been obvious to MacArthur that Truman would not tolerate a public disagreement with his policies.

MacArthur's decision and its aftermath ended any hopes he had to become president. That prize went instead to General Eisenhower, who at one time had been MacArthur's subordinate.

An affair began between Petraeus and his "biographer." Bad enough, but Petraeus gave her a diary with classified information which contained the names of covert agents. Worse yet, he lied to the FBI about it. Lying to the FBI was the great sin of the Mueller investigation.

The FBI recommended a felony indictment but the Justice Department allowed Petraeus to enter a plea in April 2015 to the vague misdemeanor of mishandling classified information. Petraeus lost his position as Director of the CIA.

Let's take a look at another general who lied to the FBI. I speak of Lt. General Michael Flynn, who President Trump appointed as his National Security Advisor. Before a month elapsed, he was gone.

Why?

Before I answer that, consider Flynn's background. His life was the military – over 30 years. He served multiple tours in Iraq and Afghanistan. He was the Director of Intelligence for the United States Central

Command, he was the Director of Intelligence for both American and international forces in Afghanistan. After retiring from active duty, he became the director of the Defense Intelligence Agency (2012-14). Obama appointed Flynn to that position. Obviously, a lot of high-level people considered Flynn to be very intelligent.

In one sense he remained very intelligent, placing his bet on a Trump victory when nearly all the experts figured Trump would self-immolate. The admiration was mutual, and Flynn became a part of Trump's inner circle. Flynn's interest in politics was recent, as was his interest in making money.

Turkey paid him over a $500,000 for his lobbying work. He was paid $45,000 for a speech he gave in Moscow at an event where he was seated with Putin. He lied in federal filings about his lobbying activities, concealing his financial ties to both Turkey and Russia. He failed to register as a foreign agent, as required by law.

Flynn had made speeches during the campaign screaming – "Lock her up." Hundreds of journalists and political opponents were searching for ways to make Trump and members of his team look bad. How could Flynn have believed that his omissions and lies would not be discovered?

In December 2016, Flynn spoke to the Russian ambassador about sanctions which had been imposed by the Obama administration in response to Russia's interference in the Ukraine. It is likely that he told the ambassador the sanctions would be lifted or at least eased after Trump was sworn in. When Vice President Pence asked Flynn about his conversation with the ambassador, Flynn denied that sanctions were discussed. He told the same lie to the FBI, a crime to which he pled guilty.

It disgusts me when I see the Trump haters enjoying Flynn's downfall. Whatever his faults, he is a man who risked his life serving his fellow citizens. If not for Flynn and the men and women who serve in our military, the talking heads on television would not have the freedom to smirk and ridicule.

And then there is the case of General Stanley McChrystal, probably the most impressive military figure in America's war against terror, the leader of special forces units which killed more terrorists than any other branch of the military. I provide more details about him in my chapter on Afghanistan.

What stupid thing did this brilliant strategist do? He granted an interview with a reporter from Rolling Stone Magazine in which he mocked President Obama and some of Obama's closest advisers. Obama felt he had no choice but to fire him.

Did McChrystal not understand that journalists love juicy quotes and thrive on conflict, especially so between a president and a top general. He was suckered to believe that the writer had become his friend, very impressed with the macho image of a combat warrior.

So he let his guard down, expressing an honest opinion about his commander in chief.

THE PRESIDENTS

President Nixon was the comeback kid, not Bill Clinton. He lost the election to Kennedy in 1960 by a whisker and then went on to lose to Pat Brown running for governor of California. After that loss, he blasted the liberal media saying they wouldn't have Nixon to kick around anymore. Yet he came back, was elected President, and then re-elected in a landslide. He was viewed as one of the shrewdest political operatives in American history.

Nixon did not have a winning, lovable personality such as Kennedy, Reagan or Clinton. He was ill at ease in one-on-one settings and he was often ill at ease speaking before crowds. This showed in his television debate with Kennedy who was the essence of cool and self-assured. Nixon's smile was almost always forced and unnatural.

He handed his enemies the means to destroy him. I refer to the taping system he installed in the White House. Without that system he would not have resigned the presidency. He should have destroyed the tapes as soon as the burglary of Democratic headquarters at the Watergate complex became public. More fundamentally it was very dumb and very sneaky to install the taping system in the first place.

People that Nixon interacted with did not realize they were being recorded. Presidents become obsessed with their legacies, their libraries, and how history will judge them. Nixon figured he would have plenty of time to edit the tapes to make himself look good. How does a man who achieved his dream of becoming president live with the fact that his own decision caused the threat of impeachment and his forced resignation?

The tapes were his property, he would have been severely criticized but he never would have been impeached on the naked word of John Dean. What killed Nixon was his involvement in the cover-up which was confirmed by his voice on the tapes. What killed him was the fact that he was a micromanager – he should have walked away from the aftermath of the burglary; instead he immersed himself in the details.

Nixon did not need dirty tricks. He didn't even need standard political intelligence – his Democratic opponent was George McGovern. McGovern won a single state (Massachusetts) and the District of Columbia. Nixon could have stayed at home on Key Biscayne or in San Clemente, and he still would have crushed McGovern – perhaps the most liberal member of the United States Senate.

Another incredibly stupid decision by Nixon: selecting Spiro Agnew as his Vice-Presidential running mate. Nearly all the insiders in Maryland politics knew that Governor Agnew was a bribe taker. I have to believe Nixon did not know this because it would have been crazy to have someone on your ticket who was that vulnerable. But on the other hand, how could he not have known? How could his vetting process have been that superficial? Agnew had to resign before Nixon did.

It was Ford who replaced Agnew, becoming president when Nixon resigned. He served one term, losing to Jimmy Carter who had zero experience in foreign affairs or at the national level. That same deficiency applied to Clinton and Bush II. All three had been governors, with none of them being viewed as particularly outstanding in those roles. It was their political talents that were outstanding.

McGovern's vetting process was even worse. He selected as his running mate Senator Thomas Eagleton of Missouri. It was discovered that Eagleton had received electroshock therapy for depression and that he had been hospitalized for nervous exhaustion and fatigue at least three times. Back then, Americans were much less tolerant and less understanding of mental and emotional problems.

McGovern's initial response was that he remained "one thousand percent" committed to his running mate. Then reality kicked in and Eagleton was replaced by Sargent Shriver, the founder of the Peace Corps, and a brother-in-law of President Kennedy.

How about Agnew's stupidity? Once you are vice president of the United States, even if you were once totally corrupt, there is no reason to continue to accept bribes. A former vice president is guaranteed to become a millionaire through a book deal and paid speeches. He can be appointed to all kinds of corporate boards where the pay is very good for doing no work.

Agnew continued to accept bribes after he became vice president; it had become part of his political DNA. He was Nixon's hatchet man, making very tough speeches against liberals in the media and politics. His enemies rejoiced when he went down.

How about President Kennedy? He was brilliant, a speed reader, well informed, sophisticated – a man who surrounded himself with loyal and competent advisers. Yet he did not understand that if America backs an invasion of a tiny country, the world's number one superpower must win.

I refer to the Bay of Pigs fiasco, where the objective was to get rid of Fidel Castro. Our CIA was training some incredibly brave Cubans who were willing to risk their lives to free Cuba. This was somewhat of a myth because Batista and his predecessors were hardly paragons of democracy. They were capitalist dictators which was fine with us, whereas Castro was a communist dictator.

Kennedy apparently believed he could keep America's involvement secret which was an absurd belief. The enterprise was doomed because Castro had a loyal military with experience, good equipment and intimate knowledge of the terrain. Kennedy sealed the doom of the invaders when he failed to provide them with air cover. Kennedy bought into the myth that the Cuban people would rise up against the dictator. He did not understand that Castro was incredibly popular with the "masses."

Castro was able to brag that he had defeated the American colossus. Many of our Cuban fighters were killed, and others were imprisoned for decades. The Cuban victory at the Bay of Pigs conferred an iconic status on Castro and that is a major reason why he and his brother were able to maintain their hold on power for well over a half-century.

GARY HART

Hart was a tragic figure in American politics. The two term Colorado Senator was often compared to President Kennedy both in looks and style. He was young, handsome, with an athletic build. Women swooned; he was an effective speaker and was the favorite to get the Democratic nomination for president in 1988.

He had been a contender in 1984 when Vice President Walter Mondale got the nomination. Mondale was crushed by Reagan. But in 1988, Hart was the favorite. The chink in his armor was that although he had been in a long-term marriage, he was a womanizer. His advisors told him the obvious as the political season was in full gear – keep your zipper up.

Hart was incredibly reckless and incredibly stupid. He knew that Kennedy and Johnson during their presidencies had multiple affairs, yet the mainstream media did not go there. He figured they would treat him the same way. How could he not have recognized that times had changed, that the media had changed?

In the heat of the political campaign he brought a Miami model, Donna Rice, to his townhouse in DC. In an interview he gave to the New York Times when questioned about his "ladies man" reputation he said in a very cocky way – "Follow me, you'll be bored." The Miami Herald followed him and it was not boring. They confirmed the tryst.

As it happened, a woman who knew Donna Rice called the Miami Herald and told an editor/reporter about the affair. Hell hath no fury like a woman scorned. Maybe Hart preferred Rice over the caller, maybe the caller was jealous of Rice or hated her. Whatever her motive, she conveyed accurate information.

Hart had the audacity to allow a photograph of Rice sitting on his lap on a boat called "Monkey Business" on Bimini. The body language and facial expressions shouted out – sex!

How does a man of Hart's stature or Clinton's stature subject their wives and children to such humiliations? It is a character issue which ultimately is the key to assessing any political figure.

Once the cat was out of the bag, a media frenzy ensued. Hart tried to ride it out, but could not. At one of the press conferences he was asked whether he considered adultery to be immoral and after a long pause he said – Yes! When asked whether he had ever committed adultery he refused to answer. The frenzy did not dissipate and Hart dropped out of the race.

Seven months after he withdrew, he got back in the race for the nomination. He finished last in the first two contests of the primary season – the Iowa caucuses and the New Hampshire primary. He quit again and his political career was over.

Figure it out – the public forgave Clinton for his philandering, but they refused to forgive Hart. Michael Dukakis, Governor of Massachusetts, got the 1988 nomination and was crushed by Reagan's vice president – George Bush. Hart would have had a much better shot.

CHAPTER 10

HAD HILLARY CLINTON WON IN 2016, SHE WOULD HAVE BEEN ONLY THE SECOND FEMALE PRESIDENT

Who was the first? Woodrow Wilson's second wife – Edith Bolling Galt. Wilson's first wife, Ellen, died on August 6, 1914. He married Galt, a 42-year-old widow of a wealthy jeweler, on December 18, 1915.

At the end of World War I, Wilson's cherished dream was for America to join the League of Nations. There was strong Senate opposition to America joining the League by those who did not want our sovereignty to be diminished.

Wilson went to Paris to negotiate the peace treaty (the Treaty of Versailles) with the other winners – England and France. He was very popular with the European crowds. In Europe there was great enthusiasm for establishing the League. Wilson figured that the American people would be equally enthusiastic.

To help create support for the League, Wilson embarked on an exhausting speaking tour, crisscrossing the nation. He had to overcome the Senate opposition led by Henry Cabot Lodge.

Touring by train, he made 42 speeches in 22 days during September 1919. Wilson also was selling his peace program contained in his famous "14 points." That schedule ruined his health.

Wilson suffered a minor stroke in September. On October 2, 1919, he suffered a major stroke caused by a cerebral thrombosis which created a blockage of blood flow to his brain. He was unconscious for several days. The stroke left him paralyzed on his left side and completely blind in his right eye. He never recovered the use of his left arm. The left side of his face drooped, his speech was impaired, and he had to use a wheelchair. He never regained his previous mental capacity, and that fact was hidden from the American people. It was also hidden from members of Congress and even from his cabinet. Few Americans understood that Wilson had suffered a major stroke, and fewer still had any appreciation of how disabling it was.

It always surprised me how easily Americans accept secrecy when transparency should be insisted upon. Franklin Roosevelt was elected four times – 1932, 1936, 1940 and 1944. Throughout his presidency he was unable to walk unaided. He had been the victim of polio, infantile paralysis. Sitting down or standing while making a speech, he projected an image of vigor.

Most Americans had no idea of his physical limitations. As we did not probe about Wilson's condition, we did not probe about Roosevelt's. Journalists were not digging for the truth in either instance.

A few weeks after his stroke, Wilson suffered a urinary tract infection that nearly killed him. After recovering from that scare, he contracted influenza in January 1920. After World War I, influenza had killed millions.

Since the president was not making any public appearances, the big lie had to be invented – which was that Wilson was merely suffering from nervous exhaustion brought on by his strenuous efforts on behalf of the League. The public was told that although Wilson was temporarily weakened, his mind was unimpaired.

Amazingly, no member of Congress or the Cabinet insisted on independent medical examinations by a panel of highly qualified physicians. Why didn't leaders of the Republican Party make such a demand? The whole country was being deferential to the office of the presidency rather than focusing on a search for the facts.

The captain of the big lie conspiracy was Wilson's personal physician, Admiral Dr. Cary Grayson. Other physicians were part of the conspiracy as well.

No one sought to invoke Article II, Section 1 of the Constitution, dealing with the –

"Inability of the president to discharge the powers and duties of his office."

The 25th Amendment was not ratified until February 1967. Like Article 2, it deals with a situation where it is asserted that a president is –

"Unable to discharge the powers and duties of his office."

Under the Amendment, if the president rebuts that contention, it is up to Congress to resolve the dispute. It would take a two-thirds vote of both Houses to remove a president.

Although the vice president, Thomas Marshall, sought to meet with Wilson, his wife would not allow it. Yes, she decided who could see the president and for how long. Very few were granted this privilege.

Could you imagine a vice president like Theodore Roosevelt or Lyndon Johnson tolerating such a situation? They would have granted interviews exposing the absurdity of Mrs. Wilson's power.

On December 4, 1919, Secretary of State Robert Lansing announced that no one in the cabinet had spoken with or seen Wilson for over 60 days. How could seasoned political figures tolerate such a situation?

Lansing, as well as other cabinet members, plus congressional leaders of both parties, were pushing Marshall to take actions that would have enabled him to assume the presidency. Marshall was beyond weak and a very rare bird: a vice president who did not lust to become president.

Marshall informed the cabinet that he would assume the presidency only in response to a joint resolution of Congress calling on him to do so, or an official communication from Wilson or his staff asserting his inability to perform his duties. He had to know that neither one was going to happen.

Of course, Mrs. Wilson and the other insiders were consistent in perpetrating the fiction that the president was functional and capable of absorbing information and making decisions. Unintentionally, Mrs. Wilson told at least part of the truth in her 1938 autobiography.

She said that she studied every paper sent from different cabinet members or senators and tried to digest and present to her husband in tabloid form the things that she felt he needed to see.

"The only decision that was mine was what was important and what was not, and the very important decision of when to present matters to my husband." That amounts to a confession about Wilson's true disability.

Yes, the jeweler's widow became the de facto president. She was not highly educated and had no background at all in decision making at the highest level. Before marrying Wilson, she had no interest in national or international affairs. Yet she decided what was important to show the president, she decided what not to show him, she decided who could see him and for how long. She was the de facto president. History has basically ignored her takeover.

How's that for democracy? How's that for a country not demanding to know the truth about their president's mental and physical health?

SOME BACKGROUND ON PRESIDENT WILSON

He had been President of Princeton University and Governor of New Jersey. When he sought re-election in 1916, he had a very impressive opponent – Charles Evans Hughes who had been Governor of New York and an Associate Justice of the U.S. Supreme Court.

The race was close but Wilson won. His popular vote was 9,126,868 to Hughes 8,548,728. 49.2% to 46.1%. In the 1912 Electoral College, it was Wilson 277 to Hughes 254.

So how was it that Democrat Wilson was first elected in 1912 after a succession of Republican Presidents? The answer lies in the feud between Theodore Roosevelt and William Howard Taft which I will detail in the next chapter.

Wilson became the first Democratic President elected to a second consecutive term since Andrew Jackson in 1832.

Wilson's slogan during the 1916 campaign was – "He kept us out of war."

On April 2, 1917, less than a month after his second inauguration, Wilson delivered a war message to Congress. The new pitch was – "The world must be made safe for Democracy." During World War I, two million American young men went to Europe to do battle.

Wilson was very naïve, a terrible quality in a president. He thought the League of Nations had the potential to abolish wars. The League was a failure and obviously could not prevent the rise of Nazi Germany and the devastation of World War II.

Wilson's other pipe dream was the spread of democracy. Myths can have a very long life. That is a very basic policy goal of President Biden – as foolish now as it was back then.

We have had other naïve presidents – even Franklin Roosevelt when he met with Stalin at Yalta. He believed Stalin's lies about not wishing to take over the countries of eastern Europe and transforming them into satellites of the Soviet Union. Or how about Obama, who believed Iran's lies about developing a nuclear capacity for peaceful purposes. Iran's number one goal is possession of atomic, nuclear bombs.

Americans, by and large, tend to be naïve. Like the very high hopes for the United Nations. The U.N. did no better than the League in abolishing wars. One's head would spin at the number of wars inflicted in the human race since the creation of the United Nations.

Wilson's second term ended March 4, 1921. He and his wife bought a home in Washington and remained there until his death on February 3, 1924. Wilson was buried at the National Cathedral in Washington, D.C. He never regained either physical or mental normalcy.

CHAPTER 11

THE SUPER-RICH CONTROL AMERICAN POLITICS

That control is okay with both Congress and our Supreme Court. The rich hide their multi-million-dollar contributions to non-profit organizations which are not required by law to disclose the identity of their donors. Also, how this money is spent is totally secret.

Under our tax code, these organizations are referred to as social welfare organizations. They qualify by presenting themselves as –

"Promoting the common good and general welfare of the community as a whole." That is the subterfuge. All the insiders know that it is a subterfuge but they have no problem with it.

Many of these "non-profits" are in reality political machines which promote a party or cause without naming a specific candidate. They are not permitted to directly engage in politics. But they engage heavily indirectly. They present themselves as local, grassroots, advocacy organizations focused on issues rather than on elections.

The Supreme Court of the United States opened the flood gates for the super-rich to dominate elections. In the "Citizens United" case, decided in a 5-4 opinion, issued January 31, 2010, the Court held that corporations and unions have the same First Amendment rights as do individuals.

"Congress shall make no law abridging the freedom of speech."

There is no limit on how much money a corporation can spend to advance its political agenda. The Court ruled that restrictions on corporate and union expenditures are unconstitutional. In reaching this conclusion, the Justices had to ignore their own precedents.

The public knows nothing about the various non-profit groups which operate under dozens of trade names so they can appear to be separate grassroots organizations. Often there is a coalition of groups which coordinate their efforts. Dark money can be funneled through non-profits to hide the identity of contributions to Supers PACs. Shell companies and other limited liability companies can also be used to achieve that objective.

Super PACs (political action committees) are different from the non-profits. The identity of donors to super PACs must be disclosed. There are no limits on the amount of money which can be contributed to these PACs. There is a fiction connected to the PACs, a fiction that is perfectly okay with Congress. PACs can raise unlimited amounts of money for their favorite candidates so long as they do not coordinate their spending. Of course, that is precisely what they do under cover. Similar to the technique used by non-profits.

The prohibition against coordination, in practical terms, is unenforceable and the Federal Election Commission is both undermanned and toothless.

The non-profits and the PACs and the manipulations which fuel them are the gateway to corruption and inequality.

Jeb Bush, the former two term governor of Florida, attended many fundraisers enabling his PAC to spend about $130 million in his quest for the Republican nomination. He dropped out of the race in late February 2016 after losing in South Carolina without having won a single state.

Bush had been an effective governor of a major state. He was the son and brother of presidents. He was into decorum and he could not grapple with an opponent who mocked him as – "Mr. Low Energy." Bush is just one example where a truck full of cash did not guarantee victory. Another was John Connally, a former governor of Texas and treasury secretary under Nixon, a man highly regarded for competence and savvy, who made moves toward a presidential run, but won nothing.

THE ABSOLUTE CHAMPION OF SPENDING HUGE AND COMING UP EMPTY WAS MICHAEL BLOOMBERG

He spent a billion dollars and did not win a single state. Bloomberg despised Trump, yet they had a lot in common – arrogant know-it-all's, who had never held political office before becoming mayor and president – very ambitious with sky high opinions of themselves.

Being a three term Mayor of New York wasn't enough for Bloomberg. He wanted to be president and thought he could be in 2020. He spent $11 million for a 1-minute commercial during the Super Bowl.

Bloomberg's plan was to skip the early primary contests. He also skipped the debates between the Democratic primary candidates during January and February. His plan was to establish himself as the most formidable candidate by doing well on Super Tuesday – March 3 – when the voters in 14 states went to the polls. These states included California, Texas, Colorado, Massachusetts, Minnesota and North Carolina. He didn't win any of them.

By February 2020, Bloomberg had thousands of people working for him – yes thousands. He was able to staff offices in over 125 cities across the nation. He paid his people way more than the other candidates. He was paying entry-level field organizing staffers $72,000 annually.

How did Bloomberg come to be worth about $60 billion? Not by curing cancer or AIDS – not by eradicating poverty and homelessness. He had done well as a Wall Street trader but his Midas touch allowed him to come up with the idea of desktop terminals that provided up-to-date financial information to the American investor class.

Yes, a computer system that gives subscribers real time access to large quantities of financial data – traders using these terminals can react to market events moments faster than those lacking the terminals. That plus a news organization – Bloomberg News.

Bloomberg was the Mayor of New York from 2002 through 2013. He believed in term limits. He liked the power and adulation of the job and decided he would like a third term. So he bullied the city council into changing the law which had been reaffirmed in two referendums limiting the Mayor to two terms.

To win that third term, Bloomberg spent over $100 million to eke out a 50.6% victory over a competent opponent, but one most New Yorkers knew nothing about. With that squeaker in the rear-view mirror, how does he convince himself that he has a shot to become president? Never underestimate the arrogance and ambition of a billionaire who believes that if you spend enough money, you can manipulate the beliefs of millions.

One cannot become the Democratic nominee for President without strong backing from African Americans. Bloomberg had a problem with that constituency. During his 12 years as Mayor, he had been a strong proponent of –

"Stop and Frisk."

If the police thought that someone looked suspicious or if for any reason they didn't like the looks of a given person, they could stop that individual and search him. The vast majority of those who were stopped and frisked were Black or Hispanic.

Individual cops had enormous discretion and could hassle anyone they pleased. In the year 2011, over 685,000 of these stops were recorded. Bloomberg not only strongly supported "Stop and Frisk" while Mayor, he supported it for years after leaving. One of his many quotes on the subject –

"Throw them up against the wall and frisk them." The "them" he was referring to were not his buddies in the investor class. His tough guy stance against the unconnected was supposed to make him look strong – you know, "tough on crime."

Okay – so how do you get support from the minorities opposed to the policy that Bloomberg had championed? The answer is phony public relations – a staple of political witchcraft.

Bloomberg addressed the congregation of a major Black church in Brooklyn. He pretended that he did not understand the impact that the policy had on young Blacks and Hispanics, many of whom were stopped multiple times.

He told the congregation – "I was wrong and I am sorry." He had continued to be wrong year after year after year.

His first call after leaving the church was to the Reverend Al Sharpton. That alone speaks volumes. How did I do, Al? Do you think they believed me?

He disguised his problem with female employees getting them to sign non-disclosure agreements. No, he wasn't assaulting them but he constantly made wiseguy comments about their appearances, their sex appeal or lack of same, their attire. The exact same type of comments that got a lot of big shots in trouble during the height of the "Me Too" movement.

Bloomberg demeaned farmers and industrial workers by saying that it does not require much intelligence to perform their tasks. To him the fields that require high levels of intelligence are finance, trading and policy. Yeah – like all the geniuses who had no clue that the crash of 2008 was about to happen or that inflation was about to skyrocket.

Bloomberg had been a Republican, a Democrat and an Independent. Over the years, he has given billions of dollars to political and charitable causes. He spent $100 million helping Democrats take control of the House of Representatives in the mid-term 2018 elections. He has supported many in State races as well, with hundreds of politicians beholden to him. He thought they would put him over the top.

Overall, he spent about a $1 billion and the only thing he won was American Samoa. Beyond embarrassing!

Equally embarrassing was his debate performance. Senator Elizabeth Warren blasted him in very strident language for his mistreatment of women employees. He was stunned, befuddled. Nobody screams at billionaires, and nobody insults a billionaire to his face. Almost everyone kisses up to billionaires.

If he couldn't handle Warren, how was he going to do against Putin and the Chinese and North Korean dictators?

A CALIFORNIA EXAMPLE OF THE OBSCENE AMOUNT OF MONEY SPENT ON POLITICAL CAMPAIGNS

There was an effort to recall Governor Gavin Newsom in California. He was able to raise $70 million. California has no limit on such donations. The chief executive of Netflix contributed three million; Zuckerberg's wife sent in $750,000. There were several other half-million-dollar donations. Needless to say, Newson was not recalled.

Money may not be the root of all evil but it most certainly is the root of nearly all political evil. $14 billion was spent on federal races (President, House and Senate) in 2020 – double the amount spent in 2016.

The big money comes from America's Oligarchs – the hedge fund and private equity people, venture capitalists, real estate developers. Congress knows exactly how this game is played but they do nothing to stop it. Why?

Because those are the people who fund their campaigns. The lobbyists, lawyers, accountants and consultants make sure that Congress knows who to reward. Congress does not seek to dismantle the tax code or clamp down on the abuses of Big Tech because their contributions come from the tax cheats and Oligarchs.

THE SOLUTION TO THE CONTROL OF THE SUPER-WEALTHY

My solution is a fantasy – the vested interests will never allow it to happen.

Fantasy number one – limit by law the amount of money that can be raised or spent on political campaigns. Limit the number of ads on television and other media.

Require that candidates state their positions very specifically on all the key domestic and foreign issues. Evasive answers would be penalized, so would generalizations.

Our political system is very superficial. Crowds that cheer wildly for their favorite candidate could not say where they stand on specific issues. Here are a few of the topics which would have to be answered under my system.

What would you do to relieve the inequities in our society between the wealthy and the middle and lower classes? What would you do to relieve poverty and homelessness?

What should America do, if anything, if China invades Taiwan?

What should America do to prevent Iran from acquiring nuclear weapons? Would you go to war against Iran to prevent that from happening?

State clearly your position with respect to Russia, the Ukraine, Israel, and the Middle East in general.

Do you agree that had America not pushed for Ukraine to join NATO, that Russia never would have invaded?

Should we continue our support of Ukraine indefinitely?

Sad to say but the average voter has no idea how their preferred candidate would respond to any of the above. Also sad to say that requiring answers is a fantasy.

CHAPTER 12

POVERTY AND INEQUALITY

In 1964, President Lyndon Johnson declared, very dramatically, that America was declaring an "unconditional war on poverty."

Over 60 years later, America has not won that war. And 60 years later, inequality is much worse. The richest 1% of Americans have as much wealth as 90% of the rest of the population.

Janet Yellen, Biden's treasury secretary and former head of the federal reserve, said in February 2021, that –

"We have 24 Million adults and 12 Million kids that are going hungry every day."

There is an organization backed by the Service Employees International Union called –

"Fight for $15.00" – a title which speaks for itself.

It has been battling for that goal for years. There are millions of Americans who don't make $15.00 an hour. Yes – millions of housekeepers, nurse's aides, clerks, cashiers, fast food workers, janitors, baggage handlers, childcare and homecare workers who do not make $15.00 an hour. But Hillary Clinton gets $250,000 for a one-hour speech to Goldman Sachs. And partners in the top Wall Street law firms charge $1000 an hour telling their wealthy clients how to avoid paying their fair share of taxes.

According to a Federal Reserve Survey of Household Economics released in May 2021, 36% of American adults would have difficulty paying for a $400 emergency expense right now. The report also says that 26% of people with jobs have no retirement savings. These are the working poor, many of whom rely on food stamps. Many are homeless.

Another point made by the federal reserve – that nearly one-third of American adults are – "struggling to get by or just getting by." The Congressman Budget Office pointed out that the income of the top 1% rose 275% from 1979 to 2007. The income of the bottom 20% rose a mere 18% during the same time period.

According to the US Department of Agriculture in 2021, there were over 41 million Americans on food stamps. According to the Census Bureau data in 2020, there were over 37 million Americans in poverty. Things have only gotten worse since 2020 and 2021. How incredibly sad six decades after Johnson's war.

Joseph Stiglitz is a winner of the Nobel Prize in economics, and has been the chairman of the Council of Economic Advisors. This is what he had to say about our economy under President Trump –

"Despite the lowest unemployment rates since the late 1960s, the American economy is failing its citizens. Some 90% have seen their incomes stagnate or decline in the past 30 years."

Part of the explanation for this is the declining power of unions. Unions that would strive for higher pay and safer working conditions. Over 90% of private sector workers do not belong to unions. And the beloved Amazon, and the beloved Starbucks along with many other companies, fire workers for activism toward establishing union representation.

Years ago, the American Federation of Labor, the Congress of Industrial Organizations, and the United Automobile Workers were powerhouses that mega rich companies had to deal with.

When negotiations broke down between 13,000 unionized air traffic controllers and the Federal Aviation Administration, President Reagan fired them all. Union busting became a badge of honor among many conservative politicians.

Matthew Desmond wrote a hard-hitting book in 2016 called – "Evicted: Poverty and Profit in the American City."

Desmond has been a Harvard and Princeton professor of sociology. But he is no ivory tower academic. In researching his book, he lived among poor families in Milwaukee for long stretches and in deplorable conditions –

He has said –

"Some people make a lot of money off low-income families and directly contribute to their poverty. No holy teaching can be summoned to defend what we have allowed our country to become."

Desmond followed his eviction book with an even tougher book in 2023 called – "Poverty by America."

Among his points –

The American people are complicit in the perpetuation of poverty. By exploiting the poor, we obtain cheap goods and services. It is our abuse of cheap labor that makes the low prices possible.

Desmond provides examples of how the poor get shafted, how it is actually expensive to be poor. They have to pay to get their checks cashed. Many do not have checking accounts or any relations with banks. Those that do, get socked with outrageous overdraft fees.

The poor are excluded from traditional banking and credit systems. Many have no credit score at all and have to deal with pawn brokers and loan sharks.

Desmond is critical of the American middle class and certainly of the rich. His bottom line is that we have the means to abolish poverty, to wipe it out completely. What is missing is the public and political will to accomplish that.

Let's look at a single example of how entrepreneurs get rich on the backs of the poor. I refer to the payday loan industry. Millions of employed Americans live from paycheck to paycheck, with no real savings. These are people whose credit scores are so low that they lack access to banks and traditional forms of consumer credit. Most of them are unable to obtain a credit card.

The majority are unable to repay the loan quickly, so they get caught up in the cycle of rolling their loans over and over into new loans; the interest rate can become astronomical. This is such a profitable business that there have been as many as 24,000 lenders, both online and in storefront locations.

Of course, the payday lenders have a trade group (lobbying group) which tells the public how wonderful they are. Their web site says –

"More than 19 million American households count a payday loan among their choice of short-term credit products."

Like they really have a "choice." Think of the money to be made on the backs of so many borrowers. Think of how pathetic it is to be so short on resources that you need one of these loans. It has been estimated that payday lenders collect some $7 billion a year in fees. In April 2017 the trade group held their annual retreat at the Trump National Doral Golf Club.

Here is another example of how those lacking in funds get shafted. Thousands have remained in jail simply because they did not have the cash to bond out. These are not criminals; they may have been cited for an expired driver's license or tag. Our cities rely on these fines and fees to meet their budget obligations. The multi-billion-dollar bail bond industry, of course, has a lobbying arm – the Professional Bail Agents of the United States.

The people languishing in jail are not a flight risk, nor are they a danger to the public. They are there simply because they are unable to afford bail. And you thought debtors' prisons had been outlawed generations earlier.

Subprime loans are like payday loans made to people with lousy credit scores, who are charged higher interest rates than those with better credit histories. The borrower misses one or two payments – no problem for the dealership or finance company making the loan. Simply repossess the car and make a profit on the bad luck of the victims, who will probably lose their jobs because they are unable to drive to work.

There are employers who never pay overtime to the working poor. There are hospitals that sue over medical debt, that garnish wages.

Worse yet there are hospitals that withhold care from patients with unpaid medical bills.

HOMELESSNESS

According to the U.S. Department of Housing and Urban Development (HUD)'s 2020 Annual Homelessness Assessment Report Part 1 to Congress, 580,466 people experienced homelessness in the United States on a single night in 2020. Of this number, there were 37,252 homeless veterans – about 8% of all homeless adults.

Between 2022 and 2023, there was a rise of 70,000 additional homeless – the most ever over a single year. Nationwide, the total of homeless was the astounding number of over 653,000.

The rise was attributed to the lack of affordable housing, to the sharp rise in rents. Also to influx of migrants. Included were all age groups. Homelessness was pervasive in large cities, small cities and rural areas.

During the pandemic there was a moratorium on evictions. That ended as did other forms of aid.

It is beyond unconscionable that an American who served in Vietnam or Afghanistan or Iraq is sleeping on a bench or on the grass or in a car. They are often awakened by a cop who tells them they have to move. To move where? To another concrete or wooden bench with a lot of splinters.

The homeless include people with disabilities, with mental health problems and of course those with various forms of addiction.

According to a November 2021 report, "Student Homelessness in New York City," put out by Advocates for Children of New York, more than 101,000 New York City students were identified as homeless during the 2020-2021 school year, a 42% increase since the start of the decade and the sixth consecutive school year that more than 100,000 New York City students experienced homelessness.

By 2022, the number had zoomed to over 119,000. Migrant children were part of this mix. Parents felt terrible about not being able to provide for their children. Tensions and conflicts between the generations are inevitable. The system is overwhelmed and children with learning disabilities and mental health problems are ignored.

Many kids simply stop attending school. Where do they do their homework? What is their attitude toward those kids who are well fed, well dressed, and housed?

What kind of people are we to tolerate these disgraceful numbers? Forget government – Bezos, Musk, Buffett, Gates, Soros, Zuckerberg could solve homelessness in a flash as could the Facebook, Google, hedge fund and private equity billionaires. If they gave a damn, no American child would suffer from hunger.

Instead their focus and their contributions go to museums and libraries where they are feted at black-tie extravaganzas and praised for their devotion to culture.

Think of how humiliating it is to be evicted, to be thrown out of the place where you and your family eat and sleep. To have your meager belongings sitting in a pile on the sidewalk, because you couldn't make a rent payment, because you had an unexpected medical bill or car repair bill.

Think of how humiliating it is to have to "donate" your blood to get some much-needed cash. These donations endanger your own health, lessen your ability to fight off infections. The United States allows an individual to sell their blood (plasma) over 100 times a year. Few other countries allow payment for blood, recognizing what a rotten system that is.

THE LIES WE TELL ABOUT INEQUALITY

How is a man or woman making minimum wage—or less—supposed to feel when they read about a hedge fund manager who took in over a $1 billion in a single year? How are they supposed to feel when they see full-page ads promoting residences on a 53-acre island in Abacos, Bahamas? Homes or penthouses priced from $8.1 million and more. And they know there are a ton of people sitting at their computers who have the money to buy in the Bahamas. Also a good place to hide their assets to avoid paying taxes.

They have to pretend that they are not resentful, they don't want to be accused of being envious. Some are so brainwashed that they believe the hedge fund owners and the private equity owners deserve their riches.

We are not a revolutionary people. If we were, there would be a revolution against the unfairness of pervasive inequality. The insiders preach about the majesty of free markets and the wonders of capitalism, and a passive public buys into that. Capitalism could be a lot fairer if the investing class cared about the working class.

Private equity firms like Blackrock and PIMCO oversee more than $1 trillion in global assets. They along with JP Morgan and the other major investment banks and the hedge funds are America's oligarchs. Oh, you didn't know that to a large extent we are ruled by oligarchs?

Think of the working poor that will never walk into one of these stores – Prada, Hermes, Valentino, Ferragamo, Tiffany, Chanel, Brioni, Gucci. Think of the millions who don't have the skills or education or temperament to succeed in the new tech world. They will never become app developers. Think of the millions who know they will never achieve the fabled American dream.

Such thoughts should make us more than skeptical about our political cheerleaders who keep telling us how great we are. We can achieve greatness when homelessness is eradicated, when poverty is eradicated, when our society becomes fairer, and when we become concerned for the unconnected outsider.

CHAPTER 13

THE FALSE PROMISES OF INDEPENDENCE AND DEMOCRACY

More wars have been fought to promote or prevent independence movements than for any other reason. More graveyards have been filled with the victims of independence movements than from any other cause.

In the majority of cases when independence is actually achieved, the only difference to the average citizen is that a new group of insiders, a new elite is in charge. This chapter will demonstrate the universality of the desire for independence and the consequences that have flowed from that desire. It would take a battalion of psychologists to figure out the passion that this idea arouses in millions.

With the breakup of the Ottoman Empire and the Austro-Hungarian Empire after World War I, all the provinces yearned for independence and sovereignty. President Woodrow Wilson naively encouraged independence movements after World War I, praising self-determination, national liberation, and autonomous development of national minorities.

Gandhi of India is one of the all-time icons of the dream of independence. A believer in non-violence and willing to endure all kinds of sacrifices, he strived for independence from Great Britain for decades. It was finally achieved in 1947.

Britain had been able to prevent all-out war between the majority Hindus and the Muslims in India. After independence a full-scale slaughter ensued. The Muslims wanted to secede from India and form their own independent nation, which they did – Pakistan. Pakistan and India fought several wars.

Part of the population of Pakistan wanted to secede and form their own independent nation, which they did – Bangladesh. More wars, killings, and millions of deaths resulting from these three independence movements.

WHAT PROPELLED AMERICA'S INDEPENDENCE MOVEMENT?

The answer is actually very simple. The policies of an arrogant and stubborn king.

Had the English king been fair and just the colonies would not have opted for independence. This is clear from our Declaration of Independence propounded on July 4, 1776.

The king is described as a tyrant, a despot, an oppressive and unjust ruler. The framers wanted the world to understand – "the causes which impel them to the separation." The Declaration refers to – "a long train of abuses and usurpations." It lays out the specifics.

"The history of the present king of Great Britain is a history of repeated injuries and usurpations, all having in direct object the establishment of an absolute tyranny over these states. To prove this, let facts be submitted to a candid world."

"He has dissolved representative houses repeatedly …"

"He has obstructed the administration of justice – he has made judges dependent on his will alone."

"For quartering large bodies of armed troops among us."

"For imposing taxes on us without our consent."

"For depriving us, in many cases, of the benefits of trial by jury."

"For taking away our charters, abolishing our most valuable laws, and altering fundamentally the forms of our governments."

"For suspending our own legislatures, and declaring themselves invested with power to legislate for us in all cases whatsoever."

"He has plundered our seas, ravaged our coasts, burned our towns, and destroyed the lives of our people."

"In every stage of these oppressions we have petitioned for redress in the humblest terms: Our repeated petitions have been answered only by repeated injury."

Had the "petitions" been responded to fairly there would have been no Declaration of Independence. The failure to respond – "Absolves us from all allegiance to the British Crown."

The king is a – "tyrant unfit to be the ruler of a free people." Under such conditions – "it is the right of the people to alter or to abolish it, and to initiate new government...it is their right, it is their duty to throw off such government..." How could the king have been so stupid? His mistreatment of the colonies made the break inevitable.

THERE ONCE WAS A COUNTRY CALLED YUGOSLAVIA

Yugoslavia came into being after World War I as a monarchy. Before it was given the name Yugoslavia it was called the Kingdom of Serbs, Croats, and Slovenes. After World War II, Yugoslavia, like many countries in eastern Europe, became Communist. As is usually the case, the wartime leader became president – Josip Broz Tito.

The component parts of Yugoslavia (the republics) were – Serbia, Croatia, Slovenia, Bosnia Herzegovina, Macedonia, Montenegro, and Kosovo. Tito was an autocrat – only a strong leader could hold such disparate and competitive republics together.

Although himself a Croat, Tito crushed a movement for Croatian independence. He was opposed to any form of nationalism which could lead to the breakup of Yugoslavia. It had been the action of a Serb nationalist assassinating the Archduke of the Austrian/Hungarian empire, that was the catalyst for World War I.

Tito broke with Stalin in 1948, not wishing to be dominated by the Soviet Union. He remained a life-long Communist. He did something very smart, becoming the leader of a group of nations during the Cold War calling themselves "non-aligned," meaning they would not automatically be part of the Soviet bloc or the Western bloc. Both blocs would court Yugoslavia, India and the other members, enticing them to join their side. The non-alignment stand often resulted in generous military and economic aid.

What led America into the quagmire of Vietnam was the mistaken belief that communism was a monolithic force controlled by the Soviet Union. As Tito broke with Stalin, so did Mao of China. Vietnam attacked Communist Cambodia to rid that country of the murderous Khmer Rouge Regime.

Tito remained in power until his death in 1980. There are no term limits for dictators. Tito gave the republics broad autonomy and measured self-government. There would be murmurings about independence from time to time, but they never amounted to a viable threat against the central government.

That all changed in 1991, as the virus of independence infected the whole country. On June 25, 1991, two component parts of Yugoslavia declared independence – Croatia and Slovenia. The Yugoslav National Army, composed mainly of Serbs, attacked both. The war against Slovenia lasted about 2 weeks, the war against Croatia went on for years. By the end of 1992, Yugoslavia had ceased to exist.

The same phenomenon was occurring in the Soviet Union. All 15 republics of the USSR were bitten by the bug of independence.

Many silly Americans thought the Soviet states would embrace democracy after having been set free. Not a single one of them did so. Nearly all were ruled by dictators who remained in power for decades. Not a single Republic of the former Yugoslavia embraced true democracy.

BOSNIA HERZEGOVINA

Bosnia Herzegovina had been a province of the Ottoman Empire. Merely a province, not an independent entity. In 1877, it became part of the Austro-Hungarian Empire, an empire that was dismembered as a result of being on the losing side in World War I. In 1945, Bosnia joined the nation of Yugoslavia. The Muslims in Bosnia sought independence which led to war and tragedy.

The Bosnian Serbs had boycotted the referendum on independence, which took place on October 15, 1991. The Serbs and Croats attacked the Muslims. When Yugoslavia was intact these three ethnic groups basically got along.

The independence issue caused Bosnia to become a killing field. The killers and the victims had been neighbors. The quest for independence and the movement to prevent it can turn normal people into monsters. The monsters prevailed in Srebrenica.

Ethnic cleansing reached its apex in the city of Srebrenica in 1995, when 8,000 Muslim men and boys were murdered by the police and army of the Bosnian Serbs. How does one become convinced that a political goal, a territorial goal can justify the commission of such atrocities? The psychologists have no convincing answer.

Srebrenica had been designated as a United Nations safe haven; with 400 lightly armed Dutch soldiers as the peacekeeping force. In one of the darkest chapters in the history of the United Nations, when the Bosnian Serbs told them to leave, they complied, even though they knew what was in store for thousands of unarmed Muslims.

The crimes were so horrendous that the Security Counsel of the United Nations felt compelled to establish a war crimes tribunal for the former Yugoslavia headquartered at The Hague. This was the first such international tribunal since the military tribunals of Nuremberg and Tokyo at the end of World War II.

Radovan Karadzic was the political leader of the Bosnian Serbs and Ratko Mladic was the military leader who ordered the Srebrenica massacre. It took years to capture both men but they were eventually punished. They had been sheltered by their Serb followers.

The war lasted from 1992 through 1995. The human cost was devastating, with civilian deaths in the range of 200,000, plus two million displaced from their homes.

The war ended with something called the Dayton Peace Treaty in December 1995.

The deal was for partition, recognizing that the mutual hatreds could never truly be bridged. One part was a Muslim, Croat Federation, the other part was a Serb Republic. The regions were to be autonomous, each having a prime minister and legislature.

The presidents of Bosnia, Croatia and Serbia all were signatories at Dayton. A NATO-led force, the so-called Stabilization Force, including 20,000 American troops, were deployed to guard against a breakdown.

An international administration was responsible for making sure that the terms of the Dayton Accords were not violated. That, plus the Stabilization Force, made any claim of being a truly independent nation a mockery.

Had reason prevailed, a partition deal could have been agreed upon to avoid bloodshed.

KOSOVO

Slobodan Milosevic, the president of a reduced Yugoslavia, consisting of Serbia and Montenegro, was totally opposed to independence for Kosovo, which was a province of Serbia. Serbia and Kosovo had been part of the Muslim Ottoman Empire for centuries as provinces, not as independent states. During the Balkan wars of 1912-13 Serbia gained control of Kosovo. Both became Republics of Yugoslavia. You need a scorecard to sort all this out.

Milosevic was a Serbian nationalist fanatic who dreamt of a greater Serbia which would be dominant throughout the Balkans. Almost 90% of the population of Kosovo were Muslim Albanians, the rest were Orthodox Christian Serbs.

Serbia attacked Kosovo in 1998 to prevent their move toward independence. The Albanians responded with the fierce and effective Kosovo Liberation Army; an all-out war ensued, resulting in tens of thousands of deaths.

NATO and the United States intervened on the side of the Albanians. They bombed Serb targets for 78 days. A rational Milosevic would have realized that NATO was determined, and he would have called for a halt to the bombing much earlier.

Milosevic was in power from 1989 to 2000. He was eventually brought to trial for war crimes at the International War Crimes Tribunal at The Hague. He died in prison in 2006 before the inevitable verdict could be reached.

The former President and Prime Minister of Kosovo, Hashim Thaci, has also been charged with crimes against humanity. In mid-2023 the Thaci trial was ongoing and it could continue for months, even years. Thaci had been the Commander of the Kosovo Liberation Army.

Kosovo had achieved independence in 2008. The United States recognized that status almost immediately. Of course, Serbia did not, nor did Russia and many other countries. Kosovo's independence was always limited. The United Nations administered the country for years, and a NATO peacekeeping force remained on the ground for nearly two decades. Almost the exact same situation as existed in Bosnia after their peace agreement. The UN had a protectorate, a guardianship over Kosovo. There is a Serbian enclave within Kosovo, and the mutual hatred has not abated. Orthodox Christian/Muslim enmity goes back centuries to the Ottoman Empire (a Muslim Empire) when wars were fought between the two.

In Kosovo, corruption is endemic – so is violence and criminality. Likewise, inequality and a huge level of people without jobs. A bright spot is the elevation of women. Many serve in Parliament – a woman has served as President, another as Speaker of Parliament. Before Yugoslavia was torn asunder there were instances of children having a Serb father and a Croat mother. Or one parent being a Muslim and the other a Christian. The American cheerleaders for independence claim that it brings people together. Kosovo and Bosnia are prime examples of the opposite.

THERE ONCE WAS A COUNTRY CALLED THE SOVIET UNION

Most Americans believed that the Soviet Union was just another name for Russia. The reality was that Russia was merely one of 15 Republics of the Union of Soviet Socialist Republics.

The other Republics were Estonia, Latvia, Ukraine, Georgia, Lithuania, Armenia, Moldova and Azerbaijan plus 6 Muslim Republics in central Asia.

By the end of 1991 the Soviet Union was no more. The Supreme Soviet council, which had ruled since 1917, dissolved itself. The last leader of the Soviet Union, who came to power in 1985, Mikhail Gorbachev, tried to liberalize the government. A faction opposed to his concessions ousted him in a coup. He was rescued by Boris Yeltsin who actually favored the dismantling of the Soviet state. Gorbachev wanted to preserve the Union, but he had become irrelevant.

Yeltsin became President of Russia and remained until 1999 when he appointed Vladimir Putin to succeed him. Putin was in charge for the next 20 plus years.

As was the case with the Republics of Yugoslavia, all the states that had been part of the Soviet Union opted for independence. None of them became democracies. Nearly all the new rulers were autocrats who remained in power for decades.

The Russian Federation was itself composed of many semi-autonomous Republics. The most troublesome one was Muslim Chechnya, which sought independence. To prevent that breakaway, Russia under Boris Yeltsin invaded in 1994. The fighting was fierce and casualties on both sides were very high. Nearly 100,000 died, mostly civilians. A peace agreement was signed in 1997 granting Chechnya broad autonomy, which was still not enough for the militants.

Russia invaded again in 1999. There were atrocities on both sides. As one horrific example, the rebels took over an elementary school threatening a massacre. Russian troops stormed the school. Some 330 children and their teachers were killed. The Chechnyan "freedom fighters" set fire to a Moscow theater, killing about 120 patrons. Just two examples of the lunacy that drives many independence movements. Kill innocent, uninvolved people, even children so that a "charismatic" leader can become the president of a new country. A new country which in all likelihood will be a failure.

On the other side of the ledger there is equal lunacy by those seeking to prevent separatists from leaving the Mother Country.

The murderers of the children had previously been normal people looking after their families and holding down regular jobs. If one of the "rebels" had shouted – "We can't do this, this is terrible, these are innocent children" – he probably would have been shot as a traitor.

If one of the Serbs at Srebrenica had refused to participate in that genocide he probably would have been shot on the spot. Fanaticism is interwoven in most independence movements. After all the deaths, after all the atrocities, Chechnya remains part of Russia.

TUNISIA AND THE ARAB SPRING

There was an occurrence in the North African nation of Tunisia in 2011 which led many naïve optimists to believe that several Arab nations were on the brink of embracing democracy. That occurrence involved the plight of an ordinary worker.

The police confiscated the fruit stand of a street vendor because he was lacking a proper permit. That had happened several times to him before. He was probably lacking the permit because he didn't have the money to bribe the official empowered to grant permits. The peddler was so depressed about the unfairness and hopelessness of his situation that he set himself on fire and died. That protest struck a nerve in the Arab World.

It unleashed a cascade of unforeseen consequences which brought down the rule of several Arab dictators. Demonstrations and protests were massive, unrelenting, and violent. Hosni Mubarak had ruled Egypt for decades; even he was brought down by the protests.

The 2011 protests had nothing to do with the Palestinians or the Israelis proving that that conflict has never been the core issue in the Middle East.

No – the demonstrations were against their own leaders – their mismanagement and dysfunction, ignoring the needs of everyday people. They were protesting against corruption, poverty, inequality and unemployment. They were protesting against the insiders, the oligarchs, their own militaries. The protest signs screamed for freedom, dignity and bread.

Many befuddled politicians tried to sell the fake narrative that if peace could be achieved between Israel and the Palestinians, that peace would blossom in the region. Our ignorance about how Arab regimes function is profound. We are a nation entranced by sound bites.

Tunisia's own dictator, Ben Ali, fell after 23 years in power. The same with dictators in Yemen and Libya. Qadaffi had ruled Libya for 42 years. Ben Ali, unlike Qadaffi and Saddam Hussein, had a getaway plan so he was able to escape the wrath of the crowd. Saddam was caught, imprisoned, and executed. Qadaffi was found hiding in a sewer and killed by the very people he believed still idolized him.

Egypt had a "democratic" election after the fall of Mubarak. The winner was a member of the Muslim Brotherhood, Mohammad Morsi. He did not last very long; the public gave his governing skills very low marks. General Al Sisi removed him, and the people applauded, even though his elevation meant the return to a military dictatorship. Tunisia was regarded as a success story by the United States and Europe, the only country to emerge from the Arab Spring as a democracy –that magic word.

A moderate Muslim political party, Ennahda, dominated parliament. The economy did not improve, and corruption persisted. Ennahda was ineffective and received most of the blame for a decade of government dysfunction. There had been ten prime ministers in ten years. Terrorist attacks remained a frequent occurrence.

Along came a savior who was finally going to straighten things out. And what a savior – a professor of constitutional law named Kais Saied, a supposed lover of democracy and the rule of law.

In very short order, the professor showed his true colors. He dissolved parliament, suspended much of the constitution, promulgated a new constitution which gave him enormous power and discretion. He ruled by decree.

No protests – just the opposite. His moves were applauded. He was elected in a landslide. His new constitution was approved in a referendum with over 90% of the vote. The people wanted solutions, and if that meant a new dictator to accomplish that and bring stability, they were willing to pay the price.

Stability and order are a much higher priority than democracy in many societies. American politicians never openly admit that basic fact. They pretend that the whole world is thirsting for democracy and that somehow it is America's mission to lobby for that.

Years after the Soviet Union collapsed, the great writer, Solzhenitsyn, returned. America and Europe were praising the fall of Communism, the reforms of Boris Yeltsin and acting as though Russia had a shot to become liberal, even democratic. Solzhenitsyn dampened that fairy tale by saying that the new Russia was ruled by an oligarchy concealed by a sham democracy.

By late 2022, much of the public had soured on Saied. The economy had not improved, inflation continued to surge, the nation was as corrupt as it had been when Ennahda was dominant. Jobs were scarce, there was a surge of Tunisians fleeing to Europe.

There had been a strike by the powerful Tunisian General Labor Union. People were angry that subsidies were lessened and wages were cut. The reason for that was the insistence by the International Monetary Fund before it would grant a loan of several billion dollars. The IMF believed such measures were necessary in order to straighten out a teetering economy.

Because of Saied's interference in the judicial realm, even judges went on strike. His response to these developments –at one time he fired over fifty judges, accusing them of corruption. Starting in February 2022, Saied fired dozens of politicians and journalists. In April 2023, Saied had the leader of Ennahda arrested along with three other officials of that party.

Yes, power corrupts but he survived because the public believed the possible alternatives would be worse. They were against the return of Ennahda to power.

I can guarantee you that whatever form of government follows Saied, it will not be a democracy. But it might be a sham democracy.

THE SUDAN

In early 2019 there was a popular uprising lasting for months against a brutal dictator who had ruled Sudan for over 30 years - Omar Hassan

Al Bashir. The protesters represented every segment of society - young, old, rural, urban - even Bashir's military had turned against him. The goal of the movement was to install a civilian government and move toward elections. The population was fed up with decades of military rule and multiple coups. Sudan installed a civilian prime minister in a transitional government that was to lay the foundation for democracy.

Well, the inevitable happened - there was a military coup staged by two generals in November 2021. Army Chief Abdel Fattah Al Burhan and his deputy, Mohamed Hamdan. The generals said they were only in charge temporarily and that by April 2023 they would restore the civilian government. Probably Biden and his Secretary of State believed them.

By April 2023 the two generals were at war against each other.

Hamdan was the leader of a paramilitary organization called the Rapid Support Forces. He had been appointed to that position by Bashir. They were an outgrowth of the Janjaweed militia which had committed thousands of atrocities in the Darfur region of Sudan. Hamdan had been the commander of the Janjaweed.

The Janjaweed killers were Arab Muslims, the victims were black African Christians, mostly farmers. The Bashir takeover had been an Arab coup; Sudan has been a member of the Arab League. The International Criminal Court charged Bashir with genocide, but never acquired jurisdiction over him. Both Burhan and Hamdan supported Bashir for decades. That tells you everything about their commitment to a transition to democracy.

The United Nations has reported that the Janjaweed had killed some 300,000 residents of Darfur during its 20-year domination of the region. The black Africans did not want to be governed by Sharia law.

By mid-April 2023, Burhan's fighter jets were firing rockets into civilian areas of Khartoum, the capital. Indiscriminate shelling was directed at pockets of Hamdan's fighters.

One would have figured that the general in charge of the army would have secured an early victory, but the Rapid Support Forces under Hamdan were preventing that. As of November 2023 – 8 months after the start of the civil war, he controlled the capital – Khartoum. They were killing Black Africans in Darfur just as they had done 20 years earlier.

By November, over one million had fled the country. Several million were internally displaced. Millions were trapped in their homes without electricity or water. A respected medical union warned that – "the rates of deaths and injuries are increasing at an exponential pace."

That great organization – "Doctors Without Borders" – were not permitted to retrieve bodies or transport the injured. The World Health Organization warned that the hospitals in Khartoum were running out of blood, IV fluids and other lifesaving medical supplies.

Well President Biden and Secretary Blinken, I don't think that the winner of this war is going to have any interest in transitioning to democracy.

Sudan's economy was a mess under Bashir, and it remained a mess after him. Runaway inflation was a plague for decades. According to the World Food Program, one out of three Sudanese were suffering from hunger even before the generals took over.

The International Monetary Fund froze a six-billion-dollar loan that the country desperately needed. The World Bank and the African Development Bank also imposed restrictions. These measures impact the general population, not the elites.

> If the Sudan had a normal functioning government, it would have the potential to be a

success story. The country is rich in oil and valuable minerals, and it is loaded with gold mines. Its ports are strategic, providing a gateway for all kinds of products, including oil, to and from land locked African nations. The United Arab Emirates had signed on to a six-billion- dollar deal to build a new port facility on Sudan's Red Sea coast.

There was a practical reason why the generals wanted the military to remain in power. Corruption was rife within the military, and many officers had become rich. The military controlled companies that were dominant in agriculture, mining, etc. A civilian government could have uncovered the extent of the corruption and inflicted punishments.

SOUTH SUDAN AND ITS QUEST FOR INDEPENDENCE

Hard to believe, but Sudan fought a war for 22 years against the South. The issue - the South wanted to secede and become independent. It achieved that goal in July 2011 with the signing of a peace treaty.

Salva Kiir and Rick Machar led the "liberation movement," so naturally, Kiir became president and Machar became vice president. As happened with the two generals in Sudan, Kiir and Machar had a falling out, which led to a war between them, beginning in December 2013. A war that caused at least 50,000 deaths.

Kiir was a member of the Dinka ethnic group; Machar was part of the Nuer ethnic group. American leaders know nothing about the histories, about the conflicts between the two. Just as we knew nothing about the Hutu/Tutsi dynamics in Rwanda, which led to nearly a million deaths. It is that lack of knowledge which leads to fantasy beliefs that democratic regimes are on the horizon. Our ignorance and arrogance in believing that we can lead such countries into accepting our values has caused thousands of American deaths.

IRELAND

There are two Irelands. The Republic of Ireland and Northern Ireland, which remains part of the United Kingdom. The capital of the Republic is Dublin, the capital of Northern Ireland is Belfast. Both Irelands had been under British rule for centuries.

Ireland was partitioned in 1921 – the Irish free state in the south consisting of 26 counties became the Republic of Ireland – an independent nation. The six northern counties with a Protestant majority became Northern Ireland and would remain in the United Kingdom. That's what the Protestants wanted. The Catholics in Northern Ireland wanted to unite with the Republic.

These conflicting desires led to thousands of deaths. The Protestants were labeled as unionists, the Catholics as nationalists. From the beginning there were battles between the Irish Republican Army – IRA – (Catholic) and the Protestants. Those conditions continued to escalate and in 1968, got worse – a period known as – "THE TROUBLES" which continued for 30 years.

Atrocities and murders committed by both sides resulted in some 3,600 deaths. Hundreds of British soldiers were killed by the IRA; the British killed hundreds of IRA members.

There was one event in particular which hardened the resolve of the IRA, referred to as – "BLOODY SUNDAY." On that particular Sunday, January 30, 1972, in Derry, Northern Ireland, British soldiers fired on a crowd of mostly peaceful Catholic protesters, killing 13.

The Catholics and Protestants believe in Jesus, as the Sunni and Shiite Muslims believe in Allah. But that unity did not deter the mutual slaughter. Christians killing Christians! How could any rational person believe that the issue which separated them was worth all the deaths, all the crippling injuries, and the creation of so many fatherless children?

Finally, in April 1998, reason prevailed when the "Good Friday Agreement" was signed. It was a peace agreement designed to end the violence and establish a power-sharing government.

President Clinton's envoy to Northern Ireland, George Mitchell, a former United States Senator, deserved much credit for his persistence and creativity in achieving the historic breakthrough. Sinn Fein, the political wing of the Irish Republican Army, became a recognized political party in the Assembly.

There have been incidents of violence over the years but thankfully, never a return to organized, full-scale killing. Yet a quarter of century later, schools and neighborhoods remain largely segregated. In some schools, there is not a single Protestant child, while in others, there is not a single Catholic child. In some cities and towns, there are walls separating the unionists from the nationalists. Different flags represent the two religions in cities and towns.

A major Protestant party had refused to participate in the shared power arrangement; the Assembly (Parliament) was not functioning for several years. Political paralysis often prevailed with real power sharing being a fiction. There are concerns about the formation of new paramilitary groups. On the other hand, there is a thirst for normalcy, to put the era of "the troubles" behind them forever.

President Biden visited both Irelands in April 2023 in celebration of the 25th anniversary of the Good Friday Agreement. He was also celebrating his own strong Irish roots.

Times and conditions change. People can change as well, as evidenced by the fact that the right to abortion and the legalization of same-sex marriages were approved in two referendums in 2015 and 2018. Problems persist but there have been 25 years of peace in Northern Ireland. Hopefully the art of compromise will flourish in the future.

HOW HAS CHINA DEALT WITH THE ISSUE OF INDEPENDENCE/SEPARATISM?
TAIWAN

Taiwan is an island about a hundred miles from China across the Strait of Formosa. It had been a Japanese colony until Japan was defeated in World War II. In 1945, Taiwan became a province of China, which was then under the control of the Chinese Nationalist Party (Kuomintang) led by Chiang Kai Shek.

When the communists defeated Chiang's forces in 1949, the losers fled to Taiwan and established the fiction of the – "Republic of China." The accompanying fiction was that they would, one day, retake the mainland. Many American political figures bought into this nonsense.

To the communist government, the Peoples Republic of China, Taiwan was simply a breakaway province. For years there was a hot nonsensical issue between the Republican and Democratic parties – "Who lost China?" The answer was simple – Chiang Kai-Shek. But our politicians wanted to play the blame game to conform to their agendas.

Chiang, like Mao, was a dictator, but he was America's kind of dictator. Chiang's wife was classy, educated and beloved by certain elements of the American political spectrum. The Taiwan government had a very effective and sophisticated lobbying arm in America.

The Chiang regime instituted martial law (the opposite of democracy) which endured for four decades. Estimates vary, but during the period of martial law, about 100,000 people were arrested and tortured, with some 1,000 having been executed.

When Chiang died in 1975, his son took over. The son died in 1988 – so for 39 years father and son ruled the country. In the late 1980s, Taiwan began acquiring some basic features of a democracy. Taiwan has evolved into a full-fledged democracy.

In 1971, the United Nations admitted China and expelled Taiwan. Up until that time, the United Nations endorsed the fiction that Taiwan was China. 1971 was also the year that many countries broke off diplomatic relations with Taiwan. That was also the year that National Security Advisor Henry Kissinger secretly visited China, laying the groundwork for President Nixon's visit.

In 1979, the United States broke off official ties with the government of Taiwan, recognizing the reality and permanence of the real China. In that same year, the United States established full diplomatic relations with China.

There is a new burning political question in America – Will China invade Taiwan and, if so, will the United States get involved? President Biden has made the moronic statement that if China invades our troops will defend Taiwan. Why moronic? In 20 years, with 150,000 troops in Afghanistan, we couldn't defeat the Taliban but we are going to be able to prevent a superpower from taking over the island of Taiwan?

There are a few normal people in the Biden Administration who are always confronted with the task of walking back some of his pronouncements. Their strategy is a purposeful ambiguity about what America would do should the Chinese unleash a war.

There is a lot of silly symbolism in America trying to show our strong support for Taiwan. In 2022, Nancy Pelosi, then the Speaker of the House, visited Taiwan. She was the highest-ranking American politician to visit in 25 years. China responded with anger and threats and by displaying its military prowess very close to the island.

President Tsai of Taiwan was in America in April 2023. She met with many members of Congress.

Ironically, at the same time of her visit, a former president of Taiwan was being received by Xi Jinping on a 12-day visit to the mainland. The party of President Ma (the Nationalist Party) supports closer ties with China. Ma was president from 2008 to 2016.

His party lost in a landslide in 2020, the year that Tsai won her re-election bid. There are term limits in Taiwan so Tsai cannot run again in January 2024.

China regards Taiwan as an inviolable part of their country and sees reunification as inevitable. The real dilemma is the fact that millions have been born and grew up in Taiwan since 1949. Their identity is Taiwanese, definitely not Chinese.

HONG KONG

Hong Kong had been a colony of Great Britain, China and the Japanese. Britain resumed control after the defeat of Japan in World War II. In 1997 Britain returned Hong Kong to China. A communist dictatorship became sovereign over one of the most vibrant and successful capitalistic societies in the world. Hong Kong had become the home to the regional headquarters of major global and even Chinese companies.

A Sino-British joint declaration promised Hong Kong a high degree of autonomy. Freedom of speech, press, and assembly were to be respected. Hong Kong was to be a self-governing city within a – "one country, two systems" framework. It would have an independent judiciary, and civil liberties were to be respected.

Whenever China tried to limit autonomy, a pro-democracy movement would surface.

In 2014, there were 79 days of protests labeled as the "Umbrella Movement." To sustain a protest for that long demonstrates the tenacity and passion of the movement. Yet the massive protests of 2014 were a mere prelude to the protests which began in June 2019.

They went on for 6 months, and they intensified. Had the protestors forgotten about the massacre in Beijing's Tiananmen Square in 1989? And that that massacre occurred under the leadership of Deng Xiaoping who was considered to be a liberal with capitalist leanings? China was not going to allow the protests to continue indefinitely! The activists for democracy had overplayed their hand, and China crushed the movement.

On May 21, 2020, China's National People's Congress announced a security law which would infringe significantly on Hong Kong's autonomy. There was a drastic overhaul of election rules. Only "patriots" could hold office. Of course, patriots were those who totally accepted the dominance of China. China bypassed Hong Kong's National People's Congress.

The Chinese army, police, and the security agencies operated openly to enforce the new order.

The justification for the new security measures were the excesses that took place during the 2019 protests when the Chinese flag was burned, and the mainland office was stormed. Violators were charged with conspiracy to commit subversion. They were denounced as separatists, guilty of sedition and partnering with foreign infiltrators.

The Chinese leadership believes that it was liberalization which led to the collapse of the Soviet Union.

China has been fiercely repressive against its Muslim population – the eleven million Uighurs who would like to be independent or at least autonomous. They have been charged with the "crime of separatism" and sent to reeducation camps (brainwashing camps) so that they will become more Chinese and less Muslim. The Muslim World has ignored this trampling of Muslim rights.

TIBET

Almost immediately after Mao's victory in the Chinese civil war, he invaded Tibet. Hundreds of thousands of Tibetans were killed during the 1950s and '60s. They were guilty of "inciting separatism." Since 2009, over 140 monks and ordinary Tibetans have self-immolated, set themselves on fire.

The most famous monk, a beloved worldwide figure, is the Dalai Lama – a Tibetan Buddhist. He is the 14th Dalai Lama, in a tradition going back some 600 years. The population believes that he possesses divine qualities – he is both the spiritual and temporal leader.

To save his life, the Dalai Lama fled to India in 1959, where he has resided ever since. About 80,000 Tibetans joined him there. Approximately 6 million still reside in Tibet. For these many decades, the Dalai

Lama has preached a philosophy of peace, love and nonviolence. He was awarded the Nobel Peace Prize in 1989.

For decades, he has made clear that he would accept Chinese sovereignty in exchange for an autonomy which would allow religious freedom, cultural and language rights. If reason prevailed, it would be simple to reach an accommodation.

SPAIN

Spain has had to contend with several independence movements in spite of the fact that it has granted broad autonomy to several regions such as Galicia and Andalusia. For decades, the Basques fought for independence, never quite achieving it. The Basques engaged in terror.

The region of Catalonia declared independence in October 2017 after a successful referendum. Spain contended that the referendum was unconstitutional. Catalonia did this in spite of having their own parliament and president and broad powers over their local affairs. The capital of Catalonia is Barcelona, one of the most prosperous and upscale cities in Spain. The leader of the independence movement fled the country. Nearly 20 of the other activists were charged with rebellion and sedition, several ending up in prison.

Spain was able to transition into democracy in the late 1970s, after enduring decades of dictatorship under Franco.

The issue of Catalan independence came roaring back in November 2023. A Socialist Prime Minister, Pedro Sanchez, needed the support of small independence party to remain in power. He offered a blanket amnesty to all those involved in the movement for independence. The strategy worked, and Parliament backed him for a new term. Sanchez, who had previously promised never to grant amnesty, headed a fragile coalition which might not last very long.

The conservative majority were furious about the grant of amnesty. Huge crowds gathered in protest. They regarded the move as unconstitutional. The Supreme Court had said the referendum was illegal and the effort was criminal.

Stay tuned!

MYANMAR

What the independent Buddhist nation of Myanmar (formerly Burma) has done to their Muslim minority, Rohingya, deserves special mention for horrible cruelty. They kicked out over a million, creating the world's largest refugee camp in Bangladesh. Again, the Muslim World has taken no action against these injustices.

Why Bangladesh? Although the Rohingya had lived in Burma/Myanmar for centuries, the Buddhist monk militants regarded them as Bengali interlopers from Bangladesh. They were denied citizenship and prevented from getting decent employment or education.

Massacres, mass rapes, executions, and arson were the order of the day. Whole families died in their homes which had been set ablaze. There are over a half-million Rohingyas still in Myanmar, living in unsanitary camps since most of their homes had been destroyed.

When most Americans think of Buddhism, if they ever do, they think of the Dalai Lama's brand – meditation, peace, withdrawal from the material world. The outrages are encouraged by monks and carried out by the military along with civilian allies.

For the first 50 years of Myanmar's independence, the military ruled the country directly. There was a democracy movement led by Aung San Suu Kyi, the daughter of the man who led the independence movement against Great Britain decades earlier. He was assassinated in 1948. Kyi became a threat to the regime because of her popularity.

She was placed under house arrest for 15 years. When the American media dealt with her periodically, they gushed, placing her in the exalted company of the Dalai Lama and Martin Luther King Jr. She was awarded the Nobel peace prize in 1991.

The military decided they would introduce the façade of democracy, so they released her in 2010. She was elected president in 2015. Tourists, investments, and foreign aid poured in for a while. The gullible ones believed there would be a transition to civilian rule and full-fledged democracy.

To the disappointment of all the gushers, Kyi was silent about the mistreatment of the Rohingya. She did not criticize the military. Yes, there was a new constitution, but the military had drafted it.

The former United Nations high commissioner for human rights wrote an article saying that Kyi had become the – "spokesperson for mass atrocity."

A United Nations' report from a specially appointed panel of August 2019 was highly critical of Kyi and spoke of genocide. An incredible reversal of her previous worldwide image.

The military could not abide Kyi's continuing popularity particularly after her landslide victory in the 2020 election – a victory against the party that was backed by the military. The military took over directly in February 2021. They charged Kyi with election fraud and other "crimes" and of course she was found guilty. In spite of her downgraded image, she remained popular because the population was okay with the awful treatment of Rohingya.

International observers concluded that the 2020 election had been free and fair. The observers from the U.S.-based Carter Center agreed. The "independent" leadership of Myanmar was far more repressive than the British had ever been during colonial days. The military dissolved Kyi's party as well as other political parties opposed to the regime.

The conditions in Bangladesh were awful in spite of it being a Muslim county. Like Myanmar it too wanted the Rohingya to be gone. To escape, many embarked on perilous sea journeys. For many, their destination was Malaysia where they thought they could get work. Malaysia denied the rickety boats' entrance, and so did other countries. Hatred for "others" knows no bounds.

Many of these boats were adrift for weeks. The Rohingyas were starving, and dehydrated; those who died were tossed overboard. The American left was largely silent. Our media and editorial writers, who for decades have been obsessed with the plight of the Palestinians, ignored these Muslims. Unlike Hamas and the PLO, the Rohingya have never produced suicide bombers or terrorists.

Even worse than the inaction of the liberal left was the inaction of the 57 Nation Organization of Islamic Cooperation. The Rohingya do not seek independence. They want to be left alone to practice their religion, to embrace their traditions and seek employment so that they can provide for their families. They also want educational opportunities.

A NEVER-ENDING STREAM OF INDEPENDENCE MOVEMENTS

Quebec is a province in Canada. In 1995, they held a referendum on independence for those who sought to become a French-speaking nation. It did not succeed.

Scotland had been in a union with the United Kingdom for over 300 years, yet it held a referendum on independence in 2014, where the vote was 55% to 45% against leaving. The British Supreme Court ruled there could not be a second referendum unless the government agreed. That hasn't happened.

The positive thing about Scotland, Quebec and Catalonia (Spain) is that they did not go to war over the independence issue.

In Sri Lanka, formerly Ceylon, a Buddhist nation, the Hindu Tamils sought independence. Their war lasted 26 years, characterized by terror, thousands upon thousands of deaths, and a history of cruel atrocities. Sri Lanka is a messed-up country surviving on loans from China and the International Monetary Fund. In 2023, their inflation rate was at 50%.

It was the Tamils who assassinated the prime minister of India, Indira Ghandi's son. His mother had been assassinated by her Sikh bodyguards years earlier. As India's long-serving Prime Minister, she had authorized an army raid on the Sikh's holiest temple and her death was portrayed as revenge. There remains, after many decades, a Sikh yearning for independence.

Kashmir, India's only majority Muslim state, is shared between India and Pakistan. The Kashmir issue has led to wars between these two countries. For over 70 years, Kashmir has sought independence. Prime Minister Modi of India, a fervent Hindu nationalist, has taken measures to restrict Kashmir's autonomy.

East Timor fought a 25-year war against Indonesia before it actually won independence.

In the Philippines, the Mindanao sought independence for nearly 50 years. After some 100,000 deaths, they said they would be satisfied with broad autonomy and meaningful self-government.

Ataturk and Erdogan of Turkey could have saved well over 50,000 lives had they granted broad and meaningful autonomy to the Kurds. The Kurds have never won independence, and they are spread out in several countries, including Iraq and Iran. The Kurds have been valuable allies of the United States, sacrificing many lives to help us defeat ISIS. In spite of that, the United States has never advocated for their independence. Instead, our advocacy has only focused on birthing a Palestinian state.

In Africa, there have been many instances of regions which want to break away from the mother country. I have already dealt with South Sudan leaving Sudan. After a protracted war. Eritrea broke away from Ethiopia to establish a new country – yes, a country immersed in wars and harsh dictatorship.

Biafra wanted to secede from Nigeria; Katanga wanted to secede from the Congo. In my chapter on Africa, I catalog the horrific examples of failed countries after having gained independence from their colonial European masters.

There was a region of Azerbaijan that wanted to be independent. A region called Nagorno Karabakh has a huge Armenian population. Armenia and Azerbaijan had both been Republics of the Soviet Union.

The two countries fought several wars over this region – wars that began in the late 1980s. Wars that resulted in thousands of deaths and thousands of displacements. Nagorno Karabakh is internationally recognized as part of Azerbaijan. Armenia, backed by Russia, won one of the wars.

Azerbaijan attacked in September 2023 and won a very convincing victory. So convincing that there will be no future wars between the two. Before this issue arose, the Orthodox Armenians and the Muslim Azerbaijanis got along very well for decades as neighbors. Nagorno Karabakh is and will remain a part of Azerbaijan. Was it worth it?

Cypress is an island in the Mediterranean which had been shared between Greeks and Turks for generations. It became a British crown colony in 1925 and gained independence in 1960. There was a militant Greek movement the aim of which was to unify Cypress with Greece. That led to a Turkish invasion in 1974, which in turn led to the partition of the country.

The Turks controlled about 40% of the island, and in 1983 declared that North Cypress was independent. Turkey is the only country that recognizes that status. The Greek part of the island, the Republic of Cypress, enjoys international recognition and joined the European Union in 2003. Thousands of Turkish troops have remained in Cypress for decades. These two ethnicities became segregated after having gotten along for generations.

THE FATAL FLAW OF INDEPENDENCE MOVEMENTS

I think I may have figured out the passions that drive independence movements and the sacrifices that millions have been willing to endure. The answer is the hatred of being dominated by others – not only dominated but looked down upon by those who consider themselves superior. That plus the inequity and unfairness between the haves and have-nots.

Instead of accommodating minority rights, central governments have sought to suppress them. Franco ruled Spain for 36 years; he banned minority cultures and languages. It is selfish, arrogant, and short sighted to obliterate identity, culture, and language.

The very worst offender has been the United States. For 100 years, our policy was to snatch very young children away from their Indian families, isolate them from their parents and send them to boarding schools. The dreaded policy with an innocent name was ASSIMILATION.

They were to become Americanized. The children were punished if they spoke their native language. All kinds of horrific abuses occurred at these schools. Our policy screwed up generations of Indians, never allowing them to realize their potential. Because of abuse many of these children died without their parents even being notified. Yeah – make

America great again! See my chapter on American Indians and shudder in shame.

Most of the independence wars and the millions of deaths could have been avoided if the central power granted meaningful autonomy. An autonomy which respected identity, traditions, customs, religions and language rights. An autonomy in which the Government would not seek to absorb the minority culture into the dominant one.

The central government would be in charge of defense and foreign affairs, but the nuts and bolts of everyday governance would function at the local level similar to the state/federal relationship that exists in the United States.

CHAPTER 14

AFRICA – INDEPENDENCE YES – DEMOCRACY NO

By the 1960s, nearly every African country had achieved independence. There are 55 countries in Africa with a population of about 1.2 billion. The countries had gotten rid of the colonialists after many decades of European rule – by the British, the French, the Portuguese, the Belgians and the Germans.

No colonial power ever prepared the newly independent states for self-government, and certainly not for democracy. The arrogance of colonialism is breathtaking. One country which considers itself vastly superior simply subjugates another country's people and exploits the resources of the captive nation to enhance its own economy.

Yes – the African countries got independence, but they also got leaders like Idi Amin of Uganda, Robert Mugabe of Zimbabwe, Charles Taylor of Liberia, and Omar Bashir of Sudan. These leaders oppressed their people even more severely than had the Europeans. The new dictators remained in power for decades. Some examples -

Zimbabwe (formerly Rhodesia) – in 2016 Robert Mugabe, age 92, was celebrating his 36th year in power. He was finally forced to resign in 2017.

Uganda – Yoweri Museveni, 40 years in power. He came to power in 1986 after a 5-year war which resulted in a half-million deaths. He overthrew his predecessor dictator – Milton Obote. And remember the reign of Idi Amin one of the all-time mass killers who fled to Saudi Arabia when his time was up.

Burkina Faso – President Blaise Compaore had been in power 26 years, but that wasn't enough for him. Protests to his continuing in office drove him into exile in 2014. Compaore had overthrown and executed the previous leader. That's called regime change in Africa.

Chad – President Idris Deby in 2016 was in office for 26 years. Yes – he had overthrown the previous leader. Before assuming the presidency, Deby was the leader of the army. That is a very common background of the new dictators. After Deby left, his son took over. That is a very common order of succession in Africa.

Kenneth Kaunda was president of Zambia for 27 years. Ahmed Sekou Toure, the first president of Guinea, ruled for 26 years. In Togo, a father-son combo ruled for over half a century. Malani had the same president for over 30 years – Tanzania 24 years – Liberia 27 years – Eritrea 23 years – Angola 38 years – Cameron 40 years – Gambia 22 years. No one was talking about term limits.

In addition to the prevalence of multi-decade dictatorships, there have been other consistent themes in the governance of African countries. Civil wars, military coups, political violence, searing inequality, endemic corruption, nepotism, massive unemployment and dysfunctional economies.

The United States is heavily engaged in Africa. As but one example – President Biden hosted a United States/Africa summit in Washington.

Our Secretary of State, Antony Blinken, visited several African countries during August 2022. Unbelievably he said that America's main goal was promoting democratic governance across the continent. He said that democratic promotion was a primary focus of President Biden's foreign policy. Welcome to fantasy land!

Have we learned nothing? It was President Bush's obsession about spreading democracy which got us into our 20-year losing wars in Afghanistan and Iraq.

It is simply beyond absurd to talk about democracy promotion in Africa. Since 2020 there have been at least seven military takeovers – coups. Countries led by military dictators including Niger, Gabon, Sudan, Mali, Burkina Faso and Guinea. Americans know nothing about these countries.

It has been over 60 years since most of Africa gained independence, and these recent takeovers illustrate the lack of democratic norms across the continent. Yet the idiot-talk persists. Blinken gave a speech in South Africa in August 2022 when he mentioned "democracy" eleven times and repeated that democracy promotion is a pillar of U.S. policy in Africa.

Here's a couple of vivid examples of our ignorance about what our government is doing in Africa.

Senator John McCain, head of the Armed Services Committee, said that neither the administration nor the Pentagon had explained to his committee the level of America's involvement in Africa. Senator Lindsey Graham said – "We don't know exactly where we're at in the world militarily and what we're doing."

The starkest example of our ignorance about ethnic, tribal, clan and religious conflicts on the African continent is provided by the nation of Rwanda.

RWANDA

In Rwanda, the Hutus represented about 90% of the population and the Tutsis about 10%; it was the Hutus who held the political power. Genocide was carried out by the Hutus against the Tutsis. Men, women, children – old, young, disabled, pregnant women, babies. The day before the massacres began, the killers were considered to be normal people and there were many instances of Hutus/Tutsis friendships and even marriages.

The killing of over 800,000 human beings cannot be accomplished in a week or several weeks. The spree took 4 months, and the Clinton administration did nothing to stop it. Had the United States sent in special forces to separate the killers from the victims, had the United States acted resolutely, we could have saved hundreds of thousands of lives. Years later, Clinton apologized for this indelible stain on his record. Yet he remains very popular with Black Americans – yes, African Americans. For the most part American blacks were silent about the genocide. No marches, no demonstrations.

To understand the background of the genocide you have to know something about the nation of Burundi. Like Rwanda the population is a mix of Hutus and Tutsis. Although the Hutus in Burundi make up about 85% of the population and the Tutsis only 15%, it was the Tutsis who ruled. Our political leaders knew less about Burundi than they knew about Rwanda.

For the very first time, a Hutu became president in July 1993. He was assassinated in October 1993, to be replaced by another Hutu. The new president, along with the Hutu president of Rwanda were killed in a mysterious plane crash on April 6, 1994. That was the spark which ignited the genocide. Without proof, Hutus blamed the Tutsis for the crash.

Even by African standards, Burundi had a horrible history. Massacres in 1972 and 1973 caused about a quarter of a million deaths. A civil war which began in 1993 and lasted about 10 years resulted in some 300,000 deaths.

In October 2017, Burundi withdrew from the International Criminal Court at The Hague (Netherlands) after a United Nations report found evidence of murders, torture and sexual violence by the army and security forces. The court was created in 2002 to deal with allegations of genocide, war crimes and crimes against humanity.

The Tutsis, under the military leadership of Paul Kagame, defeated the Hutus and took over the government of Rwanda. Naturally, Kagame became president in 2000 – the first Tutsi to hold that office since independence. In 2023, he was still the President.

Kagame called for a constitutional referendum in 2016, which easily passed allowing him to seek a third term and opening up the possibility of his remaining in office until 2034. He won his third 7-year term in August 2017 with 99% of the vote. Yes, he is popular but nobody is that popular. Considering Rwanda's history, Kagame has been a remarkably effective leader, yet he follows in the footsteps of so many other dictators in terms of his governance. To his credit, Kagame seeks to create a Rwandan identity to offset tribal, clan and ethnic hatreds.

ANGOLA

Jose Eduardo dos Santos was the dictator for 38 years. His daughter became a billionaire running the state oil company. Angola is the second largest oil producer in Africa after Nigeria. His son was in charge of the country's sovereign wealth fund.

Almost without exception, the African dictators have been very much into luxury and accumulating wealth.

The same political party has been in power since independence from Portugal in 1975.

In the early fight against colonialism, there were two national liberation groups, both wanting to get rid of Portugal, but each seeking to lead the new nation and exclude its rival. A civil war erupted between the two groups which lasted for decades.

THE DEMOCRATIC REPUBLIC OF THE CONGO

After Congo gained independence from Belgium in 1960, its first leader was Patrice Lumumba whose reign was short. He was overthrown and executed in January 1961. A new leader, Mobuto Sese Seko, came to power in a military coup in 1965 and, of course, had a long reign – 32 years. Laurent Kabila got rid of Mobuto in 1997. He was assassinated in 2001 and that's when the son, Joseph, took over at the age of 29.

After being elected and re-elected, Joseph was required by the constitution to leave in December 2016. He refused and kept postponing elections. Many African constitutions provide for term limits, but the dictators ignore them which usually leads to protests, violence and many deaths.

The Congo, formerly known as Zaire, both before and after independence probably holds the title for the most violent deaths of any African country – in multiples of millions.

As awful as many of the European colonials were, the very worst was King Leopold of Belgium. He exploited the natural resources of the Congo, mainly rubber, and in doing so enslaved and murdered millions.

The great tragedy of Africa post-independence is that considering the abundance of oil, diamonds, gold, copper, fertile land, giant forests, enviable tourist attractions – few countries have been able to translate their natural wealth into stable, peaceful nations with flourishing economies.

Twenty thousand United Nations peacekeepers were unable to bring peace to the Congo. As was the case in many African countries, there was a region of the Congo that wanted to secede –to be independent – Katanga led by Moise Tshombe. In 1961, the Secretary General of the United Nations, Dag Hammarskjold, was on a mission to try to end Congo's civil war. His plane crashed killing him and 15 others. The cause of the crash remains a mystery; there was suspicion of sabotage.

There are about 200 ethnic groups within the Congo's population of about 90 million. Most have their own languages and unique means of communicating. There are well over 100 armed groups in the Congo, a country much larger than Texas. There can be no effective central government with so many ethnic differences and so many armed militias. Yes – Biden and Blinken – let's wave a magic wand and transform the Congo into a democracy.

ZIMBABWE

The independence movement of Zimbabwe was unusual in that the white minority of Rhodesia (which became Zimbabwe) had itself revolted against British rule declaring itself to be an independent nation.

The United States and nearly all members of the United Nations did not recognize this status. The new nation continued to rule over the blacks. The black majority fought a 7-year guerilla war against the Ian Smith government of Southern Rhodesia. There were two main guerilla groups; one led by Joshua Nkomo and the other by Robert Mugabe. The Mugabe faction prevailed and the new nation of Zimbabwe became independent in 1980.

Mugabe ruled from 1980 until 2017– 37 years. There were rigged elections and one-party rule. Like other African countries Zimbabwe had a constitution and a parliament and an executive branch and other accouterments of democracy – but Mugabe was a dictator.

Zimbabwe incurred huge debt to international donors such as the World Bank, the European Investment Bank, the African Development Bank and the International Monetary Fund. All because of economic mismanagement and corruption that is the common plight of many African countries. They need to be propped up by international donors.

Even though Mugabe was 93 in 2017 he did not make a rational decision to retire. He had never designated a successor, but he had a plan. Like most of his plans it was a lousy one. The plan was that his wife, Grace, 41 years his junior, would succeed him.

The problem with that plan was that Grace was widely despised because she was viewed as manipulative, overly ambitious and a flaunter of luxury in an impoverished country.

Mugabe fired his vice president, Mnangagwa, age 75, who had been his closet associate and chief enforcer for decades. He had been Mugabe's chief of state security as well as defense minister. Mugabe also overlooked the fact that his vice president had strong allies in the upper echelons of the military. That turned out to be his undoing when the military turned against him.

The new president was Mnangagwa. Mnangagwa only received 50.8% of the vote. European Union observers said there was rampant fraud in the election. The opposition Movement for Democratic Change rejected the result saying that the public did not want a clone of Mugabe. Many alleged that the "winner" had a leading role in rigging past elections.

Very uncharacteristically in Africa, the new government granted Mugabe a very generous "retirement" package. A huge mansion, several deluxe cars, a staff, a furnished office, free medical treatment, and free first-class international travel. Deposed leaders are usually imprisoned or murdered.

GABON

Let's have a look at a country where the leader was deposed in a coup as recently as 2023. A father and son ruled Gabon for 56 years. The father died in 2009 and the son – Ali Bongo Ondimba – took over.

The coup occurred within hours after an election, of course won by Bongo. Many previous elections ended in violence but the regime remained intact. The takeover was led by Bongo's cousin, the head of the elite guard whose duty it was to protect the president.

France had been the colonial power. After independence in 1960, Gabon maintained a close relationship with France. In spite of great oil wealth, the rate of unemployment was huge. The usual disparity between the super-rich insiders and the rest of the population.

KENYA

In the 2022 election one of the candidates was Raila Odinga, a major political figure for decades. He was the son of the original vice president of the country. Before assuming that position, his father was a leader in the struggle for independence. The outgoing president was Uhuru Kenyatta, son of Kenya's founding father, Jomo Kenyatta. Nepotism is simply a way of life in Africa.

Uhuru had defeated Odinga in previous elections but they were allies in 2022. William Ruto had been Kenyatta's running mate in an earlier election. Shifting political alliances are very common in Africa. The August 2022 election result was suspect, with 4 of the 7 national election commissioners refusing to verify the vote.

William Ruto defeated Odinga by the tiniest of margins – 50.5% to 48.9%. At age 77 this was Odinga's fifth losing bid for the presidency. He challenged the outcome before Kenya's Supreme Court.

Following an election in 2007, political violence outdid itself, it went on for months causing thousands of deaths with some half million being displaced from their homes. Kenyatta and Ruto were accused by the International Criminal Court of crimes against humanity relating to their role in the killings following the 2007 election. The case collapsed and neither politician was punished.

In the 2007 election, Kenyatta defeated Odinga but Odinga claimed fraud. That is the claim made after nearly every African election and in most cases that claim is true. In 2013 there was another election between the same two rivals with the same result. Odinga again claimed fraud. More protests but fewer deaths than there had been in 2007.

Odinga is a member of the Luo tribe, Kenyatta is Kikuyu, and Ruto is Kalenjin. Americans and their leaders know zero about the differences between them. President Obama's father was a Luo which means Obama himself was Luo. That fact was not stressed by Obama's opponents in the two elections he won against McCain and Romney.

Jomo Kenyatta was Kenya's first president. In the 1950s he led the Mau Mau rebellion which was designed to terrorize the whites. It was a terrorist group which killed many Europeans. Jomo spent the last 10 years of British colonial rule in prison which only strengthened his claim to the presidency. His chosen successor was Daniel Arap Moi who served for 24 years.

TERRORISTS HAVE BECOME DOMINANT IN AFRICA – AS BUT ONE EXAMPLE – NIGERIA

The terrorist group, Boko Haram, kidnapped schoolgirls in 2014.

In February 2018, Boko Haram struck again – this time kidnapping 110 girls, some as young as 11, from a government girls' school of science and technology.

A violent feud between Boko Haram and an ISIS affiliate began in 2016 and has resulted in hundreds of deaths, maybe thousands. ISIS controls hundreds of square miles of Nigeria. In December 2018, ISIS struck a heavily fortified military base, and also a naval base. ISIS has overrun and looted a dozen military bases killing many soldiers. Both terror groups have repeatedly bested Nigeria's military. The terrorists have been able to eject the army from several fortified bases.

Negotiations took place to free about 100 of the girls captured in 2014 in exchange for five Boko Haram commanders and about $4 million. As late as 2019, the terrorists were still holding about 100 girls that had been taken in 2014. One can only imagine what their lives have been like since then, how often they have been abused, raped and forced into servitude.

Whether it is 300 girls or 100 they have to be housed and fed presumably in a building of some kind. Yet the government can't find them let alone rescue them. For a while the west was optimistic about Nigeria. An incumbent president, Goodluck Johnson, was defeated in the election of 2015 and the new president, Muhammad Buhari, assumed his office peacefully.

Buhari had been a general who ruled Nigeria for only a year or so in the early 1980s. He took over in a military coup and was ousted in yet another coup. Decades later many voters believed a strong leader would bring stability. 2015 marked the first peaceful transfer of power between civilians of different parties since independence from Britain in 1960.

Buhari was re-elected in February 2019 in spite of Nigeria remaining in a deep recession. The unemployment rate was about 25%. The World Bank said over half the population was living in poverty.

Nigeria is Africa's most populous nation and its largest producer of oil. It is blessed with vast natural resources; it was known to have the region's best universities. Yet because of terrorism and the inability to govern effectively, the economy remains in need of foreign donations.

Term limits were respected so Buhari could not run for a third term. He had become a mystery man, spending much time out of the country. The rumors had it that he was in poor health, being treated for undisclosed illnesses in London.

There was an election in February 2023 won by multi-millionaire Bola Tinubu. He had been an effective Governor of Lagos, Nigeria's largest city, from 1999 to 2007. He was viewed as corrupt.

There were the usual claims that his presidential victory was fraudulent followed by the usual violent protests. But he assumed the office. Bola is a Muslim, as was his running mate. Usually the running mate is a Christian to satisfy that segment of the population.

The fact that Nigeria has a government school of science and technology for girls demonstrates the aspirations of parents who want their children to be successful and thrive. The goal of the terrorists is to destroy that hope.

LIBERIA

Liberia, a Christian country founded by freed American slaves has an awful history. In 2018, it had its first peaceful transition of power in over 70 years. The country had also made history in electing the first female president in African history -- Ellen Johnson Sirleaf, who served two terms, 12 years, before leaving office peacefully.

Sirleaf had a Harvard background showing that Africans will vote for an intelligent qualified woman as their leader. She was recipient of the Nobel Peace Prize in 2011 (a shared prize) in recognition of her contributions to democracy.

Some past history of Liberia –

Two civil wars lasting 14 years overall with a death toll of one-quarter million.

The assassination of two presidents -- William Tolbert in 1980 and Samuel Doe in 1990. The entire cabinet of one president was executed.

Another president, Charles Taylor, has been convicted of war crimes and is currently serving a 50-year sentence. Considering that past, the elevation of Sirleaf was extraordinary.

SOUTH AFRICA

The African country most familiar to Americans is South Africa. The reason for that has been the media attention and the international attention to the unjust system of apartheid. Few Americans could name the leaders of any of the other 50-plus African nations but everyone was familiar with the name of Nelson Mandela.

Mandela was imprisoned by the government in 1964. There finally came on the political scene a leader who understood that white minority rule could not last forever. F. W. de Klerk became president in 1989 and instituted a reform program. Mandela was released from prison in February 1990 after 27 years. In 1991 the apartheid laws were repealed. In May of 1994 under black majority rule, Mandela was elected president.

Mandela, like Lincoln, wanted to bind up the nation's wounds. He preached forgiveness and reconciliation; he agreed to protect private property. It takes a very big man not to seek revenge after spending nearly 3 decades in prison.

The president after Mandela was Thabo Mbeki who began in June 1999. Both Mandela and Mbeki, as well as Mbeki's successor, were members of the African National Congress Party, which has ruled since the end of apartheid.

The end of apartheid did not begin an era of racial harmony, social justice or economic fairness. The country and the economy were run by a white establishment and black insiders. Although only about 15% of the population, the whites controlled most of industry as well as most of the arable land. The black insiders, by and large, were no more attuned to the needs of the masses than the apartheid leaders had been. South Africa remains a society whose main feature is massive inequality.

A report by the World Bank and International Bank for Reconstruction and Development said in April 2018 that South Africa remains "one of the most unequal countries in the world."

Shantytowns, a housing crisis, huge unemployment suffered by the masses. For the blacks that are connected, it's mansions, expensive cars, and upscale restaurants.

Corruption scandals have plagued the African National Congress. There are huge levels of poverty and crime, there is high unemployment, which among the young and unskilled approaches 50%. South Africa has one of the highest HIV/AIDS infection rates in the world. Mandela's own son died of AIDS. Mbeki had some crazy theories about AIDS transmission and refused to accept the medical and scientific consensus on the subject. For blacks, there is limited access to decent health care and quality education

There was an event in August 2013 which brought back memories of the worst excesses of apartheid. In a 2013 confrontation, black police killed 34 black platinum miners who were protesting in a wildcat strike. Hard to believe that black police would kill their mirror images over a labor dispute.

There have been battles between the ANC and the Zulu Inkatha movement resulting in many deaths. The ANC leader who followed Mbeki was Jacob Zuma, who took office in May 2009.

There was an impeachment motion against him in April 2016 which was defeated 233 – 143. What was the issue? Zuma had made improvements in his private home – a pool, a helipad etc. costing about $16 million – and of course Zuma didn't go into his pocket to pay for the extras; rather, he used public funds.

This was very much in the zone of small potatoes compared to other corruption charges against him. He was accused of granting multi-billion-dollar government contracts to wealthy insiders who had so much power over him that they could direct cabinet appointments.

Many members of Zuma's own party were thoroughly fed up with him. This was demonstrated in the municipal elections in July 2016 when the ANC lost major cities to the Democratic Alliance Party in Pretoria (the capital) and Johannesburg (the economic hub). The corruption had become so brazen that the Secretary General of the ANC said it could turn South Africa into a "mafia state."

Former President de Klerk complained that party loyalists were appointed to key posts for which they were unqualified. South Africa's bond rating had been downgraded to junk. He was saddened that, considering the huge mineral resources of the country, the economy was in shambles and that the vast majority of blacks remained mired in poverty. Squatter camps and shantytowns proliferated.

Zuma was a major figure in the liberation struggle; he was in prison for a decade on Robben Island along with Mandela. He had been the Intelligence Chief of the ANC. It was those credentials which allowed him to gain the presidency and hold onto it in spite of his deficiencies.

But finally his own party forced him to resign on February 14, 2018, even though he had a year-and-a-half left on his term. He had become too much of a liability and the party feared defeat in the 2019 national elections.

Replacing Zuma was Cyril Ramaphosa who had been his deputy president for 4 years and had earlier replaced Zuma as the head of the party. Cyril had been a union organizer and a protégé of Mandela. He had left politics to go into business and became a multi-millionaire. During the Zuma years he was silent on the corruption issue.

Ramaphosa's cabinet contains people accused of corruption. The most glaring example is his selection of David Mabuza to be deputy president. Mabuza was accused of graft, payoffs and bribes while he was education minister. Schools are in awful physical shape and the entire educational system is held in low repute.

It has been over a quarter century since the end of apartheid – enough time to create a stable, democratic country with decent economic prospects for its citizens. That was Mandela's dream as he languished in prison.

ETHIOPIA AND ERITREA

Ethiopia was a feudal monarchy led by Emperor Haile Selassie who came to power in 1916. Selassie looked the part of an emperor and people who are old enough remember him as a tragic, regal figure begging the League of Nations to prevent Italy from taking over his country in 1936. The League was even more ineffective than the United Nations.

The Emperor was deposed in 1974 and died in custody in 1975, probably murdered. By 1977 a committed communist, Colonel Mengistu, gained power. Mengistu ended up killing some 100,000 of his opponents as he consolidated power. Ethiopia was subjected to years of his brutal and sadistic dictatorship. Communist leaders, almost without exception, become mass murderers once they gain power – Pol Pot in Cambodia, Stalin, Mao.

The dominant ethnic group in Ethiopia was the Tigrayan, the group mainly responsible for getting rid of the communist regime in 1991. A coalition of four parties dominated by the Tigrayan ran the country for decades. This ethnic group only represents about 6% of the population yet it controlled the military, the security forces and the economy. Ethiopia is the second most populous country in Africa (after Nigeria) with a population of about 120 million.

For years the Oromo ethnic group, comprising about one third of the population, had protested against the dominance of the Tigrayan. One has to understand the history of a nation and the dynamics and interactions of various groups to understand how a minority comes to rule over a majority. Think of Saddam Hussein in Iraq, a minority Sunni Muslim who ruled over the majority Shiites, or Burundi, where the minority Tutsis ruled over the majority Hutus.

In April 2018, a revolutionary event occurred when, for the first time in modern Ethiopian history, an Oromo became the country's leader – Prime Minister Abiy Ahmed. His policies were revolutionary as well.

He freed political prisoners and allowed opposition leaders to return from exile. He removed the ban on political parties, the entrenched one-party system would cease to exist, and he lifted the ban on some outlawed separatist groups. He would permit peaceful dissent.

In a monumental accomplishment, Ahmed ended the 20-year war between Ethiopia and Eritrea. Eritrea became a British protectorate in 1941. In 1962 it was annexed by Ethiopia as a province. A referendum was eventually held and the people of Eritrea voted overwhelmingly in favor of independence, achieving that status in 1993.

Tens of thousands of deaths were endured during the war, a war fought over disputed borders and territory. In June 2018, Ahmed agreed to hand over to Eritrea a border town which had been a sticking point for some 20 years. By July 2018 there was a formal declaration of peace between the combatants. Ahmed was being praised as a new type of leader in Africa. Hopes were high; many thought democracy was around the corner. It was not to be.

Eritrea, like South Sudan, has not been an independence success story. For years Eritrea had no constitution, no judicial system and no formal educational system. The country was plagued with the usual African attributes –illiteracy, unemployment, poverty, corruption and violence. According to a United Nations report issued in June 2017, the government has killed, tortured and arrested thousands. The 500-page report from the United Nations Office of the High Commissioner for Human Rights describes terrible living conditions where cruel abuses are an every-day occurrence.

In a depressingly familiar African scenario, there was a coup attempt against Ahmed in June 2019 which began in the semi-autonomous region of Amhara. Amhara is home to Ethiopia's second largest ethnic group of the same name. During the siege, the Army Chief of staff was killed along with the president and Attorney General of Amhara. The coup attempt did not succeed.

In October 2019, Ahmed was awarded the Nobel peace prize for ending the war with Eritrea.

There are dozens of ethnic groups in Ethiopia and many of them were pushing for greater regional sovereignty, whereas Ahmed sought to forge a national identity. There are nine semi- autonomous regions in Ethiopia, yet the protestors seek even greater control. Local politicians want more resources and land for their own regions. Resources, territory, borders and what group will be in control are always the issues which lead to wars. There have been ethnic massacres in various regions.

In November 2020, Ahmed went to war against the Tigray region. He received the peace prize for allowing Eritrea to become independent, he would not allow the Tigrayans to do the same. For long periods he would not allow food and medical supplies to get to the population.

According to the United Nations, food shortages left nearly half of Tigray's six million people on the verge of starvation.

Eritrea was an ally of Ethiopia in the war against Tigray. They massacred many hundreds of civilians – teachers and farmers who were in no way a threat. Parents would be shot in front of their children. The atrocities committed by both Ethiopia and Eritrea were mind boggling. Ethnic cleansing was the policy against Tigray. Has a Nobel Peace Prize ever been revoked?

The war ended in November 2022 with Ethiopia the clear victor. It is estimated that a half-million Africans lost their lives, plus millions displaced. And for what?

The bottom-line issue is always the same. What leader – what sect or tribe or ethnic group is going to be in charge, in control? Who's going to be the new dictator and how long will he last? No thought is ever given to raising the standard of living or reducing inequality.

AMERICA'S INVOLVEMENT IN AFRICA IS FOCUSED ON OUR BATTLE AGAINST TERRORISM

Our military (mainly Special Forces) had been training the militaries of several African countries for years. How many Americans know of our base in Djibouti –a drone base home to about 4,000 American troops. How many Americans ever heard of this country? Yet Djibouti is the primary American base for the operations of our Africa Command.

In June 2019 there were approximately 800 American military personnel in Niger – and they were doing a great deal more than merely advising, assisting and training. The United States has constructed a large drone base in Niger.

We also have a drone base in Cameroon where we have trained their military for years. In 2013, President Obama sent troops to Mali to assist the French who were battling Al Qaeda. In May 2018, there was an African Land Forces Summit Conference attended by 126 United States Army officers and their counterparts from some 40 African nations. That demonstrates just how deeply America is involved in Africa.

SOMALIA – AN AMERICAN TRAGEDY AND THEIR FIGHT AGAINST TERROR –

In a standard African military coup, in 1969 the president of Somalia was assassinated, and also standard African for an takeover, the leader of the coup, Siad Barre, became the new president.

There was relative stability under Barre yet he had to fight off militias, separatists and warlords. By 1991 Barre had to flee the country after 22 years in power. For nearly three decades there were intermittent civil wars. A central government did not exist; various warlords controlled different sections of the country.

The United States entered the picture in 1992 to support United Nations humanitarian aid efforts. We were defeated not by a national army but by a gang loyal to the warlord who controlled the capital of Mogadishu.

Eighteen brave Americans lost their lives – some of their bodies were dragged through the streets to the cheers of large crowds. Clinton was our Commander in Chief during this humiliation. Hollywood made a movie of the fiasco, "Black Hawk Down," which recounted how

Mohammed Aidid's men shot down four American helicopters with rocket propelled grenades.

In spite of our humiliation, our military has been heavily engaged in Somalia. Primarily against the Al Shabab terrorists who have sworn allegiance to Al Qaeda. ISIS made its appearance in Somalia in 2016.

In November 2017, a United States airstrike killed over 100 at a Shabab training camp. Under Obama in March 2016, we killed about 150 at a Shabab graduation ceremony. One of our drone strikes killed their leader, Ahmed Godane. As was the case with the deaths of other terrorist leaders, Shabab continued its attacks.

In October 2017, they set off a double truck bombing in Mogadishu where the death toll reached nearly 500. In January 2016, Shabab struck a military base in Kenya killing some 130 soldiers. A military base should be the most secure facility in any country. How is it possible for a gang to penetrate such a base and kill so many soldiers possessed of superior weaponry? Back in 2015, Shabab killed 147 students and staff at the University of Garissa in Kenya. The terrorist groups cross borders. They compete with each other. The higher the body count, the higher the prestige. AND ALWAYS REMEMBER THAT THE KILLERS AND THEIR VICTIMS ARE BOTH BLACK AFRICANS.

Shabab strikes other countries to punish them because their soldiers are active in peacekeeping efforts of the African Union. One of Shabab's biggest "prizes" was attacking the upscale Westgate shopping mall in Nairobi, Kenya, killing 67 shoppers – men, women, children.

Shabab did not exist when Al Qaeda attacked America on September 11, 2001. Sad to say President Bush, but your Global War on Terrorism has failed miserably.

Other terrorist organizations have emerged in Africa which likewise did not exist before 9/11. There is Boko Haram which is based in Nigeria, and Al Qaeda in the Islamic Maghreb based in Mali. If you asked them how mass killings could bring about a worldwide Islamic caliphate they would mumble some incoherent slogan.

African Union peacekeepers were first deployed in Somalia in 2007. There have been as many as 20,000 soldiers and police from six countries serving in that mission. In spite of that and American airstrikes, Shabab, although having lost territory, continues to grow and attack.

Boko Haram has hit targets in Chad, Niger and Cameroon in addition to those in Nigeria. In March 2016, Al Qaeda in the Islamic Maghreb struck hotels in Mali, Ivory Coast and Burkina Faso. At one time they ruled over an area the size of Texas in northern Mali. African Union forces, United Nations peacekeepers with America leading the way, have been successful in uprooting the terrorists from many areas they once controlled. The terrorists concentrate on soft targets like hotels occupied by Europeans and journalists. And they are very patient, slowly re-infiltrating areas which they had previously lost.

Going back to 1998, Al Qaeda struck American embassies in Kenya and Tanzania, resulting in over 200 deaths.

Boko Haram kidnapped about 275 schoolgirls in 2014 from Chibok, a village in Nigeria. They are noted for brainwashing women and pre-teen boys and girls into becoming suicide bombers. UNICEF said they used 151 suicide bombers in 2015, about one third of them children, mostly in Nigeria but also in Cameroon, Chad and Niger. Between 2009 and 2015, Boko Haram destroyed hundreds of schools. Their very name means that western education is a sin. They have killed hundreds of teachers and prevented hundreds of thousands of children from getting an education.

The children, their parents, and their teachers deserve great admiration for their persistence in risking their lives so that they can acquire an education. There are many heroic figures in Africa who seek to improve health and education, who battle corruption and tyranny –and all while risking their lives. If only they had a political leadership that was worthy of them.

How do you hide so many girls from drones, from special forces, from African Union armies, from United Nations peace-keeping missions?

We simply don't know who we can trust in these countries. The terrorists are very good at infiltrating armies and security forces. There have been instances of military commanders joining the terrorists. Yes

– commanders and their units which have been trained by American Special Forces.

Aside from America and our superb Special Forces, the most active country fighting terror in Africa has been France. They have had military bases in several countries. The French were persistent – they battled terrorists for years in Niger, Mali and Burkina Faso. The military junta in Niger cut its ties with France; the French were kicked out of Burkina Faso. The populations wanted them gone because the attacks persisted in spite of the French efforts.

There is a terrorist group that has been floating around Africa for decades called the Lord's Resistance Army. They have done much damage, committed many atrocities and forced hundreds if not thousands of children to fight for them. Africa has many great trackers intimately familiar with the jungles and forests. Why can't the Lord's Resistance, Boko Haram, and Shabab be located and destroyed? Is it because they all have confederates within the military and security forces? Is it because so many of the armed forces are corrupt, poorly led and ineffective?

Anthony Banbury, a United Nations Assistant Secretary-General for Field Support, announced that he was leaving after nearly three decades. Why? Because he said the United Nations sent 10,000 soldiers and police to Mali and accomplished nothing, and because African soldiers which the United Nations supposedly vetted committed a torrent of rapes. He accused his beloved organization of – "failing in the creation of stable, democratic institutions."

RUSSIA AND CHINA ARE THE NEW COLONIALISTS

Unstable nations with abundant national resources are such inviting targets. In October 2019 Putin held a summit for dozens of African leaders at the Black Sea resort of Sochi. Russia and China have been seeking trade and political partnerships. China has become South Africa's largest trading partner.

China is building infrastructure all across Africa – roads, ports, etc. When the countries are unable to repay massive loans, which is often, China gains control of these projects. African countries get enmeshed in debt traps. China's tentacles are everywhere. Russia's ambitions are everywhere.

In many ways, this is a replay of the Cold War, where the United States and the Soviet Union competed for allies in Africa. The old refrain of winners and losers. Even back then there was a lot of cheap, dishonest talk but neither side had any interest in promoting democracy. Both sides were happy to back ruthless dictators.

SOME POINTS TO PONDER

The European colonialists laid the groundwork for all of the government malfeasances which I have described. It was the labor and resources of the captive nations that fueled the rise of the European Nations, and it was that exploitation which fueled the downward spiral of the newly independent African nations.

The newly independent states, with very few exceptions, were unable to implement the democratic norms of compromise, cooperation, accommodation and settling differences without resorting to violence.

The Africans simply could not adjust to the concept of power sharing. In Angola and Zimbabwe, for example, there were rival liberation groups, guerilla groups – all of whom fought the colonists, all of whom fought for independence. Their goals were the same. Why couldn't they cooperate and share power? Instead they were killing each other until one side prevailed.

Even the terrorists refuse to share power, which is actually a good thing. If they cooperated, they would be more effective. Boko Haram and ISIS are enemies in Nigeria. ISIS and Shabab are enemies in Somalia. Yet all the terrorists have the same unattainable goal – a worldwide Islamic caliphate governed by Sharia law.

The core problem in Africa is the lack of any national identity. People identify with their tribe, with their ethnic group, with their religion, or with their language group. They may identify with a particular militia or warlord. The goal has to be for people to consider themselves Nigerians or Kenyans or Rwandans. Americans have varied identifications – state, city, religion, ethnic group, teams they root for – but they consider themselves to be Americans.

Unemployment, poverty, corruption and violence are so widespread that millions have sought to migrate to Europe even though success in an unfamiliar and often hostile environment is unlikely. Thousands of Africans have drowned in an attempt to make this crossing; that's how desperate they are.

If there ever develops a leadership committed to the eradication of terror, violence and corruption –a leadership committed to clean elections and term limits and peaceful protests – billions of dollars would come pouring in from international donors, and certainly the United States.

There could then be a joint effort to use the vast natural resources of the continent to improve the economies and raise everyone's standard of living. Even genuine democracies would be within reach.

Obviously, I have focused on some of the most troubled countries in Africa. There are some bright spots, a potential for some enlightened leaders but I will leave them to the optimists.

CHAPTER 15

THE TOTALLY AVOIDABLE DEATH OF GEORGE FLOYD

The image of a policeman's knee on Floyd's neck, as he lay immobile on the concrete pavement, made an indelible impression on America's psyche. Not immobile for a few seconds but for nine full minutes – nine minutes which resulted in Floyd's death.

Why were the police involved with Floyd on May 25, 2020? Floyd had gone to a neighborhood convenience store in Minneapolis, Minnesota to buy a pack of cigarettes. A teenage clerk reported that Floyd paid for the cigarettes with a counterfeit $20 bill. That call led to a chain of events which impacted American history.

Hard to believe, but four cops arrived to deal with this "crime." The police officer in charge was Derek Chauvin, who had been on the Minneapolis force for 19 years. Part of his responsibilities involved training new recruits. He had never been suspended, and in fact, had been the recipient of several awards.

Floyd was frightened to be confronted by four cops who wanted to place him in a police vehicle. He begged not to be restrained, and not to be forced into the police car. It looked like he was having an anxiety attack, being claustrophobic, and fearful of being placed into a confined space.

He was six feet, 4 inches and would have been scrunched in the police car.

Floyd did not have a weapon, he was never aggressive toward any of the police, he was not even verbally aggressive. Chauvin was angry because Floyd did not immediately obey his command to get in the police car. That's part of the cop mentality – my commands must be obeyed even when the commands are trivial or make no sense. That's how Floyd ended up on the concrete. He said again and again that he could not breathe; he was calling for his recently deceased mother. Chauvin did not care; he was going to show who was in charge. A crowd had started to gather.

Two of the other cops pinned down Floyd's back, and legs. Remember that we are talking about a lousy pack of cigarettes.

Why didn't one of the other cops say something like – "Look, I know that you are my superior, but you are endangering this man's life. He is unarmed, and poses no threat. It's not like we are dealing with an armed robber or murderer." That would have been a normal reaction to an intolerable situation.

All someone in the crowd had to scream was –

"Your knee on his neck is being filmed. This will be on the nightly news, not only locally, but nationally. You are killing this guy, damn it, get your knee off his neck."

When that video circulated online, a revolution was born. You would expect protests in Minneapolis – but not all over America.

THE PROTESTS OCCURRED IN MORE THAN 2,000 CITIES, AND TOWNS ACROSS ALL 50 STATES.

Thousands of people were marching every day in very close proximity to each other, and this was happening at the height of the pandemic. The protests were everywhere – rich areas, poor areas, Republican strongholds, Democratic strongholds, white areas, black areas. The video of a white cop killing a black man without cause energized America.

Many of the protests were not peaceful. Thousands of buildings were damaged, many destroyed by fire, business establishments wiped out. A number of deaths. Anger at police in general – understandable but unfair.

I have no doubt that if the nine horrible minutes had not been filmed, the police would have concocted a phony story. Their immediate response to Floyd's death was a lie about a "medical incident."

A jury found Chauvin guilty of murder and he was given a 21-year sentence. The three other officers will serve time in prison as well. All because of a lousy pack of cigarettes and the horrible judgment of a seasoned police officer.

CHAPTER 16

THE TRAGEDY AT THE ROBB ELEMENTARY SCHOOL IN UVALDE, TEXAS

An 18-year-old killer walked into the school armed with a high-powered AR-15 style rifle and murdered 19 fourth graders and 2 teachers. The precious bodies of these 9 and 10-year-olds were shredded by the weapon. Several of these incredibly brave children had called 911 pleading to be saved. They called as they were seeing their classmates murdered.

FROM THE TIME THE KILLER ENTERED THE SCHOOL UNTIL HE WAS KILLED, 77 MINUTES ELAPSED. BY THE TIME THE SHOOTER WAS KILLED, NEARLY 400 LAW ENFORCEMENT PERSONNEL WERE AT THE SCHOOL.

First on the scene were officers from the Uvalde School District Police Force, and its chief Pete Arredondo. His officers assumed that he was the "incident commander," but he said he was not. To hell with the label, confront the killer and kill him.

During the 77 minutes, officers from these other agencies arrived – The United States Border Patrol –

The Texas Department of Public Safety, which includes Rangers –
State Troopers –

The local sheriff's office –

The police force from the City of Uvalde. These agencies were loaded with macho Texas tough guys who had been around guns all their lives. Some were excellent marksmen. They were not afraid to confront the killer. They were stymied by thoughts about procedure, chain of command and a fear of being criticized.

Finally, US Border Control agents went into the classrooms and killed the killer. But by then, 19 children were dead.

During the 77 minutes there were moronic debates about –

Who was the "incident commander?" Was there a need for a "command post" and – Were they dealing with an active shooter situation or a barricaded suspect situation?

There was talk of waiting for a key from a janitor. No cop simply attempted to open the door and of course they could have simply broken down the door. They learned later the door could have been easily opened; there was no need for a key.

One video showed a cop using a hand sanitizer dispenser. Video from a hallway camera showed cops simply milling about.

The 18-year-old killer was able to legally purchase two AR-15 rifles. Was he asked why he needed them? The killer had worked at Wendy's and saved his money for the purchase. He had a plan. He had attended this very same elementary school and probably harbored some sick grievance against it.

There had been some online clues about his mental state but naturally no one took-action to weed him out. After all, his Constitutional rights had to be respected. There were probably discussions about "due process."

Another bad decision allowed this demented person to enter the school. The killer crashed his truck outside the school, as he walked toward the school he started shooting into the school while still outside. A city cop armed with his own AR rifle saw all this, he knew that the killer was going into the school to kill children – yet he didn't shoot him. Why? He was concerned that he might hit a bystander. He was worried about being criticized.

Some parents wanted to rush into the school to save their children. Unbelievably the police held them back. How could it be that not a single cop said – "This is no time for a discussion, for a debate. An armed lunatic killer is in there with our children. I'm going in to kill that bastard. Who's going with me?"

The political cover-up began almost immediately. Governor Greg Abbott arrived at the scene and was fed the lie that the police – "showed amazing courage." When he learned the truth about the delay and the failure of 400 police to act, he was "livid."

The innocence and promise of those wonderful children were taken away in a place where they had every right to believe that they would be protected. The pain of the parents, grandparents, and siblings has to be unbearable.

When one looks at class pictures of the smiling, happy, healthy faces of the 19 children and consider how they died, any normal person would want to cry. Seeing their classmates ripped apart and waiting their turn. And I am sure many who focused on those beautiful photos actually did cry.

The Justice Department investigated all the screwups and issued a nearly 600-page report on January 18, 2024. The murders had occurred on May 24, 2022. The bottom line of the report made it clear that gross negligence and gross stupidity were involved. As was a misguided focus on procedure and labels.

They could hear gunshots. How could it have been anything other than an active shooter situation? The investigation uncovered some facts about the killer. He was bullied and very messed up. Some gave him a nickname of "school shooter." He was considered by some to pose a deadly threat. But no one took the initiative to say – take him out of circulation, make sure he does not have access to weapons.

Instead he was able to purchase two semi-automatic weapons and thousands of rounds of ammunition. He talked openly about being depressed and contemplating suicide. Before his rampage he shot his grandmother. He texted a girl in Germany that he planned to "shoot-up" an elementary school.

He was a walking, talking time bomb. He was obviously a potential danger and ordinary, observant people could see this.

How does a deranged person like this acquire an arsenal of weapons legally?

America is blessed with so many brilliant and courageous people. How could this avoidable tragedy have happened? I ask the same question about the death of George Floyd!

CHAPTER 17

THE ME TOO MOVEMENT- THE DOWNFALL OF A HOLLYWOOD GIANT

The Me Too movement publicized behavior which has been part of the American scene for generations. Sexual abuse has been prevalent in every corner of America. It has been present in universities, in the media, in the military, in business offices, in lawyer's offices, and in doctor's offices. The abusers included the wealthy and the highly educated.

Very few women ever complained. Even when the abuse included assault and rape, and was reported to the police, law enforcement seldom took action and especially so if the accused was prominent and connected. If the victim dressed sexy or had a few drinks, the cops would laugh it off. Many men had the attitude – "She was asking for it."

Rape victims were subjected to tough cross examinations exposing their sexual histories. "Me Too" encouraged women to come forward – at last they were listened to and taken seriously.

In the old culture, which has not disappeared entirely, high school boys and grown men would brag about their conquests, giving no thought to harming a girl's reputation. This "locker room talk" was usually exaggerated and there would be competitions as to who were the most successful abusers. Deflowering virgins was a particular point of pride.

The mistreatment and exploitation of women is a deep character flaw in American men. The exposure of Harvey Weinstein's decades-long pattern of abuse changed everything.

Because of his power in Hollywood, Weinstein was able to advance the careers of women. It was the dream of so many to become movie stars. Many would have flocked to him consensually in spite of him not being handsome or good company.

Studio bosses were even less handsome or interesting yet they had their pick of beautiful and ambitious women. For decades everyone (men and women, too) laughed at jokes about the "Casting Couch."

Trump thought he was having a private conversation when he was bragging about what a big shot, a "star" could get away with in their treatment of women. When you are a star you can grab a woman, kiss her, press up against her, fondle her breasts (or worse) and there would be no consequences. The women would not complain – who the hell were they going to complain to? The bragging was leaked to the public but it did not prevent Trump from becoming President.

What Trump said was basically true – an example of what women had to put up with before "Me Too" kicked in.

Getting back to Harvey –

How could someone so smart be so dumb? Over 90 women accused him of sexual misconduct. He would have to get caught. That many women would eventually compare notes and some would come forward. The 90 number demonstrates how confident Weinstein was that he would never be called to account.

Weinstein was tried in New York, convicted and sentenced to 23 years. Later on, he was tried in California, convicted on rape and other charges, and in February 2023 sentenced to 16 years. The Governor of California's wife, Jennifer Newson, claimed Weinstein had raped her years earlier. His lawyer told the jury that Mrs. Newsom was – "Just another bimbo who slept with him to get ahead." That was a standard line for defense lawyers.

Bill O'Reilly had a huge audience for his Fox Television cable program. Presidents would agree to be interviewed by him. The top executives knew that he was a serial harasser, pressuring women to engage in sex with him. Fox had paid millions to several women in exchange for their silence. How humiliating that has to be. They did not fire O'Reilly because he made money for them. Advertisers flocked to his highly rated show.

O'Reilly was eventually fired only after several women went public and the settlements were publicized. Any man with an ounce of pride would not take advantage of a woman who was not attracted to him, and who would only acquiesce under duress, or fear of losing her job.

Bill Cosby was a different story. Unlike O'Reilly, who was only a good talker, Cosby was a huge, legitimate talent – both as a comedian and actor. In his prime, he was very handsome with the physique of a professional athlete. He could have had a different woman every night, totally consensual. He had been on the cover of hundreds of magazines. He was one of the most recognizable entertainers in the world.

Yet he resorted to drugging women and assaulting them when they were barely conscious. Psychiatrists could have a field day trying to figure that out. There were some insiders who knew of Cosby's routine but they all kept their mouths shut.

For years, Cosby was the star of a situation comedy where he played a doctor and family man, with a beautiful wife and lovable kids. The show was a tremendous success. His blackness was beside the point; white America became very comfortable with him. He paved the way for Obama – a handsome, articulate, likeable black man.

It was a shock to see Cosby with the help of an aide (he had become blind) walking to his sentencing and imprisonment. Contrast that picture with the beloved television commercials for Jello, etc. that he would do surrounded by children. The kids loved him – as he made adults laugh that magic had worked with children as well.

Charlie Rose came across as a big-time intellectual on PBS and CBS's 60 minutes, asking guests questions relating to national and international issues. According to multiple women he was a big-time abuser. So too, was Leslie Moonves, the chief executive of CBS – one of the biggest jobs in the news and entertainment world. He was fired in September 2018.

Many people knew of the reputations of Rose and Moonves but they all kept their mouths shut. Before "Me Too," that was the pattern in every field; silence was golden. A whistleblower would have been ostracized.

There was groping and harassment in the United States Department of Justice, in the death penalty unit yet – presumably loaded with serious and competent lawyers. Sexual misconduct was exposed at universities by esteemed professors, at research institutions.

How about our military? A survey released by the Defense Department in 2019 said that 13,000 women had been assaulted in 2018. We are talking about our Army, Navy, Marines, and Air Force. A separate report said assaults at service academies had risen by 50% since 2016. The Pentagon concluded that – "sexual violence is a national crisis." A crisis that was ignored for decades. Many women's lives were ruined; many others spent decades in therapy. And our macho guys didn't give a damn. Yes, I call that a character flaw.

National Public Radio – loaded with highly educated liberals. An abusive work environment, bullying, treating lower-level employees like dirt. Even criticism of the revered Garrison Keiller (Mr. Mellow). NPR's top news executive resigned, as did the chief news editor. No one said – cut the crap, stop acting like punks or I'm going to fire your ass. Your behavior is juvenile, grow up! No, it was all tolerated until "Me Too" found a national audience.

How about Nike, the world's largest sports footwear and apparel company? All the big shots at Nike are millionaires; those at the very top are probably billionaires. Yet, ordinary guys walk around with T-shirts emblazoned with the Nike symbol.

Eleven senior managers who tolerated sexual harassment and worse for years at Nike are gone, and of course the bosses had no idea that this was the workplace culture. One of the Nike executives who is gone was the head of diversity and inclusion. The hypocrisy and phoniness is stunning. Did anyone stop buying their sneakers after learning of the Nike "culture"? I doubt it!

NBC conducted a 5-month in-house investigation which concluded that no higher up knew about Matt Lauer's track record. If you believe that, you believe in the tooth fairy. If the big shots didn't know specifics, it's because they didn't want to know. Lauer had been very popular on the Today Show; he was paid millions for early-morning chit-chats.

The Attorney General of the State of New York cultivated a reputation as a woman's champion. He had sued Harvey Weinstein, and of course was outraged at Harvey's conduct. Eric Schneiderman physically assaulted women with whom he was having consensual sex. That was his idea of role playing. One day he was Brando, on another he was Lancaster.

Schneiderman resigned in record-breaking time. His assaults on four women were laid out in an article in the New Yorker magazine and the very day it appeared, he was gone.

How about another former attorney general of New York? This one was elected to the No. 1 position – Governor. I speak of Eliot Spitzer. While Governor, married to a very attractive and accomplished lawyer, he would travel with a prostitute to Washington, D.C. They would both walk into a hotel frequented by political and lobbying insiders. Spitzer was easily recognized, and I'm sure there was a lot of giggling and finger-pointing. This probably should be in my section on smart people making incredibly dumb decisions. Brilliant!

AMERICANS KEEPING SILENT WHEN THEY SHOULD HAVE BEEN SCREAMING FROM THE ROOFTOPS

The most vivid example of this syndrome has been decades of silence about Catholic priests abusing thousands of children, including rapes. This was a worldwide phenomenon.

Nearly every diocese was a fortress of secrecy. Instead of the church hierarchy being outraged at what priests had done to young Catholics, the strategy was to cover up and transfer. Priests were sent to other locations without these new jurisdictions being told of their sordid history. As to be expected, the transferred priests continued to prey on new victims.

The chronic abuse was first reported by the Boston Globe in 2002 – initiated by a mother whose son had been victimized. She started asking questions and making accusations.

There were as many as 250 priests that were accused in the greater Boston area alone, there was credible evidence of hundreds of rapes which spanned 4 decades. The nation's most senior prelate, Cardinal Bernard Law, resigned as Archbishop of Boston, because he was involved both in the cover-ups and in the transfers.

State after state revealed the same pattern. Missouri found that 163 priests were accused of sexual abuse against minors. The Missouri Attorney General made a comment which applied nationwide and worldwide –

"For decades, faced with credible reports of abuse the church refused to acknowledge the victims and instead focused their efforts on protecting priests."

I could never understand why some rugged Italian or Irish father did not confront or assault a priest who had molested or raped their sons. Were most Catholic kids taught from birth that priests were holy and could do no wrong? Did the kids fear that they would not be believed? A grand jury report in Pennsylvania found that Bishops covered up abuses of hundreds of priests which had occurred over several decades. Yes, several decades in Boston, several decades in Pennsylvania and throughout America – and almost nobody opened their mouths.

On May 23, 2023, the office of the Attorney General of Illinois issued an astounding report saying that 450 credibly accused child sex abusers have ministered in the Catholic Church in Illinois over almost seven decades. At least 1997 children had been abused since 1950 in the state's six dioceses. Until the Boston exposure, the outrages were kept secret for generations.

Where was the media, where were the investigative reporters to expose this sordid history? They should have been shouting from the rooftops.

What was the process for vetting candidates for priesthood? It was obviously lousy. The requirement of celibacy I'm sure played a major role in screwing up the psyche of so many priests. As celibacy is unnatural so is the sexual predation of the priests.

One of America's most beloved college football coaches, with a great winning record and very lengthy tenure, kept his mouth shut about abuse. I refer to Joe Paterno of Penn State, who averted his eyes from the conduct of a valued assistant coach who had been with him for many years. The motivation always is to protect the reputation of the institution and to hell with the victims. Coach Paterno resigned under pressure, leaving a stain on what would have otherwise been a legendary legacy.

Dr. Lawrence Nassar of Michigan State University was for two decades the team physician for USA Gymnastics, which oversees the Olympic world championship teams.

During his examinations of hundreds of young women, he would employ totally improper touching and insertions. No one spoke up for years, although the girls spoke to each other and knew that his conduct was reprehensible. One Hundred Fifty-Six women made victim statements when the matter finally went to court. Some coaches were suspicious for years, but nobody confronted Nassar or reported him. He will spend the rest of his life in prison. In 2018, Michigan State agreed to pay $500 million to over 300 of Nassar's victims.

Several of Nassar's victims had reported the abuse to the FBI's Indianapolis Field Office in 2015. The agents were not impressed and took no action. For generations that was the dominant male attitude toward female complaints. The Inspector General of the Justice Department, Michael Horowitz, blasted those agents; several were fired.

In January 2022, the University of Michigan agreed to pay $490 million to settle with over 1,000 students and athletes who had been abused by Dr. Robert Anderson, a physician in the athletic department. Unbelievable – 1,000 students abused, and Anderson was allowed to remain in his post for 37 years. There were numerous complaints over the decades, but no one in authority stepped up to end the abuse and punish the abuser. Imagine what happens at marginal colleges and prep schools where teenagers do not live at home.

The greatest sin was allowing the abuse to continue, enveloping a wider range of new victims. There never was a movement encouraging children and women to speak up and telling those in authority that complaints had to be taken seriously.

At Rockefeller University in New York, a respected specialist in pediatric endocrinology had abused children for decades. A law firm was hired to investigate and found that complaints about the doctor's behavior were reported to various authorities as early as the 1960s, but the doctor remained. The University issued a statement profoundly apologizing for its failure to take action years earlier. How is it that upper echelon academics allow the abuse to continue when their focus should be protecting their students?

Dr. Richard Strauss was the team physician at Ohio State University for wrestling, gymnastics, and swimming. The law firm hired to investigate his conduct conducted some 500 interviews and issued a lengthy report describing egregious conduct.

Ohio State's own investigation found that Strauss had abused at least 177 men from the 1970s to the 1990s, and that dozens of university employees failed to take action against him. No wrestler or football player ever beat the crap out of Strauss. We are talking about totally unnecessary genital examinations. Nobody wanted to besmirch the moneymaking machine of the Ohio State athletic department. The state medical board investigated, but took no action. Strauss committed suicide in 2005.

In January 2022, 56 former students at the University of North Carolina's School of the Arts filed a lawsuit saying that dozens of teachers over a span of 40 years inflicted sexual, physical, and emotional abuse, and that the school took no action in spite of repeated complaints. Some of the students were ages 12 to 14, enrolled in summer programs to gain skill in dance and the performing arts.

For decades, the Boy Scouts of America (a revered institution promoting our highest values) provided a harvest for thousands of pedophiles. And for decades, the usual American response – ignoring the criminal behavior and protecting the Institution.

The organization was founded in 1910 and its mission was to embrace the ideals of patriotism, courage, loyalty and self-reliance. Get ready for this astounding number – there have been 82,200 individual claims of sexual abuse by Scout leaders. The Scouts filed for bankruptcy, coming up with a plan to distribute $2.5 billion. The Scouts' own valuable camping and recreational facilities as well as other real estate.

What follows are some more examples of mouths being shut when they should have been screaming for justice and accountability.

There were some 700 accusers against a campus gynecologist at the University of Southern California – Dr. George Tyndall. Complaints had been made to university officials as early as the 1990s. There was no report made to the state medical board. Tyndall was not suspended until 2016. The cover-up was made public by the Los Angeles Times in 2018. The president of the university resigned.

James Heaps was a gynecologist at the University of California (UCLA) from 1983 to 2018. He was accused by hundreds of women over the years. An abundance of silence and coverups!

The Southern Baptist Convention, in May 2022, published a list of ministers and other church workers who were "credibly accused" of sexual abuse. The list went on for 205 pages; it covered offenses going back decades. Complaints were ignored for over 20 years.

The Convention is the largest Protestant denomination in the country with almost 14 million members.

How about the National Women's Soccer League? After ignoring complaints for many years, an investigation was conducted and a report issued on October 3, 2022. The conclusion –

"Our investigation has revealed a league in which abuse and misconduct – verbal and emotional abuse and sexual misconduct – had become systemic, spanning multiple teams, coaches and victims."

Owners and executives knew all about this and did nothing. The soccer players, to their great credit, protested publicly. The New York Times and Washington Post reported the abuse. Players were coerced into sexual relationships. Abusive coaches would be transferred to other teams with their histories kept secret.

It can't be repeated often enough – What the hell is wrong with us? How can such behavior be tolerated?

The Pentagon admitted that they were negligent in supervising the Junior Reserve Officers Training Corps Program as dozens of veterans who taught in high schools were accused of sexually abusing their students.

The theory of the program was that it provided training in leadership and civic responsibility. Of course, the Pentagon hoped that the program would be a pipeline to enlistment. In an all-voluntary military, recruitment often lagged behind expectations. Decorated veterans were able to prey on teenagers in about 3500 high schools around the country. Many have been criminally charged. Neither the military nor the schools had in place a system to monitor the conduct of the instructors.

Numerous universities covered up abuses by campus fraternities for decades. Female visitors at parties would be drugged and assaulted. It was all a big joke to those who spouted – the "boys will be boys" line. Finally in 2021, there were student protests against the assaults at Nebraska, Iowa, the University of Massachusetts, Northwestern, Syracuse, Kansas, etc. School officials who ignored the complaints should hang their heads in shame.

For over two decades, a pediatrician named Stanley Weber worked for the Indian Health Service on two reservations in South Dakota and Montana. For years, he had been accused of multiple sexual assaults including rape. The Indian Health Service joined universities, hospitals, churches, and governments in covering up and protecting the abusers.

It was not our government which finally outed Weber. Rather, it was the joint efforts of the Wall Street Journal and the investigative program, "Frontline," on the Public Broadcasting Service. Weber was sentenced to five life terms in 2020. 20 years and hundreds of victims too late.

Taking advantage of and exploiting the disadvantaged and vulnerable is powerful evidence of moral decay and a total lack of empathy. A lack of interest in the suffering and long-term consequences to the victims. Think of the many thousands of lives adversely impacted, sometimes for a lifetime, by the traumas that were inflicted by men who didn't give a damn.

Those who were told about the abuse and kept their mouths shut share the guilt of the actual offenders.

CHAPTER 18

THE MYTH THAT AMERICANS ARE BASICALLY HONEST THE COLLEGE ADMISSIONS CHEATING SCANDAL

If you were to ask this question to millions of Americans chosen at random – "Do you believe that Americans are basically honest?" – probably 95% would answer "yes." What follows is evidence that they would be wrong. Every parent who paid bribes to get one of their kids into a prestigious university is both educated and wealthy. They all understood that what they were doing was dishonest and crooked. They all believed they would not get caught.

Parents wanted to brag that their kids were accepted to the top tier universities. That their kids were smarter than your kids.

They bribed coaches to designate their children as recruited athletes for sports in which their children had no skills. Sports such as soccer, tennis, volleyball, water polo and rowing.

Bribes were also paid to those who were monitoring college entrance exams – SAT, ACT. The scores of their children would be falsely raised or a stand-in would be hired to actually take the test for them. Wrong answers would be scratched, to be replaced with the correct ones.

Coaches had connections to the admissions departments and they had the discretion to recommend recruits. The scheme went on for several years and was the brainchild of William Rick Singer, who presented himself as a private admissions consultant. He put out podcasts with college entrance tips; he did YouTube videos. He was the middleman to bribe the coaches and the test administrators.

52 parents were criminally charged. Among them was a managing partner of a major law firm, a radiation oncologist, a professor of dentistry, two successful actresses, and prominent business executives. Most parents pled guilty.

Singer would brag about his "side door" approach to getting unqualified kids admitted. His business card said –

"Future Stars – Academic and Athletic Scholarship Services."

The pay-off parents were sophisticated in the worlds of finance, hedge funds, and real estate. They understood just how crooked Singer and his "side door" were.

Some of the guilty pleas –

The Women's Soccer Coach at Yale who had served honorably for over 20 years.

The Sailing Coach at Stanford –

The Men's Tennis Coach at the University of Texas.

The Senior Athletic Department Administrator at the University of Southern California expressed great remorse for what she had done. She made a very telling statement at her sentencing.

"It was just so much pressure to raise money at my institution."

Yes, it is the connection between fundraising and admissions that causes many good people to engage in criminal activity.

The competition to get admitted to the elite schools is fierce. Straight "A" students are often turned down. For example in 2018, the

University of Southern California admitted only 13% of those who applied. In 2019, the university had nearly 66,000 applicants.

The admit rates are even more discouraging at Harvard (4.5%), at Yale (about 6%), and at Stanford (4.5%).

Many people, including students, had to be suspicious that something corrupt was going on. At some point everyone knew that Student 1 or Student 2 did not know how to play soccer or volleyball – so how the hell did they get admitted as a recruited athlete?

But everyone kept their mouths shut. Or if complaints or suspicions were voiced, they were ignored. The schools were hoping for hefty contributions from the wealthy parents.

The Department of Justice eventually uncovered Singer's scheme. He pled guilty to racketeering conspiracy in Boston federal court in March 2019. In order to reduce his sentence, he cooperated with the government by agreeing to record his calls with parents and by wearing a hidden wire. He ensnared many into incriminating themselves.

The parents could not rationalize that their so-called crimes were victimless. Fraudsters were admitted in place of deserving students. I call those ego crimes!

THOUSANDS OF AMERICANS WERE DISHONEST DURING THE COVID PANDEMIC

The COVID pandemic caused many thousands of tragic deaths. Millions lost jobs; millions of businesses closed down. The government responded very generously with relief funds.

The Inspector General of the Small Business Administration said that over $200 billion went to businesses and individuals who had committed fraud. The Small Business Administration gave over $1 trillion to small businesses and their employees. Yes, a trillion. Criminal gangs got their hands on much of this money. But many thousands of ordinary, solid middle-class Americans grabbed what they could, realizing that oversight was weak and prosecutions rare. The pot of gold was seen as a bonanza to be tapped.

Thousands of "law-abiding" citizens and business owners falsely claimed they were entitled to tax credits under the pandemic relief legislation. The Internal Revenue Service said that it had paid out over $230 billion in refunds under the tax credit program and had a backlog of over 600,000 claims. The Labor Department oversees federal unemployment insurance programs.

The Inspector General of the Labor Department revealed that there was $45 billion in fraud in a single year. The Government Accounting Office reported that the Labor Department gave out $878 billion in unemployment insurance benefits from April 2020 until September 2022. Billions of those benefits went to many thousands who fraudulently claimed that they were entitled to those benefits.

The Labor Department revealed the sad fact that even before the pandemic, chronic unemployment benefits fraud cost billions every year for many years.

There is a sordid history of banks cheating their own customers, their own depositors. The most striking example is provided by Wells Fargo, one of America's mega banks with thousands of branches. The chief executives pressured thousands of employees to meet aggressive sales goals. To achieve this, the employees simply created false accounts, of which the customers were totally unaware. Of course the big shots were totally aware.

Hoping to salvage their own jobs, those at the top fired thousands of low-level employees for opening the false accounts even though they were only following orders from on high. The chief executives were found to be complicit and two of them were toppled in this shameful scandal.

Yet Wells Fargo continued to do great. In the third quarter of 2023, they along with JP Morgan Chase and Citigroup reported over $22 billion in profits. And that's in a single quarter.

How would you or a family member like to be cared for by a nurse with a phony degree? There has been a network of nursing school operators who create bogus academic credentials and phony college transcripts allowing unqualified people to attain licensed practical nurse's degrees or registered nurses diplomas. The "students" would usually pay somewhere between $10-20,000, and there were thousands of such students. The crooks reaped huge profits.

The employees of these schools, the recruiters, and the students themselves kept quiet about the ongoing fraud and the dangers to patient care. The nursing schools are but one example of for-profit schools which promise good jobs but rarely deliver.

A FEW MORE EXAMPLES OF RAMPANT DISHONESTY

In a recent annual report the FBI said that businesses and individuals reported $10.3 billion in losses in a single year to internet crime. The Federal Trade Commission stated that consumers reported losing nearly $8.8 billion to fraudulent schemes in a single year.

It is likely that a majority of fraud victims never report the crimes. They suffer their embarrassment in silence. Many recognize that our law enforcement agencies have a poor record in prosecuting the fraudsters; there are just too many of them.

The experts predict that within online shopping during the 2023 holiday season there will be losses to the tune of about $48 billion. Many naïve victims are duped into revealing personal information such as date of birth, Social Security number and banking pass codes.

America would be a lot greater if there was an admission of the extent of fraud and dishonesty and a concerted effort to emphasize the virtue of honesty in all of our dealings with others.

CHAPTER 19

THE DRUG OVERDOSE EPIDEMIC

Perhaps you've heard of the Sackler family. If you have anything to do with fund raising at major universities, you have certainly heard of them because they have made enormous contributions to Harvard, Yale, Columbia, Oxford. They love having their name on buildings and particularly museums – the Sackler wing at the Metropolitan Museum of Art in Manhattan, the Sackler Museum at Harvard, the Guggenheim. That is the route followed by many hedge fund, private equity, investment banker people – millions to museums and universities so that everyone will know how wonderful they are and how cultured they are.

Where did the Sackler billions come from? From a prescription painkiller – Oxycontin. Their corporate entity was Purdue Pharma. The marketing strategy was to downplay and flat-out lie about the risks of addiction and to exaggerate the benefits of the drug. The pitch was that we were entering a new era of pain management – an enlightened era.

Purdue provided legions of doctors with all-expense-paid trips to exotic locations with their families so that they, too, would downplay the risks of addiction. The most-basic tenet of medical education is – "FIRST, DO NO HARM." Some of the doctors who were overprescribing could not pass up the gifts, the free meals, the most expensive wines, and the cash. In order to disguise these inducements, the doctors were paid for giving speeches on pain management and other topics. At times, the audience would consist only of the doctor's employees.

American doctors prescribed opioids at far-higher rates than did doctors in any other country. What does that say about the lack of honesty found in this educated class?

Purdue employed an army of aggressive sales representatives to promote their cash-cow drug. Some of these golden boys and girls were so good at what they did, that they could make $100,000 in bonuses in a given quarter.

The American Society of Addiction Medicine has said that 4 out of 5 who are regular users of heroin started out with prescription painkillers. There are synthetic opioids that are much more powerful than oxycontin, such as fentanyl. These drugs can be bought online on any number of dark websites by the use of special browsers. Isn't technology wonderful?

In November 2020, Purdue pled guilty to the federal felonies of defrauding health agencies and drug enforcement officials, and violating anti-kickback laws. Back in 2007, Purdue pled guilty to the felony of misbranding a drug with the intent to mislead. For these and other crimes Purdue has been fined over $600 million. A mere stubbed toe to the Sacklers.

The founder of one pharmaceutical company was sentenced by a federal judge to 5 years in prison – John Kapoor of Insys Therapeutics. The crime: bribing doctors to massively prescribe a highly addictive drug. Sad to say, the doctors knew they were causing harm but they could not pass up the easy money.

On behalf of thousands of survivors of overdose victims, a flood of lawsuits was filed against Purdue Pharma as well as other manufacturers, distributors, and retailers. Purdue filed for bankruptcy in 2019. In March 2021, Purdue submitted its restructuring plan consisting of over 300 pages. The Sacklers said they were willing to pay $4.275 billion in exchange for being granted immunity from all civil litigation against them. They eventually upped their offer to $6 billion.

Monies to the states and cities would be used to alleviate the epidemic, not to cover shortfalls in state budgets. The national tobacco settlement with the various states was severely criticized because those billions went into the general coffers of state and local governments to be used for purposes totally unconnected to the goal of reducing tobacco use and addiction.

The Sacklers garnered most of the media coverage but there were other players in the opioid supply chain such as distributors and pharmacies. Other pharmaceutical companies manufactured pain relieving drugs.

A huge player that received little media attention until 2022 was a company named Teva which manufactured both generic and branded opioids. In July 2022, Teva announced a settlement with over two thousand cities, states and Indian tribes for $4.25 billion.

Major drug distributors like McKesson, Cardinal Health and Johnson and Johnson were sued on the legal theory that they had created a "public nuisance" by allowing drugs to flood hundreds of cities. In July 2021, the states and cities (not all of them) reached a tentative settlement with these defendants for $26 billion. Under the proposed plan, consisting of hundreds of pages, the money would go to states and cities rather than to individual victims and their survivors. The monies would be used for treatment, prevention and education.

From 1999 to 2019 nearly a half-million Americans died from overdoses. The death rate jumped 30% from 2019 to 2020 according to the Centers for Disease Control and Prevention – 93,000 deaths in 2020. 2021 was the first year that overdose deaths topped 100,000 – about 108,000. The numbers were even worse during the first half of 2022. The availability of fentanyl was a strong contributor to these staggering numbers.

Another factor was the pandemic. Isolation, depression, anxiety added to the toll. Drugs represented an escape from life's hardships and inequities.

Many children became orphans when both parents died from overdoses. Some addicted pregnant women gave birth to drug dependent babies. An infant going through withdrawal. How does a parent deal with that? The drug makers, the over-prescribing doctors and the pharmacies can rationalize all they want, but they bear responsibility for these tragedies.

Distributors, by law, are supposed to monitor the amounts of prescription drug shipments. When they would ship millions of opioids to cities and towns with small populations, they had to know that the drugs were being abused. They were required to report suspicious orders.

Every opioid that was distributed originated from a doctor writing a prescription. The pharmacies had to know what was going on with the surge in prescriptions that they were filling.

In November 2021, a federal jury in Cleveland found that pharmacy chains at Walgreens, Wal-Mart and CVS had substantially contributed to the overdose crisis in two Ohio counties by ignoring suspicious massive opioid orders. It would be the counties that were receiving the money rather than individuals.

There were other settlements. The pharmacy chains at Walgreens, CVS, and Walmart settled for $13 billion. They had failed to investigate over-prescribing. The grocery chain, Kroger, agreed to pay $1.2 billion for not properly monitoring prescriptions at their retail pharmacies.

The basic defense of the pharmacies before they agreed to settle was that they were merely filling legal prescriptions written by doctors. That defense didn't hold up because they continued to dispense massive quantities of pills while ignoring evidence that the pills were being abused.

A full-page ad that appeared in the New York Times on February 14, 2022, sponsored mainly by healthcare workers, made it clear that the drug epidemic was as strong as ever. That it was definitely a "crisis." They established -

"Harmreduction.org" to alleviate the crisis through education, treatment and understanding. The ad informed the public that -

"More than 100,000 people in the United States died in the last year (2021)."

Thankfully, there are still many good people focused on dealing with the epidemic. There are solid Americans who serve on Overdose Quick Response teams ready to administer Narcan to reverse the effects. There is a division of overdose prevention at the CDC.

There is often a connection between addiction and mental health problems. In June 2022, the National Center on Addiction and Substance Abuse at Columbia University said that our addiction treatment system was a – "non-system." Many are working hard to repair that system.

There is a nexus between the overdose epidemic and millions of unhappy, struggling Americans. Americans who hate their jobs and the inequities which permeate every corner of our culture – Americans who know that they will never be participants in the oversold Great American Dream. They hate the techie and banking billionaires. Think of how filled with despair one has to be to turn to drugs as an outlet.

It is a national problem, not confined to the urban minority poor. The epidemic enveloped white, rural America-states like New Hampshire and Maine.

I am convinced that there is a nexus between the overdose epidemic and America's suicide epidemic. 2022 was a record year when nearly 50,000 Americans killed themselves. Suicide rates for Native Americans and Alaska natives are double the rates for other Americans. That will not surprise anyone who has read my chapter on Indians.

The suicide rate among those ages 10 to 24 increased 56% between 2007 and 2017. About one thousand college students kill themselves each year. There are many suicide and crisis lifelines manned by good people who do their best to alleviate the crisis.

I am sure that the pandemic, which killed over one million Americans, contributed heavily to the national mood of dependency.

And then there are the veteran suicides. Six thousand veterans committed suicide each year between 2008 and 2017. So many of them realize that the 20-year wars in Afghanistan and Iraq ended in failure, that their sacrifices were in vain and that we lost the war against terror. Disgusted, disillusioned people turn to drugs and suicide.

MCKINSEY AND COMPANY – A GLOBAL CONSULTING GIANT

The company has advised Saudi Arabia, China and a host of other countries. It is the ultimate insider with influence unknown to 99% of Americans.

Founded in 1926, McKinsey has over $10 billion in annual revenue. It is one of the world's largest private partnerships. It has about 3,000 partners and 45,000 employees worldwide. Among its alumni are Sheryl Sandberg, who was the chief operating officer at Facebook – Sundar Pichai CEO of Google – and Jane Fraser CEO of Citigroup. It has advised defense, intelligence and policing establishments in authoritarian countries.

McKinsey has advised dictators on how to remain in power. It consults with political parties and legislative bodies. It has had contracts with various American federal agencies including Immigration and Customs Enforcement (ICE) and Customs and Border Protection.

Their consultants are experts at damage control when their clients are facing corruption allegations. They are also experts at image control when they represent dictators or crooks.

So why am I writing about McKinsey in this chapter on prescription opioid overdoses? Because they advised Purdue and other manufacturers, as well as distributors, on how to aggressively market their addictive products. McKinsey helped educate Purdue and others on how to – "turbo charge their sales engine."

For giving that advice heedless of the human cost, McKinsey had to settle with the Justice Department paying a fine of nearly $600 million.

The media was very interested in interviewing some of the major decision makers, but McKinsey refused to make them available. Secrecy has been one of the keys to their nearly century-long record of success. They have a strong policy of not identifying clients or the advice that they give. Their advice to private corporations is always geared toward increasing profits. If that involves cutting costs and firing people, so be it.

Their reach is so broad that they have even been retained by our federal Food and Drug Administration. One of McKinsey's specialty areas is advising in connection with bankruptcies and restructuring companies going through that process.

The art of restructuring is very profitable. Were they advising Purdue Pharma in their bankruptcy case?

Who are these invisible, powerful players? Just another mysterious enterprise in the American landscape affecting us in unknown ways. But ways that are known to the chosen ones – to the insiders in the tech, financial and political worlds. Our politicians mouth platitudes about the need for and the virtue of transparency. How many of them have been secretly advised by McKinsey about how to win elections? A LOT!

WHATEVER HAPPENED TO THE PURDUE BANKRUPTCY DEAL?

By 2024, the "settlement" still had not been finalized. None of the $8 billion had been disbursed. No individual has received a dime.

That was surprising, since the vast majority of plaintiffs approved the deal. Nearly all the states approved the deal. Everybody wanted to get their hands on the cash. The United States Court of Appeals for the Second District approved the plan. However the Justice Department appealed to the U.S. Supreme Court which heard oral argument in December 2023.

There were legal issues involving the newfound powers of bankruptcy courts to structure mass injury settlements. And to insulate third parties from liability. THE SACKLERS NEVER DECLARED PERSONAL BANKRUPTCY.

Many legal commentators and members of the general public hated the idea that the Sacklers had already parked billions in offshore tax havens. Consistent with their ethical values they were seeking to avoid paying their fair share of taxes. And as always there is a horde of lawyers willing to help them accomplish that.

Under the plan that was approved, individuals would receive $750 million – less than one billion of the 8 billion. The cities have much more clout with better connected lawyers. The monies would be paid out over a period of 18 years. These are tax reasons for such a long payout.

By the time my book is published, the U.S. Supreme Court will have ruled.

A single word explains the drug overdose epidemic and that word is – GREED! The ego driven need to show off one's riches!

Not a quality that Americans can be proud of!

CHAPTER 20

THE UKRAINE AND THE AMERICAN PUSH TO HAVE IT JOIN THE NORTH ATLANTIC TREATY ORGANIZATION

The Ukrainian people have suffered greatly as a result of the Russian invasion in February 2022. Millions of refugees, thousands of deaths, the destruction of homes, hospitals and schools. The Ukrainian defense forces have performed magnificently. They surprised all the experts who were predicting a brief war in which Russia would be victorious.

YET IT ALL COULD HAVE BEEN AVOIDED. ALL THE UKRAINIAN LEADERS HAD TO SAY TO PUTIN WAS – "WE ARE NOT GOING TO JOIN NATO."

It was American presidents who were promoting the idea of NATO membership for the Ukraine. Let's start with President Bush II, who was obsessed with the myth of spreading democracy worldwide.

During Bush's two terms in office, Fiona Hill was the national intelligence officer for the National Intelligence Council. She was a Russian specialist and was the Council's Senior Director of Russian affairs. She made it clear to Bush that Ukraine joining NATO was a very bad idea and would likely provoke a military response from Russia. Several of our NATO allies and many in our intelligence community agreed with Hill. Bush did not follow Hill's advice.

Hill continued to serve in the Obama and Trump administrations. That's how highly her advice was valued.

Robert Gates was defense secretary under both Bush and Obama. This is what he had to say about Ukraine's potential membership in NATO -

"Trying to bring Ukraine and Georgia into NATO was truly overreaching and an especially monumental provocation."

Gates understood that if these two former republics of the Soviet Union joined NATO, Russia would go to war. How come Bush, Clinton, Obama, and Biden did not understand that?

Clinton's defense secretary, William Perry, told him that Ukraine membership in NATO was a terrible idea that would lead to tragic consequences. He viewed NATO expansion to include former Soviet republics and satellites to be a profound strategic blunder. Clinton ignored the warning.

George Kennan was a legendary figure in American diplomacy. He had served as our ambassador to the Soviet Union. It was Kennan who came up with a policy that is given major credit for avoiding a hot war between the United States and the Soviet Union. That policy was called "containment" and was devised to prevent Soviet expansion beyond its region.

Kennan called NATO expansion into Russia's sphere – "a tragic mistake." Referring to the Senate's approval of Ukraine membership in NATO, Kennan said -

"What bothers me is how superficial and ill-informed the whole Senate debate was."

Did any senator say that Ukrainian membership would cause Russia to invade? Did any senator point to Putin's track record of targeting civilians, of being oblivious to how many civilian deaths he caused? Of course, it was "superficial," because the senators, so many hack politicians among them, knew that speeches about democracy and freedom almost always resulted in unrestrained cheering. Millions believed that Afghanistan was going to be transformed into a democracy. Instead, it remained a country ruled by the Taliban.

William Burns was our ambassador to Russia; he speaks Russian. Biden later appointed him as director of the Central Intelligence Agency. During the Bush administration, Burns sent Secretary of State Condoleezza Rice a memo warning against Ukraine joining NATO -

"Ukraine's entry into NATO is the brightest of all red lines for the Russian elite –" his point being that all of Russia (not just Putin) loathed and feared NATO expansion. Obviously, Rice did not tell Bush that he was making a terrible mistake.

Robert Service is a renowned historian and expert on Russia, and a professor at Oxford. He has written books on Lenin, Stalin and Trotsky. I am sure that Bush, Clinton, Obama, Trump, and Biden never read any of them. Service blames the Russian invasion on an immense – "strategic blunder." A blunder made not by one president but by several.

John Mearsheimer is an American liberal, a professor and author who has criticized the Bush doctrine of attempting to spread democracy -

"We went around the world trying to create liberal democracies." He viewed that as a fool's errand. As early as 2015, Mearsheimer said -

"The west is leading Ukraine down the primrose path and the end result is that Ukraine is going to get wrecked."

Tragically, he was right and Ukraine did get "wrecked."

The objective people who were not scrambling to score political points recognized that Putin's position was understandable and reasonable. Ukraine had been part of Russia for centuries; it was part of Russia during the Czarist Era – well before the Soviet Union existed. Ukraine had turned over its nuclear weapons to Russia. That's how close they were. How dare America snatch it away to become an enemy of Russia?

When the Soviets placed missiles in Cuba, that could have led to World War III. Because they were encroaching on our sphere of influence as we were doing on Russia's. President Kennedy was as smart handling the Cuban Missile Crisis as he was dumb in plotting the invasion at the Bay of Pigs.

Putin had over 100,000 troops on the border of Ukraine for several months. His intentions could not have been clearer. Had the United States and Ukraine said they were abandoning any plans for NATO membership, there would have been no invasion – no millions of refugees, no hundreds of thousands of deaths, no destruction of the country's civilian infrastructure.

Over 30 countries belong to NATO. The Baltic states of Lithuania, Estonia and Latvia had been republics within the Soviet Union. They became members of NATO. Poland and Hungary were satellites of the Soviet Union for decades. They became members of NATO. Putin hated those memberships, but he did not take military action against any of them.

His red line was the Ukraine. That's why Defense Secretary Gates called the attempt -

"An especially monumental provocation that was truly overreaching."

It should have been obvious to even the most superficial observer as to what Putin's reaction would be. We knew what Putin was capable of; he had been guilty of wanton cruelty to the civilians of Aleppo and Chechnya. He took pleasure in destroying cities.

He was the man who called the collapse of the Soviet Union -

"The greatest geopolitical catastrophe of the century."

It was counter-productive to "provoke" Putin. The West led by America had become dominant. The Warsaw Pact, the military alliance between the Communist states, was dissolved. Poland and Hungary had been members of that Pact; now they were part of NATO. Putin felt humiliated, and hated America for advocating Ukraine's membership.

In November 2023, Ukrainians celebrated the ten-year anniversary of ousting their pro-Russian President Yanukovych who fled to Russia. That uprising was an earlier humiliation for Putin and he was resolved that Ukraine would never become part of America's orbit.

THE UKRAINE IS A CORRUPT COUNTRY DOMINATED BY CORRUPT OLIGARCHS

President Biden, Congress, and the media have portrayed the Ukraine in a very positive light, as a democracy led by a heroic president. Zelensky had several meetings with President Biden who thanked him profusely for accepting our billions. He addressed Congress and the United Nations. Our politicians acted as though he was the new Churchill. Members of Congress traveled to Ukraine to praise him and assure him that America would back him forever.

The truth is that Ukraine remained corrupt while thousands of its military were bravely fighting against the Russians and dying in that process. The political people who were in charge of the war were corrupt! That sentence should bring Americans to their senses. Biden and his administration are hopeless; they are committed to the myth.

On September 3, 2023, over a year-and-a-half after the Russian invasion, President Zelensky fired Ukraine's minister of defense. You heard that right - the minister of defense - Reznikov. The new defense minister had been an investment banker. How's that for being qualified?

Zelensky also dismissed six deputy ministers of defense - you get it? The whole department was corrupt. The state secretary for defense was also dismissed.

Bribes were paid by those seeking to avoid the draft. Documents were falsified so men could be labeled as unfit to serve. There were many who had vested interests in prolonging the war - it was very profitable. The chief of Ukraine's Supreme Court was arrested on bribery charges.

A deputy minister of the economy was accused of embezzlement of humanitarian aid. The director of the domestic intelligence agency and prosecutor general were dismissed because of allegations of corruption. Profiteering, embezzlement, kickbacks, money laundering - corruption in the Ukraine is endemic.

Zelensky thinks all these arrests will impress America so much that our country will continue to shuffle billions. These "reforms" will also impress NATO members, guaranteeing an invitation to join. Actually, they demonstrate the opposite – just how entrenched corruption is.

The following organizations demonstrate the depth of that entrenchment.

The Anti-Corruption Action Center.

National Anti-Corruption Bureau.

National Agency for Preventing Corruption.

Parliament also has an Anti-Corruption Committee.

Zelensky proposed a law to punish corruption as treason, hoping that the threat of death might turn things around. The law was not passed.

THE NATO DREAM MAY BE A MIRAGE

In April 2008 there was a summit held in Bucharest, Romania, where President Bush advocated for Ukrainian membership in NATO. He came very close to promising that NATO would welcome the Ukraine with open arms. He also advocated for Georgia.

A few months after the summit, Russia attacked Georgia. It was a 5-day war wherein Russia backed several separatist regions. Advocacy for causes that are none of America's business have real life, terrifying consequences.

Biden went even further with loose talk at another summit. This one was held in Vilnius, Lithuania in July 2023. A time when the war between Russia and Ukraine was going full blast. He doubled down on his favorite theme - also Bush's favorite theme - that the world must choose between democracy and autocracy.

We have learned nothing from President Woodrow Wilson's naïve promise at the end of World War I to make the world safe for democracy. Or for his childish belief that the League of Nations could abolish warfare - an organization that America refused to join.

Remember that Bush tried to sell the fable that Afghanistan and Iraq were on their way to becoming democracies. At the Lithuanian summit, Biden said -

"We will stand for liberty and freedom today, tomorrow, and for as long as it takes."

As the war dragged on, reporters often asked Biden how long we were going to back Ukraine with billions in both military and economic aid. Bidens standard answer was -

"As long as it takes."

Biden's national security advisor said that canceling or diminishing our support for Ukraine was - "not up for negotiation."

Our Defense Secretary was in the Ukraine on November 20, 2023. He doubled down on the Biden theme.

"The United States will continue to stand with Ukraine in their fight for freedom both now and into the future. We will continue to support Ukraine's urgent battlefield needs and long-term defense requirements."

By the way, former President Trump says that aid to Ukraine should be stopped. As President, he had said NATO, founded in 1949, was "obsolete." He obviously never would have advocated for Ukraine's membership.

Are you ready for the biggest irony of all? As of November 2023 (the time I am writing these words) NATO had not invited Ukraine to even apply for membership. This was very upsetting to Zelensky who said it was "absurd" not to offer a timeframe for membership.

The Ukraine may never actually become a member! When we were advocating for membership, we had no way of knowing whether the member nations would ever invite the Ukraine to join.

There is another western organization that the Ukraine is desperate to join - The European Union. Zelensky feels confident since Hungary, Poland, Lithuania, Latvia, and Estonia are members.

The Ukraine received a favorable signal when the head of the European Commission recommended that talks could begin. The bad news is that the process of joining in some instances has taken over a decade. Turkey has attempted for decades to be admitted but has always been turned down. Several Balkan nations have been waiting for years.

For an applicant to be admitted they would need unanimous approval from all 27 members of the world's largest trading bloc. The member states would have to be satisfied that the Ukraine had made major progress in rooting out corruption, limiting the power of oligarchs and protecting minority rights. That process could take years and could be the stumbling block to NATO membership as well.

At the end of 2023, Russia controlled about one fifth of the Ukraine. Zelensky had often said the war could not end until all that territory was returned. America did not tell him to get serious.

Ukraine planned a highly promoted counteroffensive during the summer of 2023. The United States and some Western partners had trained and equipped tens of thousands of military for that offensive. It was not a success.

By November 2023, Ukraine's top military officer said the war had entered a "stalemate" phase.

In 2014, Russia had taken control of the Crimea, a region Ukraine contended belonged to it. There was a mini war in the Donbas region of the Ukraine between Russian speaking separatists and the central government – a war that persisted from 2014 through the Russian invasion of February 2022. Donbas sought independence.

The Ukrainians had proven themselves to be excellent fighters so how could Putin have thought victory would come quickly. He was emboldened by his quick success in Georgia. Negotiations to end a war can be very complicated and time consuming and ultimately very unsatisfactory.

Take Korea, for example. A war that ended with a 1953 Armistice. There was no peace treaty; there was only a ceasefire. A state of war still exists between North and South Korea.

It took two years of talks, over 500 meetings to reach the Armistice deal. During those two years 45% of the American deaths occurred. Insane!

America has given Ukraine tanks, long range missiles, armored vehicles, artillery, guided rockets etc. We spent over $47 billion during the first year of the war – more than double the amount given by all nations of the European Union combined.

Russia has killed thousands of Ukrainians civilians. They have destroyed homes, hospitals, schools, churches, and factories. Millions have left their homes and livelihoods to become refugees.

The World Bank has said it would take $400 billion to rebuild the Ukraine – probably a lot more. That process will be a bonanza for all the thieves. Even during the war Ukraine had been host to an army of foreign contractors.

By the way, President Zelensky, who has been in office since 2019, announced that he was calling off the presidential election scheduled for 2024.

This chain of horrors could have been avoided by America and Ukraine saying – "the hell with NATO, we are not joining." The bogus intellectuals love to make things complicated to prove their cleverness in unravelling all the facts.

BUT IT REALLY IS THAT SIMPLE!

CHAPTER 21

AMERICAN INDIANS AND THE CRUEL POLICY OF FORCED ASSIMILATION

Our government forcibly removed Indian children from their parents to place them in boarding schools. There were over 500 of these boarding schools spread across the nation. The first such school opened in the year 1801. They were in existence for well over a century. Congress passed laws to coerce parents to send their children to these schools. Thousands of children never saw their parents again. With few exceptions, parents were not allowed to visit.

Think of a parent's reaction to the tragedy of losing a child, being unable to protect their children. Most of the schools were run by the Catholic Church. Others by Presbyterian, Episcopalian, etc.

The schools divorced children from everything related to their Indian heritage. Why? What was the reasoning behind the kidnapping of these children? The answer is ASSIMILATION – TO TRANSFORM THEM INTO AMERICANS!

They were to be separated from their culture and traditions, their Indian names were changed, they were taught to look down upon

Indian beliefs and practices as primitive, respect for tribal elders was erased. They were punished if they dared speak their native language. Their long hair was cut short, their tribal clothing was tossed.

Memories of holidays, songs, ceremonies, special foods were eradicated.

Who could the kids complain to? Who could their parents complain to? There was no one to protect them. It was an environment where pedophiles could flourish.

If someone deliberately sought to screw up the lives of thousands of Indian children and their relatives, they could come up with no better formula than the policy of forced assimilation.

How was it that the liberals, the human rights advocates, the civil rights advocates tolerated this travesty for well over a century? Most of them bought into the myth of bringing them into the American mainstream. The superior culture.

What did the policy of forced assimilation lead to? Poverty, alcoholism, a high suicide rate, particularly amongst teenagers, unemployment, poor health, an epidemic of diabetes, crime, domestic violence and drug abuse. Indian life expectancy is 30 years below the national average.

Dr. Nora Volkow, director of the National Institute on Drug Abuse, said at a national conference in April 2021 –

"When you look at mortality from methamphetamines it's chilling to realize that the risk of dying from a meth overdose is 12 times higher among American Indians and Alaskan natives than other groups."

An Indian woman, Judith Surber, living on the Hoopa Valley Reservation in California wrote an article which appeared in the New York Times November 19, 2023. In it she describes how the – "opioid epidemic spread through our tribe like wildfire."

Her husband, two sons and a grandchild were all impacted. Oxycontin, then heroin, now fentanyl. She asks – will her sons make it?

Our Justice Department has said that 80% of American Indians have been victims of violence.

A mass grave for many dozens of children was discovered on the grounds of an Indian agricultural school in Oklahoma. 189 Indian children were buried on the grounds of the Carlisle Indian School. The disappearance of these children went unnoticed by our government and the media. The deaths and burials were covered up by those who were running the schools.

What was the cause of all those deaths? Physical, psychological, sexual abuse, lousy medical care, forced labor, beatings, violence. Parents had no idea where the children were buried; most were not even notified of their deaths. Indian burial rites are a very important part of their traditions.

The Interior Department released a shocker in 2022. The admission that over 50 of these abandoned schools contained burial grounds. What would be the effect on a child knowing that a classmate died with his or her body being tossed in a mass grave? Yes – a very cruel policy of assimilation.

I have looked at many photographs of assembled children at these schools. The one constant in these pictures is that none of the children are ever smiling.

Let's have a look at another beacon of democracy to see how they treated their indigenous people. The Canadian government bought into the same crap as the Americans did. How is it that intelligent, educated people can arrive at such decisions which cause immeasurable grief and death to so many? How is it that the storied Royal Canadian Mounted Police participated in grabbing these kids?

Canada was going to civilize the "primitive heathens." They would be punished for speaking their language or engaging in their cultural and social traditions. Of course, indigenous rates of poverty, disease, addiction and violence far exceeded those of mainstream Canadians. As in America, they were ousted from productive and beautiful lands to make room for the developers.

From the 1870s until 1996 about 130 boarding schools were established for the 150,000 children who had been stolen from their parents.

Canada had its own bombshell in 2021. A mass burial site in British Columbia, containing the remains of 215 children, was discovered at a closed school. Ground penetrating radar was being used in both

Canada and the United States to discover other mass graves. None of the religious people who ran these schools and approved the "dumping" policy were ever held accountable. The same in America.

Canada's Truth and Reconciliation Commission, founded in 2008, estimated that mistreatment of children led to some 4,000 deaths and acknowledged that –

"A key component of government policy was CULTURAL GENOCIDE."

In July 2022, the Pope did something extraordinary. He went to Canada and met directly with many natives. To his great credit, he gave a full-throated apology for the policies of his church. He said – "I humbly beg forgiveness for the EVIL committed by so many Christians against the indigenous peoples."

The Pope went even further calling the assimilation project – "GENOCIDE."

He knew that a chief aim of the Catholic run schools was conversion. What the Pope said about Canada was also true across America.

President Andrew Jackson signed the Indian Removal Act in 1830. All the Indians east of the Mississippi were forced to leave their homes and sacred lands and go to what is now Oklahoma. The famous Trail of Tears.

America stole millions of acres from the Indians in spite of our promises in numerous treaties not to do so.

If you were to ask this question, way less than 1% of Americans would know the answer. "Does our Declaration of Independence say anything about Indians and, if so, what does it say?"

It refers to Indians as – "MERCILIESS INDIAN SAVAGES."

Americans are far more familiar with these oft quoted lines from our Declaration of Independence –

"We hold these truths to be self-evident, that all men are created equal, that they are endowed by their creator with certain unalienable rights, that among those our life, liberty and the pursuit of happiness." Yes, "all men" – except for Indians and Blacks. This is a striking example of the mind's ability to compartmentalize and live with totally conflicting ideas.

Our government approved and encouraged the mass killing of buffalo as part of the effort to seize land from the Indians who depended on the animal.

There was a spiritual connection between American Indians and the buffalo – the bison. 30 million of them roamed the Great Plains in 1800. Hard to believe but by 1889 only about 500 remained in existence.

Many decades later, many decent Americans felt guilt about the decimation of this majestic animal. Efforts were undertaken to save the bison from extinction. Now there are about 350,000 of them in the United States. Unfortunately most are confined like cattle and end up in slaughterhouses. Only about 20,000 are protected in federal and state preserves where they are free to roam and have access to healthy grass.

The disappearance of millions of bison allowed for the success of white expansion into the Great Plains and the West.

Here is another question that almost no American could answer – how many federally recognized tribes are there?

The astounding number is 574. Oglala Lakota, Muscogee, Creek, Cherokee, Choctaw, Chickasaw, Black Feet, Navajo, Sioux, Laguna Pueblo, Apache, Hopi, Zuni, Ute, Chippewa – to name just a few.

We know nothing about the differences between these tribes, as we know nothing about their histories, their languages or their traditions.

The 574 figure explains in part why the Indians have never had a successful civil rights movement – their inability to unify. That's why the Indians have never had a Martin Luther King-type leader. And even if such a leader had emerged, the media would not have covered him in anything approaching its coverage of the black civil rights movement.

There was an outstanding warrior, Tecumseh, who along with his brother sought to unite the tribes, hoping that they would see themselves as one race. He could not overcome their loyalty to individual tribal identity nor inter-tribal disputes over land, horses, buffalo and other resources.

Indian leaders were not invited to appear on "Meet the Press" or "Face the Nation" or "60 Minutes." They did not have super PACs or hedge fund donors or a battalion of lobbyists. There have been periodic protests, but never a sustained unified movement. The American Indian Movement, founded in 1968, cried out for justice, pointing to our government's many broken promises.

Think about it – you almost never hear Americans talking about Indians or showing any concern for them. Way less than 1% of Americans have ever spent time on an Indian reservation or ever had a conversation with a Native American.

On April 26, 2021, an article appeared in the New York Times, written by four very impressive Indian women. They refer to themselves as the Women of Bears Ears National Monument in Utah.

After reading this article, one would have an appreciation of Indian values and would be reminded of our mistreatment of them – forced assimilation, forced relocation to marginal reservations which comprised a speck of land compared to their original holdings and centuries of treaty violations.

The women wrote about the need to protect sacred ancestral lands –

"We know these lands as a mother knows her child, as a child knows her mother. We are rooted to Mother Earth just as we are rooted to our mothers."

The Obama Administration, to its credit, had set aside the land as a national monument. In December 2017, President Trump, to his discredit, slashed it by about 85%, opening it up to drilling, fracking, exploring for oil and gas.

The women continued –

"Restoring Bears Ears National Monument would restore balance, harmony and beauty among all life. We have been misrepresented by politicians who have failed repeatedly to protect sacred lands."

Indians are a very spiritual people who revere the land of their ancestors.

The Bears Ears Monument, consisting of over one million acres, actually had a happy outcome in June 2022 during the Biden administration.

The area will be managed jointly by the federal government and several tribes. National monuments are protected from development by law. They are established by presidents, as distinguished from national parks which are created by Congress.

President Biden appointed the first Native American in our history as a cabinet secretary. A 35th generation New Mexican representing her state in the House of Representatives – a member of the Laguna Pueblo Tribe, Deb Haaland. She was confirmed by the Senate 51 to 40.

The Bureau of Indian Affairs, the Bureau of Indian Education, the Bureau of Land Management, the Fish and Wildlife Service all fall within the purview of the Department of the Interior. The Department oversees about 500 million acres of public lands. It is responsible for protecting hundreds of endangered species.

Before Secretary Haaland, the department had been led by a former oil lobbyist. As to be expected of him and Trump, there was a rollback of environmental regulations and permission was granted for drilling and mining activities. There was even a rollback of habitat protection under the Endangered Species Act. Secretary Haaland put herself through college and law school, having to rely on food stamps and student loans. Her grandparents attended the dreaded boarding schools.

The most famous massacre of Indians and their families is the one that occurred at Wounded Knee on the Pine Ridge Reservation in South Dakota in December 1890. Our soldiers killed hundreds of Lakota Sioux, including women and children.

Unbelievably, our government awarded 20 Congressional Medals of Honor to the shooters.

In a 5 to 4 decision of the United States Supreme Court in July 2020 it was held that a good part of Oklahoma is actually Indian land – part of their reservation. The opinion was written by Trump appointee Neil Gorsuch who recognized that living up to treaty promises mandated this result.

From the Gorsuch opinion –

"On the far end of the trail of tears was a promise. Forced to leave their ancestral lands in Georgia and Alabama the Creek Nation received assurances that their new lands in the west would be secure forever. In exchange for ceding all their land east of the Mississippi River, the United States Government agreed by treaty that the Creek country west of the Mississippi shall be solemnly granted to the Creek Indians." In spite of this excellent opinion, I don't think the Indians will become the power brokers in Oklahoma.

The value of the opinion is the recognition of how our government consistently betrayed our obligations to the indigenous peoples.

Our mining activities on Indian lands have polluted their waterways, fouled their rivers, and decimated fish populations. We have desecrated sacred burial grounds with our Dakota access pipeline and Keystone Oil Pipeline which traverse hundreds of miles of Indian land. The protest camps against the pipelines, which lasted for months in freezing weather, were razed by pressure hoses, rubber bullets and dogs.

Feelings of guilt led Congress to pass the Indian Gaming Regulatory Act in 1988. The Seminoles opened the Hard Rock Casino and Hotel in Broward County, Florida which became a destination for high rollers. Hard Rock and other casinos have become very profitable for several tribes.

One hell of a trade-off – from a people who could roam the entire country surrounded by the beauties of nature and a multitude of animals.

In spite of the many injustices visited upon them, the Indians have never engaged in terror. No suicide bombers. Many of the kids who lived through the awful schools fought for America in all of our wars.

In 1973, Marlon Brando won the Academy Award as Best Actor for his role in "The Godfather." As a means of protest for the way Hollywood had depicted Indians, he asked an Indian friend to speak at the ceremony.

Sacheen Littlefeather, an activist and actress, started to deliver her speech. She never completed it because the crowd responded with jeers and boos. Perfectly consistent with how Americans have always treated Indians. She was dressed as an Indian, the first time a Native American woman had stood onstage at the ceremony which was in its 45th year. It only took the Academy 50 years to apologize, shortly before her death at age 75 in 2022.

In 1950, a poll was taken asking nearly 400 journalists to select the greatest all-around athlete ever. They didn't select Babe Ruth or Ty Cobb or Jack Dempsey. The winner was Jim Thorpe – a proud Indian.

He was in the Pro Football Hall of Fame, having played both offense and defense. In the 1912 summer Olympics he won both the pentathlon and decathlon. Thorpe did not become rich or successful. Like the vast majority of Indians, he had an unhappy life.

Had we treated the Indians fairly, we would have had the benefit of a great talent pool that would have enriched us as a nation. Look at the great accomplishments of Blacks once their talents were unleashed. And not only in sports and entertainment – millions became doctors, lawyers, office holders – success in the areas of business, finance and education.

The Indians would have had similar achievements had our governments allowed them the freedom to choose between joining the American mainstream or adhering to tribal values. If given that right, Indians could have been part of both worlds and enhanced both.

CHAPTER 22

STARBUCKS – A NATION OBSESSED WITH COFFEE IS NOT GOING TO WIN ANY WARS

There are over 9,000 Starbucks stores in the United States with over 250,000 employees. Worldwide about 35,000 stores. Starbucks' very successful public relations has advocated for – togetherness, connectivity – a meeting place, a hangout place, a family place. Your home away from home.

The Starbucks owner, Howard Schultz, over the years hit on every do-gooder theme – race relations, gun violence, student debt, gay rights.

THE ENVIRONMENT: on the sleeve of every cup Starbucks says –

"Same great sleeve – less waste – because we care about our planet this 85% post-consumer fiber cup sleeve uses 34% less paper than our original."

GENDER PAY EQUITY: Starbucks proudly bragged in full-page ads over several years.

"We've achieved 100 percent pay equity in the United States – we're also committed to achieving 100 percent gender pay equity to our PARTNERS in all global cooperated markets."

You get that – the billionaire is "partners" with the employees fetching your coffee.

Full health benefits for both full and part-time employees. This is a billionaire who would like to be president. Why not? Trump never held any political office either.

EDUCATION: The Starbucks college achievement plan covers tuition for an online degree program offered by Arizona State University.

In full-page ads, Starbucks offered –

"<u>Congratulations to the hundreds of Starbucks' PARTNERS from across the country who graduated from Arizona State University. You inspire us every day with your hard work and brilliance.</u>"

OUR MILITARY: More full-page ads –

"Your commitment inspires ours. In celebration of Spouse Appreciation Day we recognize military spouses, the unsung heroes of our armed forces – we honor your commitment with our own."

It turned out that my cynicism was justified. Schultz crisscrossed the country for three months on a book tour in early 2019. His book was intended to convince people that as a purveyor of coffee he was qualified to deal with China, the Middle East and terror. The public reaction was – "stick to hiring baristas." He was not about to subject himself to the debates or the primaries.

Starbucks has hired thousands of veterans and their wives. I don't think it's such a great thing for a guy who faced combat in Iraq or Afghanistan to be taking orders for a cold foam Cascara brew or Frappuccino from some yuppie tax attorney.

Remember, we are talking about coffee. But the pitch is that you will have so much more than a cup of coffee. You will have an experience, joining something much bigger than yourself. You will become part of a special "culture," part of the "soul" of Starbucks. Starbucks actually advertises that it seeks to create "a third place" between home and work – "an inclusive gathering place for all."

"Where we can all come together"

"Together" is the magic word. During the several Democratic debates in 2019 that word was uttered hundreds of times. All the candidates were experts at bringing people "together."

"Onward with love. Starbucks is like a second home where everyone takes care of each other." Yeah, all these strangers are taking care of each other.

If you don't realize that you are being manipulated by this approach you are easy prey.

Take a look at just a few full-page ads for coffees that should embarrass any normal person –

"New cold foam cascara cold brew – cold foam crowns cold coffee craft – find yourself happy." "A cloud of velvety cold foam meets smooth cold brew."

Printing on the cup says –

"Our Baristas Promise: love your beverage or let us know. We will always make it right."

"Taste the cool tropical flavors of strawberry and acai – find your happy."

"Sip a cup of magic – caramel brulee latte."

"Introducing Cloud Macchiato – bold espresso cascades through light, fluffy layers of foam, topped with a drizzle of caramel"

"Starbucks blonde is smooth but packs a punch – new blonde espresso." "New Ultra Caramel Frappuccino blended beverage – Live it up with a rich layered take on the classic."

A country that buys into this crap is not going to win any wars. A country that treats this kind of language as normal was not capable of defeating the Taliban in our 20-year war in Afghanistan.

Many employees (baristas) came to the realization that they were not and never would be "partners" with the millionaires at the top of the Starbucks chain. Many have decided that they want a union to protect their interests and deal with grievances.

Grievances? What grievances? Schultz sees himself as a great employer who provides his employees with high pay and generous benefits.

That's true. Two stores voted to unionize in Buffalo, New York in December 2021. That's when Mr. Nice Guy showed his true colors – vehemently anti-union, plus an egotistical bully.

Many employees were no longer buying into the phony argument that a union would interfere with the direct relationship between the company and its partners. As of November 2022, 250 stores had unionized over the past year.

Schultz left the company way back in the year 2000. But he kept returning and then leaving again. He had founded the company in 1987. Schultz had allowed Kevin Johnson to replace him as CEO, but Schultz returned as interim CEO in April 2022.

He got of rid of Johnson after 5 years for being too understanding about the union movement, even though the company was doing great under him with record revenues. Revenues in the multiple billions.

In March 2023, Schultz replaced Johnson with Laxman Narasimhan, a former top gun for McKinsey Consulting – the firm that advised Big Tobacco and Purdue Pharma how to keep millions hooked on cigarettes and drugs.

He and Laxman are very ambitious. China is their largest market outside the United States. They expect to have 9,000 locations in China by 2025. Also, 2,000 more stores in the U.S. by 2025. Starbucks has 35,000 stores globally, more than double the number it had in 2008.

Schultz retired for good in 2023. Schultz explained his ego driven attitude behind his anti-union stand – "If they had faith in me and my motives they wouldn't need a Union." His feelings were hurt because many of his "partners" no longer worshipped him.

Regional managers would show up at stores to intimidate workers. Union activists would be fired, certain stores would be closed. Additional benefits and wage increases would go to some non-union stores.

Many of the new locations are pure drive-throughs with no seating. Customers are not sitting around sipping their beverage and listening to jazz. There is mobile ordering and speed is prized. Millions are into complex drinks. Whipping up a cold drink Mocha Cookie Crumble Frappuccino takes a hell of a lot longer than pouring a normal cup of coffee for a normal person. Yes, the overworked baristas need a union. That's why stores in over 25 states have filed petitions for union elections.

The union represents about 9,000 workers at over 300 stores. Yet the vast majority of employees have resisted the move for membership. Starbucks tactics have been very successful.

A judge for the National Labor Relations Board concluded that Starbucks had illegally monitored, disciplined and fired employees engaged in union organizing, added workers to dilute support for the union, and promised new benefits to workers in an attempt to defuse support for unions. The judge also found active retaliation against those workers who sought union membership. A hell of a way to treat your "partners"?

The NLRB has filed over 500 complaints against Starbucks for violating Federal Labor Law.

The Board made findings of "egregious and widespread misconduct" by Starbucks against their own employees.

One would think there would have been a customer rebellion against this kind of corporate behavior. But no, the patrons did not want to give up their fancy drinks. During November 2023, there was a massive protest and walkout by thousands of members of Starbucks Workers United. Yes, thousands at over 200 stores.

Why? What was the issue?

Starbucks has an annual promotion called RED CUP DAY. If customers order certain beverages like a Sugar Cookie Almond Milk Latte they can get a bright red reuseable cup. Beyond silly, and should be beyond embarrassing.

The deluge of customers yearning for that reuseable cup made extra work for the baristas. They had to handle more orders with insufficient help and that's what led to the walkouts. Also the fact that management was insensitive to the needs of their overworked employees.

Before his decision to crush the union movement, Schultz had a positive image; he was well liked. I was struck by a protest sign at one of the demonstrations – a sign targeting the billionaire –

"UNION BUSTER IN CHIEF"

Yes, Mr. Schultz, the profits will keep rolling in but that sign represents your true legacy.

CHAPTER 23

THERANOS – ANOTHER EXAMPLE OF SMART PEOPLE MAKING STUPID DECISIONS –

A 19-year-old "visionary" named Elizabeth Holmes, with zero credentials in medicine or science, came up with the idea of a blood testing startup – an idea that made her very rich and famous. That with a simple pin prick to a finger, one could extract a couple of drops of blood and be able to screen for scores of diseases. She claimed that early detection of diseases would save millions of lives.

Did the potential investors say to themselves or others – "how come this idea wasn't developed at one of America's leading medical schools or research institutions?" Or did they say – "show me how this works on actual patients." Did they ask independent physicians or scientists whether these exaggerated claims made sense? Or did they insist on talking to actual patients whose lives were allegedly saved by early diagnosis? Did they insist on allowing experts to review the records of such patients? They did none of those things.

Due diligence would have revealed that Holmes lied about the military accepting her technology and pharmaceutical companies endorsing it. The investors did not want to lose out on the cash bonanza that was just around the corner.

The Walmart heirs tossed in about $150 million. Rupert Murdoch, the owner of Fox News and the Wall Street Journal, invested multiple millions, as did Robert Kraft the owner of the New England Patriots football team.

MORE GULLIBLE BILLIONAIRES

Larry Ellison of Oracle invested. So too, Betsy DeVos, education secretary under Trump and an heir to the Amway mega fortune.

Venture capital firms invested; so too, private equity firms and hedge funds. For several years, a venture capitalist was chairman of the Theranos Board of Directors. And what a Board it was. It included –

Henry Kissinger – national security advisor and Secretary of State under President Nixon – George Shultz, who was Secretary of State under President Regan – William Perry, who was Secretary of Defense under Clinton and James Mattis a marine general who was Secretary of Defense under Trump. America depended on the judgement of these men to keep our country safe. It is frightening to realize that men of such stature could be suckered by a Silicon Valley con artist.

Walgreens and Safeway also fell for the Holmes pitch, signing contracts with Theranos to install her magical devices in their stores. Customers had the right to assume that these retail giants were endorsing the accuracy of the tests, that they had conducted a thorough investigation.

Investors had poured in over $900 million. At one time Theranos had a valuation of $9 billion. This is Alice in Wonderland squared.

Forbes Magazine, one of the big business bibles, had Elizabeth on its cover in 2014, as did several other magazines gushing that she was the youngest self-made female billionaire ever. Gushing about how she mesmerized investors with her charisma.

So how did her empire unravel? Because of a series of articles in the Wall Street Journal in 2015. She got away with the fraud for nearly

15 years. She hid the failures of the magical devices and blocked peer review. Theranos employed hundreds of engineers and scientists. Many knew the claims being made were untrue, nearly all kept their mouths shut because the pay was very good. How could they rationalize the fact that innocent victims were being damaged?

Elizabeth Holmes was indicted on criminal fraud charges in June 2018. After several weeks of testimony, a federal jury in San Jose, California rendered its verdict on January 3, 2022.

Holmes had testified for 7 days, figuring she could charm the jurors (eight men and four women) like she charmed Kissinger and Shultz. It didn't work. She was convicted on four counts of defrauding investors.

I was stunned by another finding. The jury acquitted her on four counts related to defrauding patients. The jury cared more for the millionaire investors than they did for the everyday patients who received inaccurate blood test results.

What was wrong with these jurors who deliberated for seven days? But I realized it was not their fault. The prosecution and the judge were much more concerned about the investors than with the real victims.

The prosecution only called three patients to testify. They collectively were on the witness stand for a mere hour. The testimony of the other 26 witnesses related to the losses of the investors. I didn't give a damn about the investors who were only looking to become richer.

During Holmes' testimony, she blamed her partner and boyfriend, Ramesh Balwani, for pressuring her to lie about the accuracy of their technology. In a separate trial after the Holmes verdict, Balwani was also convicted and sentenced to 13 years in prison.

A different jury might well have had the attitude – "the hell with the rich investors. They should have done thorough due diligence and they should have been suspicious about all the exaggerated hype." A different jury could have thought – "don't give us all that visionary crap – she wanted to join the billionaires club, not improve the world." That's apparently the kind of jury she had.

Many jurors will ignore the judge's instructions if they like the defendant and her lawyer and if they have the mindset of refusing to render a verdict that will send the defendant to prison. Jurors never have to explain their reasons for reaching a particular verdict.

The jurors who acquitted O.J. Simpson of murder may have done so because they liked and admired him. They did not have to explain why they believed a certain witness, why they disbelieved another, or why they chose to ignore strongly incriminating evidence.

Yes – sometimes a case is won or lost when a given jury is sworn in, before they have heard from a single witness. Most juries take their responsibilities seriously and base their decision on the law and the evidence. Some do not. Any lawyer who denies that happens in the real world is lying to you.

The trial judge had the discretion to allow Holmes to remain free while the verdict was being appealed – a process which could take years. He declined, saying she would have to report to prison. The Ninth Circuit Court of Appeals agreed with the trial judge since they believed there was little likelihood that the verdict would be reversed on appeal. The decision surprised many considering that Holmes, at age 39, was the mother of a one-year-old and three-year-old.

She had been free from the time of the verdict on January 3, 2022 until she had to report to prison on May 30, 2023. In addition to the sentence, Judge Davila ordered Holmes and Balwani to repay the investors $452 million!

America was fascinated both by her rise and fall. There was an eight-part television series on Hulu, plus a podcast. There will be more, plus books.

My expectation is that Holmes will serve far less than her eleven-year sentence. She is hardly a threat to society. The fact that her two young children will grow up without a mother will cry out for leniency. Many considered the sentence to be unduly harsh in the first place. Others saw it as being appropriate.

CHAPTER 24

HOW THE ULTRA-RICH AND MULTINATIONAL CORPORATIONS USE TAX HAVENS TO CHEAT THEIR FELLOW AMERICANS

The tax evaders create subsidiaries in these countries and pretend that these phantom entities are earning millions. Profits made in the United States are shifted to these subsidiaries, most of which have no employees, and only a post office box address. The multinational companies can choose where to record their profits. As long as the monies stayed overseas, the American companies paid zero taxes. The 2017 tax law passed under Trump changed that, allowing foreign profits to be taxed.

There is a law firm in Bermuda called Appleby, which is one of the world's top offshore law firms. They are the royalty of tax avoidance and tax shelters. In late 2017, millions of Appleby documents were leaked –

they became available for scrutiny – and the scrutiny was conducted by a consortium of investigative journalists who were capable of connecting the dots.

Some of the great Americans who did business with Appleby were the billionaires George Soros, James Simons, Warrens Stephens, Sheldon Adelson, and Penny Pritzker. Also, the beloved Bono and Madonna. Appleby had about 31,000 American clients – a cheater's hall of fame. 31,000 Americans – none of whom, I guarantee you, have a guilty conscience about cheating the unconnected working people whose taxes are deducted from their wages and salary checks. And believe me, each of the 31,000 think of themselves as being basically honest.

It has been estimated by economists with a conscience that about 63% of foreign profits made by American multinational corporations are tucked away in subsidiaries, depriving America of about $70 billion in tax revenue each year. Think of what could be accomplished for America's infrastructure with those extra billions. How these billions could be used to alleviate poverty, homelessness, and research into the eradication of disease.

Apple was expert at the game of inverting – merging with a foreign company and relocating its headquarters to a lower-tax country. The dodge of an inversion allows a company to siphon their profits to these havens.

The techie band of geniuses at Apple wanted an even better deal than they were getting in Ireland, so they shifted some of their phantom operations to, of all places, the Isle of Jersey in the English Channel. All these maneuvers are okay with the millions who love their iPhones. Not only okay, but many admire the "cleverness" of those who know how to outsmart the regulators. Like moving intellectual property licensing rights to subsidiaries.

Google has its European headquarters in Ireland. So do Facebook and Twitter, along with scores of other American multinationals. Ireland is the European base for 24 of the world's largest pharmaceutical companies. A pharmaceutical company could choose to hold the patent rights to its most lucrative drugs in a subsidiary that conducts no normal business.

Here's but one example out of a myriad of subterfuges concocted by high-priced lawyers, accountants, lobbyists, and consultants.

A study by the Center for Research on Multinational Corporations, a nonprofit group funded in part by the Dutch Ministry of Foreign Affairs, found that Viacom CBS avoided billions of dollars in taxes. How? By inventing a complex system that involved subsidiaries in Barbados, Luxembourg, and the Netherlands. Only the sophisticates in the rarefied world of high finance have any idea about how things actually work in those countries. The "outgunned" IRS agents are unable to unravel these manipulations, and even if they could, the process would take years.

Few Americans know anything about "The Pandora Papers" – a collection of over 10 million records of hidden financial transactions. Somehow these records were leaked and examined by a consortium of investigative journalists consisting of several hundred coming from many different countries.

These journalists deserve a great deal of credit for exposing massive amounts of hidden wealth. The protectors of the system and the miscreants were focused on trying to ascertain the identity of the leakers so that they could be punished. The journalists were focused on transparency and truth.

The Pandora Papers revealed that approximately 35 current and former leaders (presidents and prime ministers) were corrupt. In some cases, their wealth came from straightforward bribes. Most of these leaders had campaigned against corruption – their hypocrisy is stunning. The complicity of bankers in helping them hide the source of their wealth was a revelation to those outside the world of finance.

One technique to obscure wealth was using a string of offshore shell companies to buy luxury real estate and keep ownership secret. Shell companies were used to launder money.

Multiple media outlets cooperated in forming an – "Organized Crime and Corruption Reporting Project." Their focus and the focus of the European Union was on Luxembourg which was pressured to publish its corporate registry. And what an eye opener that was. 140,000 active companies! Companies with owners, officers, shareholders – all okay with institutionalized thievery.

Over 1200 Americans were listed as beneficial owners of active companies, many billionaires among them. Wealth can be funneled through chains of complex, interlinked entities to obscure both the origin of the money and its exact location.

Jason Furman, a Harvard economics professor, Chairman of the White House Council of Economic Advisers (2013 – 17), made this observation – "Our system for taxing international corporate income has long been dysfunctional. It is needlessly complex."

Yes, that's why the cheaters love the system. Even a supposed good guy like Furman refuses to be honest and straightforward about the problem. That we have a system that rewards dishonesty. The real scandal is that nearly all the dishonesty is legal. And the public tolerates this "dysfunctional" and dishonest system. The cheaters are never called to account. They are protected by their lobbyists and by their political contributions. That's what Furman and all the other economists should be talking about.

Treasury Secretary Janet Yellen made this valid point–

"It just isn't right for very successful companies to be able to avoid paying their fair share to support expenditures that we need to invest in our economy, to invest in our workforce, in research and development, and a social safety net that's operational."

Barbra Angus is often quoted on tax issues. She is the global tax policy leader at Ernst & Young. She had been the chief tax counsel on the House Ways and Means Committee. I mention this to demonstrate one example out of hundreds of the inside relationships between major accounting firms and Congress and the Treasury Department.

There is a revolving door between the "Big Four" accounting forms (Ernst & Young, KPMG, Deloitte, PWC) and government – in particular with the Treasury Department. The accountants rotate in and out of Senior Tax positions at the Treasury Department where they write up the loopholes and tax shelters that benefit their private clients.

The accounting firms do thousands of audits verifying the accuracy of the financial statements of corporations. Many have a huge conflict of interest because while they are doing audits, they also advise the same clients on methods to reduce their taxes. Accounting firms actually pitch offshore strategies designed to lessen tax obligations. Accountants who have worked for the Treasury Department know how to advise on avoiding audits. The Congressional Budget Office revealed that the audit rate fell 61% from 2010 to 2018.

Speaking of Ernst & Young, and the belief that Americans are basically honest, the firm was fined $100 million by the Securities and Exchange Commission. Why? Because it was discovered that between 2017 and 2021 hundreds of auditors cheated on ethics examinations.

How's that for irony? The job of auditors is to detect cheating. The higher echelons of Ernst & Young knew of the cheating but took no action to eliminate it.

Way back in 2001, the major accounting firm of Arthur Anderson enabled the energy giant Enron to commit fraud, resulting in the collapse of both as criminal charges were followed by convictions. Both firms no longer exist. If you can't trust the auditors, who the hell can you trust?

The House Ways and Means Committee and the Senate Finance Committee often hold hearings and even conduct investigations, but they never take effective action to truly solve the root causes of corruption and evasion. Blatant inequality could be severely reduced and money would be available to pay for education, healthcare, assistance for the elderly and disabled if the cheaters paid what they actually owed.

CHAPTER 25

THE ART OF TAX AVOIDANCE

The American tax system is a cheater's paradise. Charles Rettig, the former Commissioner of the Internal Revenue Service, has said that most of the tax avoidance is accomplished by the very wealthy and by large corporations. Testifying before the Senate Finance Committee on April 13, 2021, Rettig made this astonishing statement –

"It would not be outlandish to believe that the actual tax gap could approach and probably exceed $1 trillion per year." Think of how that $1 trillion could improve the lives of millions of Americans.

The tax cheats flood members of Congress with contributions, and that's why Congress has never gone after the cheaters seriously.

Rettig was asking for billions so that the IRS could hire qualified auditors who would be able to detect high-level cheating. He said that the IRS was "outgunned" by lawyers and accountants representing corporations and the super-wealthy.

It takes expertise to untangle the intricate webs of partnerships and subsidiaries created by the Wall Street law firms and the massive accounting firms.

That's why President Biden, in his first year in office, asked Congress to give the Internal Revenue Service $80 billion over the coming decade and to add 87,000 employees so that thousands of cheaters could be exposed and punished. Simply asking for so many billions indicates how widespread the cheating is.

Of course, the proposal went nowhere. Congress actually reduced the budget of the Internal Revenue Service. From 2010 to 2019, Congress cut the enforcement budget of the IRS by over 20%. Many members of Congress, when they retire or lose an election, enter the financial world or the lobbying world. They do not want to make enemies of their future employers.

Rettig said the Service had lost 17,000 enforcement personnel over the last decade. It is no mystery as to why so many have quit, disgusted at a system that rewards crookedness.

Biden's Treasury Secretary, Janet Yellin, has said –

"Our tax revenues are already at their lowest level in generations."

Lawyers and accountants employed by the Treasury Department write the rules and regulations governing the tax code. That experience makes them very valuable to law and accounting firms and finance firms that advise wealthy clients on how to beat the system. Many high-level Treasury employees join or rejoin these firms at phenomenal salaries and as partners.

There is an army of highly educated tax experts whose mission in life is devising strategies so that the super-rich can eliminate or greatly lessen their tax obligations. Most of the members of this army are pillars of their communities.

Former Treasury Secretary, Jacob Lew, joined a private equity firm after he left the government. Timothy Geithner, Treasury Secretary under Obama, did the same thing.

The Trump administration was loaded with private equity and hedge fund veterans. His Treasury Secretary, Steven Mnuchin, came from that world and returned to it. These people are not looking out for struggling Americans. The private equity industry has employed 200 lobbyists and contributed over $600 million to political campaigns over the past decade. Every member of Congress that has taken their money is compromised.

On the rare occasions when the billionaires' tricks are challenged, their lawyers litigate in the United States Tax Court. These disputes can go on for years, and it is usually the "outgunned" government that caves by agreeing to a modest settlement.

No one except the insiders has any idea who these judges are. Neither do the members of Congress who confirm them, neither does the President who appointed them. They are recommended by the tax world's insiders. Many are honest and competent but they too are "outgunned" by those who represent the cheaters.

Our income tax code is over 70,000 pages if one includes statutes, regulations and case law, as the Standard Federal Tax Reporter does. The complexity is a bonanza for lawyers, accountants, and consultants. It has made millionaires of many of them.

Our tax code has nearly 10,000 provisions. The 16th Amendment to our Constitution was ratified February 3, 1913. It instituted the income tax.

"The Congress shall have power to lay and collect taxes on incomes, from whatever source derived..." Simple and direct. No one back then dreamt that that simplicity could lead to the massive mountain of statues and regulations that govern the present monstrosity.

Congress keeps passing laws that add to the complexity of the system. For example –

The 2017 tax cuts and Jobs Act passed under Trump.

The Inflation Reduction Act of 2022.

The Pandemic Era Cares Act.

Under the Inflation Reduction Act a tax credit is given for producers of clean hydrogen. This is a climate change provision designed to replace fossil fuels. Deciding who is entitled to the credit is complicated. The Treasury Department came up with a 128-page proposed rule relating to that credit.

A ton of lobbyists are active when it comes to taxes. They take members of Congress out to lunch, give them tickets to Broadway shoes and sporting events, trying to persuade them to vote in favor of provisions which benefit their clients.

One example out of hundreds. Hedge fund managers did not have to pay self- employment taxes, saving them millions. How do you think they got that exemption? Congress created the exemption for limited partners in 1977. So of course hedge fund managers called themselves limited partners. Nearly 50 years later a Tax Court ruled against the exemption. Naturally, there will be appeals from that ruling.

Taxes can be avoided by businesses and individuals merely by shifting labels. Labels like partnerships – limited partners –limited liability companies – Are you the sole proprietor of a business – Can your route income through an S Corporation – The IRS decides who is self-employed –

Yes, how you designate yourself or your business has tax consequences. Complexity allows "clever" lawyers and accountants to game the system and outwit the over-burdened regulators.

A tax case reached the United States Supreme Court which could have a huge impact – Moore vs. the United States. The Court heard oral argument on December 5, 2023. The Moores were challenging an IRS ruling which taxed them on unrealized gain, on an asset which increased in value but which they did not transform into income.

The rule for decades had always been that the tax kicked in only after the gain was realized, only after the taxpayer actually accepted the money – took in the gain.

One case in the tax court involved the estate of the pop star – Michael Jackson. It was litigated for seven years (yes, seven) and resulted in a 271-page opinion. The lawyers made millions. The issue involved the value of Michael's public image. The IRS said the estate underpaid multiple millions. Valuing the estates of superstars is yet another avenue for lawyers, accountants and consultants to rake in big money.

Part of the reason for the complexity is that some of our philosophers in Congress over the years decided that our tax laws should serve some broader policy purposes such as encouraging home ownership. The code should not be the instrument to achieve social goals.

Commission Rettig told Congress –

"We receive between 1 and 1 ½ million pieces of mail per week." The IRS has a backlog of millions of unanswered letters. And knowing this, Congress cuts their budget. That's great news for the cheaters and terrible news for millions of confused taxpayers.

During tax season in 2021, the IRS received over 200 million calls from frustrated citizens with questions. Very few of the calls were ever returned. As of June 2022, the IRS was so far behind it had millions of unprocessed paper returns. Paper returns take longer to process than those filed electronically. Because Congress has gutted their budget, the IRS has been unable to update antiquated technology. Yet the Biden administration laid on these stressed and overworked employees the task of distributing pandemic relief money to millions.

A columnist for the Wall Street Journal, Laura Saunders, in May 2022, described an experience with the IRS experienced by millions. On May 14, she waited five-and-a-half hours at a Taxpayer Assistance Center in Harlem. The line started to form at 6:30 am, even though the office did not open until 9:00 am. She arrived at 8:30 am and was number 48 in line.

Everyone in line shared her experience saying they had been unable to reach the IRS by phone. Makes you proud to be an American, doesn't it?

Another job given to the IRS is to regulate charities that apply to become tax exempt non-profits. Thousands of crooks and scammers set up fake charities which only enrich themselves. The IRS is unable to investigate their true status and simply approves nearly all applications, thus allowing a massive fraud to continue without consequences.

I will now cite two examples of just how insane the American tax system is – Donald Trump and Leon Black of Apollo Global Management. And yes, "insane" best describes a system which tolerates – even encourages – dishonesty.

THE TAX AVOIDANCE MASTERY OF DONALD TRUMP

Utilizing an army of journalists, researchers and tax experts, the New York Times spent months pouring over years of Trump's tax returns.

On September 28, 2020, the paper devoted six full pages to their findings. Only the Times has the resources to undertake such a project.

The bombshell conclusion – Trump had paid zero taxes in ten of the previous 15 years!!!

Nurses working long shifts in intensive care units throughout the country during the pandemic had their taxes deducted from their paychecks. Construction workers building skyscrapers in freezing weather have their taxes automatically deducted. But Trump and many in the multi-millionaire, billionaire class get away with paying zero. And we are a nation which prides itself on being into "fairness." And we are a nation which tolerates these outrages. Worse yet, many Americans admire the cleverness of those who outwit the regulators.

Trump's lawyers and accountants knew how to claim hundreds of millions of dollars in losses and how to manipulate business deductions and consulting fees.

Because of lobbying and campaign contributions, real estate investors have received many advantages under the tax code and this is especially true of owners of commercial buildings. They can use past losses to offset income. They can claim a building has depreciated in value, even as its actual value increases. During the 2016 campaign, Trump admitted that he loves depreciation. Not only was Trump a master of depreciation, he was also a master of all kinds of deductions. For his "Apprentice" television program, he deducted $70,000 for hairstyling as a business expense. Is it any wonder that thousands of IRS employees have left in disgust?

What was Trump's excuse for not revealing his tax returns during the 2016 election cycle against Hillary Clinton? That his returns were being audited. That in no way prevented him from making his returns public. He played this shell game, throughout his presidency, on the few occasions when the subject even came up. He got away with never releasing his returns.

Yet his tax paying base remained loyal. During many months of polling in 2023, Trump remained miles ahead of the other Republicans who wanted to become President. His lead remained constant in spite of several criminal indictments. He never participated in several Republican primary debates held in 2023.

Had Hillary Clinton had access to Trump's returns, she would have become president. Day after day she could have said in debates, ads and interviews –

"It's ok with you that the construction workers building your hotels in freezing weather have their taxes withheld, while you in the luxury of Trump Tower and Mar-a-Lago pay zippo. You revel in your cleverness in avoiding your responsibility to contribute to the general welfare of your fellow Americans. To you, those who simply pay their taxes are suckers."

TAX ADVICE FROM A SEX OFFENDER THAT ENABLED A BILLIONAIRE TO AVOID $2 BILLION IN TAXES

Leon Black was the chief executive and chairman of the private equity firm – Apollo Global Management. Apollo had about $455 billion under management, including from hundreds of pension funds and sovereign wealth funds.

Black, who led the company for three decades, was a billionaire many times over. But like so many of his brethren in the upper one-tenth of one percent, he wanted to avoid taxes. And all these cheaters consider themselves to be patriotic Americans. Black paid $158 million for tax advice. That is not a misprint! His tax guru was not a lawyer, nor was he an accountant. His name was Jeffrey Epstein. Yes, that Epstein.

Black paid Epstein those millions between 2012 and 2017, knowing that Epstein was a serial sex offender.

Why would Black have chosen Epstein? There are many law firms in Manhattan and elsewhere that have specialty units dealing with tax, estate and trust issues. How could Black have failed to understand that once his relationship with Epstein became known, it would kill his reputation?

Yes, billionaires can be very stupid! Consider the stupidity of Epstein. A billionaire can get all the girls he wants on a consensual basis. Why have dozens of 14-year-old girls come to your mansion for massages and other services? They will talk to each other; some will talk to their parents and friends. Exposure would be guaranteed.

Another billionaire was even dumber, Leslie Wexner, the man who owned Victoria's Secret. He actually gave Epstein power of attorney over his financial affairs for years and paid him multiple millions for his tax-avoidance advice.

All hell broke loose when the Black/Epstein relationship was outed. The upper echelon at Apollo was furious. They hired the highly respected Dechert law firm to investigate. Dechert concluded that Black got what he paid for – tax, trust and estate-planning advice. Dechert concluded that Epstein's advice may have saved Black as much as $2 billion in taxes. This gives you some idea of the convoluted complexity of our tax code. These are loopholes not available to the millions whose taxes are automatically withdrawn from their paychecks.

Epstein was a college dropout, but he obviously possessed a narrow type of genius which enabled him to understand the intricacies of tax law and how to take advantage of every loophole, how to establish sophisticated trusts and other devices to reduce income taxes and avoid gift and estate taxes.

Epstein also had a "genius" for establishing relationships with prominent and successful people like Bill Gates, the multi-billionaire founder of Microsoft. Was Epstein giving him tax advice or getting him girls? They had many dinners together. Bill Clinton was a frequent passenger on Epstein's private plane and had visited his island getaway. Was Clinton interested in Epstein's art collection? I don't think so!

Black had a personal art collection worth in the neighborhood of $1 billion. Giving or loaning a work of art to a museum can convey all kinds of tax advantages. Black was the chairman of Manhattan's prestigious Museum of Modern Art. In 2018, he gave $40 million to the museum. This is the classic route for so many financial wizards, they give away tons of money to establish their cultural bona fides. I would be shocked if Black ever spent an hour studying one of his multi-million-dollar acquisitions. It's all about bragging rights.

The Apollo board ousted Black as chief executive and chairman. Prominent artists whose works were displayed at the Museum of Modern Art threatened to remove them if he remained as chairman of the board of trustees. He did not.

In an effort at rehabilitation, Black said he would donate $200 million to promote gender equality and fight sex trafficking. He could have paid the taxes he actually owed, felt good about contributing to the general welfare, and he still would have had more wealth than he could have spent in ten lifetimes.

When a billionaire cheats the IRS, he is also cheating millions of his fellow citizens who need to cover the shortfall. "Greed" is and should be a very dirty word.

A news organization called Pro Publica outed some more billionaire greed. They discovered that in some years, Bezos, Elon Musk and George Soros paid zero in taxes. They demonstrated that the people's champion, Michael Bloomberg, had not paid his fair share using perfectly legal methods only available to the super-rich and super-connected.

The tone deafness which Bloomberg exhibited in the Democratic debates was on display once again when in righteous indignation, he insisted that all legal means should be employed to identify the leakers and – "ensure that they are held responsible." Had the public known of Bloomberg's strategies to avoid paying his fair share, he would not have dared to seek the Democratic nomination for President. He could have saved a $1 billion in a fruitless effort which only produced a single win in American Samoa.

Instead of national outrage and disgust over these revelations, the focus became – "who leaked this private information?"

At least 55 of our largest corporations paid zero federal income taxes in 2020. FedEx, Nike, Archer Daniels Midland were in the zero group. Collectively these three had $40 billion in profits in 2020. No one is refusing to buy Nike sneakers as a matter of principle.

Every member of Congress understands that our tax system rewards cheaters. Why don't the politicians who campaign endlessly on the platitudes of fairness, decency and the American way, put an end to this outrage?

The fact that most of these evasion gimmicks are legal is the real scandal. As are the tax haven countries where the billionaires park and hide their money. The real scandal is that Congress has never criminalized this anti-social behavior which spits in the face of the millions who do pay their fair share.

Think of the simplicity of the 1913 Amendment which instituted the income tax. If I were in charge, the income tax law would be about 10 pages; the rate would be fair, and anyone engaging in fraud would end up in jail.

CHAPTER 26

ROOSEVELT AND TAFT – HOW TWO PRESIDENTS WENT FROM BEING BEST FRIENDS TO BECOMING ENEMIES –

Theodore Roosevelt was elected President in 1904; William Howard Taft was elected President in 1908. They were both progressive Republicans. For many years they had been best friends, although by temperament, they were polar opposites. Roosevelt did everything he could to get Taft the nomination and then get him elected in 1908.

Roosevelt is one of the most outstanding and beloved presidents in American history. He is on Mount Rushmore along with Washington, Jefferson, and Lincoln. Yet how he became president in the first place was a fluke.

Roosevelt had been Police Commissioner in New York before he became Governor of New York. Thomas Platt, the New York political boss, who ran the Republican political machine, thought Roosevelt was too progressive and wanted to get rid of him. His solution – get Roosevelt on the ticket as vice president to William McKinley who won.

Roosevelt had reservations about becoming vice president. Vigorous, energetic, and ambitious, Roosevelt at age 42 knew that he would be bored. He would have much preferred to continue as governor of New York, an executive position where he was in charge.

But he accepted and Platt was happy. So were a lot of conservative Republicans in New York. They all knew that a vice president has little actual power.

Roosevelt was right, he was very bored as vice president. He was resentful that McKinley never assigned him to meaningful jobs that would have meshed with his exuberant vitality. McKinley understood that with Roosevelt in the limelight his own status would be diminished. The press loved Roosevelt because he was interesting, energetic, and very quotable.

McKinley was assassinated in September 1901, elevating Roosevelt to the presidency. As president, Roosevelt was a force of nature – an activist in every sense of the word.

He won his own term in 1904 against Alton Parker, Chief Judge of the New York Court of Appeals. In the popular vote, Roosevelt received 7,630,457 votes (56.4%) to Parker's 5,083,880 (37.6%). Roosevelt received 336 electoral votes to Parker's 140. Roosevelt carried 32 states to Parker's 13.

With his inexhaustible energy, Roosevelt sought to put his progressive principles into practice. For years the Republican party had been the darling of corporations and Wall Street. That's where the hefty political contributions came from.

A laissez faire philosophy had dominated politics since the Civil War. It was a philosophy which worshipped private enterprise and which opposed government interference and burdensome regulations. Roosevelt and Taft both believed that government had a responsibility to remedy social problems, to improve working conditions, and to safeguard public health.

Roosevelt repeatedly attacked the "plutocrats" and "malefactors of great wealth." He was against political bosses and the spoils system. He reformed the civil service so that employees would be selected on the basis of merit rather than on the basis of political loyalty. He did much for labor and children.

Some of Roosevelt's accomplishments –

The building of the Panama Canal –

The creation of America's magnificent national parks –

Protection of forests and wilderness sites –

Irrigation projects to provide water to millions –

Preserved over 200 million acres against commercial development –

He was awarded the Nobel Peace Prize for his mediation of the Russo Japanese War.

The Roosevelt legend was magnified by his leadership of the volunteer regiment (the Rough Riders) during the Spanish American War. America had declared war on Spain in 1898. We were fighting on behalf of Cuba, which Spain had long dominated and colonized.

Roosevelt's exploits as the leader of his regiment received massive amounts of favorable publicity. His troops admired him greatly both for his personal courage and leadership skills.

Roosevelt, throughout his career, romanticized war. He was a great believer in vigorous physical activity. He boxed, wrestled, and was an avid hunter. The opposite of Taft.

Taft was a huge man. To put it bluntly, he was fat. His main physical activity was golf which Roosevelt found boring. His disposition was conciliatory, he had the classic judicial temperament, and he loved being a judge. He had been an Ohio state judge and at age 34. President Benjamin Harrison appointed him to the United States Circuit Court which is an appellate court one step below the United States Supreme Court. He had also been appointed United States Solicitor General by Harrison. Taft much preferred quiet judging to acting as the advocate for the government.

For a time, Taft was a Professor of Constitutional Law at Yale. He felt that duty required him to resign from his judgeship to accept the position of Governor General of the Philippines. America dominated the Philippines and there was to be a transfer from a military administration to a civil one, with Taft becoming the leader of that new administration. He received very high marks for how he handled that position and was even popular among the Filipinos.

Taft was War Secretary during the Roosevelt administration. A strange job for a man who would always seek to avoid direct confrontations.

A ROOSEVELT DECISION WHICH HE REGRETTED ALL HIS LIFE

When Roosevelt ran for president in 1904, he announced that if elected he would not seek a third term. There was no reason for him to have made that promise. It is true that no president had ever served a third term but there was no prohibition against doing so. Roosevelt knew that had he run in 1908, he would have won just as Taft won. In 1908 Roosevelt was more committed to Taft getting the Republican nomination and ultimate victory than Taft himself was. Roosevelt had only been elected once. But he nearly had another full term due to McKinley's assassination.

In the 1908 election, Taft defeated William Jennings Bryan. In the popular vote, Taft received 7,678,395 (51.6%) to Bryan's 6,408,984 (43.1%). In the Electoral College it was Taft at 321 – Bryan at 162. Taft carried 29 states to Bryan's 17.

Roosevelt loved being president, Taft did not. Among the many mutual accolades and compliments exchanged between the two friends, Roosevelt had said –

"There is not in this nation a higher or finer type of public servant than Taft."

Taft often referred to Roosevelt as his very best friend. He cherished that relationship.

As it turned out, Roosevelt strongly disagreed with some of Taft's policies and decisions. For details about those differences, an excellent source is the book – "The Bully Pulpit" by Doris Kearns Goodwin.

Roosevelt had become so disenchanted with Taft that he totally changed his mind about seeking another term as president. The worst decision of his life. In 1912, Roosevelt tried to wrest the Republican nomination from a sitting president. In those states that held primaries, Roosevelt won a majority, including Taft's home state of Ohio. Taft won only New York and Massachusetts.

In those primary contests, Roosevelt attacked Taft with personal insults. Taft had to respond so he blasted Roosevelt's egotism, saying that he was only in the race –

"merely to gratify his personal ambition and vengeance."

When the delegates to the Republican convention awarded the nomination to Taft, Roosevelt said the convention was – "organized by theft." He said that Taft had become a captive of the reactionary wing of the party.

Then Roosevelt made another terrible decision: to run in the 1912 election as the candidate of a third party: the Progressive Party, dubbed the "Bull Moose Party" by the press. Often, when Roosevelt had been asked how he felt, he would say he felt as strong as a bull moose.

An incident occurred during the 1912 campaign which illustrates the uniqueness of Roosevelt. A would-be assassin shot him in the chest. Luckily, Roosevelt had folded the transcript of a speech he was about to deliver in his jacket pocket, and the thickness of that speech deflected the bullet into his ribs rather than his heart.

Roosevelt refused to go to a hospital until after he gave his speech. He spoke for an hour with the bullet still in his body.

The inevitable happened. By splitting the Republican vote, Roosevelt was responsible for electing the first Democratic president in 20 years – Woodrow Wilson. Wilson became the beneficiary of the Roosevelt/Taft Feud! The combined vote of Roosevelt and Taft exceeded Wilson by about 1.3 million. Wilson only received 41.9% of the popular vote.

Wilson received 6,296,284 votes (41.8%). Roosevelt's popular vote count was 4,122,721 (27.4%). Taft's 3,486,242 (23.2%). The Socialist Party candidate, Eugene Debs, received 901,551 votes (6%).

In the Electoral College, Wilson received 435 votes, Roosevelt 88, and Taft a mere 8. Taft only won Vermont and Utah; he did not even win his home state of Ohio.

Wilson won 40 states, and Roosevelt took only 6.

Taft's loss was humiliating to an incumbent president, yet he was almost relieved. He felt that his many accomplishments during his single term would be judged fairly by future generations. Many thought that if not for Roosevelt Taft would have defeated Wilson. The Roosevelt-Taft contest left many scars.

With the end of both their political careers, the two former friends reconciled. As to be expected, it was Taft who initiated that effort. When Roosevelt had undergone surgery in February 1918, Taft sent him a sympathetic telegram. Roosevelt's response – "Greatly touched and pleased by your message."

That was the first written exchange in six years. Later, they met in person and were very friendly. They agreed on their displeasure about Wilson's conduct of the war. They were both happy about their renewed friendship and regretted that it had taken so long.

On October 3, 1921, Taft got the job he really wanted. President Warren Harding appointed him Chief Justice of the United States Supreme Court. At age 64 Taft said –

"This is the greatest day of my life."

That says it all about Taft's mentality. Being elected President was not – "the greatest day" of his life. Taft served on the court until 1930. On March 8, 1930 he died. Roosevelt had died years earlier in his sleep from a coronary embolism on January 5, 1919.

What was the relationship between Theodore and the other branch of the Roosevelt clan also in New York. Theodore's brother was the father of Eleanor who married Franklin Delano – the 4-term president.

Eleanor's father was a troubled man, an alcoholic who died young. I don't want to play amateur psychologist but it sometimes happens that when one sibling is so outstanding, the other sibling knows that no matter what his achievements, he will always be known simply as the brother of the superstar. The inability to deal with that can lead to depression and alcoholism.

These two political giants will be forever linked. In their separate ways, they both strived to make their country a better place, a fairer place.

CHAPTER 27

SOME OTHER PRESIDENTIAL ELECTIONS – LANDSLIDES AND SQUEAKERS

President Nixon experienced both two squeakers and a landslide. In 1968, his opponent was Hubert Humphrey, who had been President Johnson's vice president. Johnson had decided not to run for reelection in 1968. George Wallace, the former governor of Alabama and ardent segregationist, was in the race as well.

Nixon and Humphrey both received over 30 million votes 43.4% vs. 42.7%. Wallace received about 10 million votes. In the Electoral College Nixon had 301, Humphrey 191, and Wallace 46. Humphrey lost by less than 1%! Think of how different American history would have been had he won.

Nixon won this squeaker but he lost another one in 1960. He and Kennedy both had over 34 million votes, but Kennedy had about 150,000 more. 49.7% against 49.5%. Nixon actually carried more states – 26 to 22. In the Electoral College vote, JFK received 303 to Nixon's 219.

In 1960, Kennedy was 43 years old, and Nixon was 47. A little different from Trump versus Biden, both of whom were in their late 70s.

Kennedy won the state of Illinois by a mere 9,000 votes, and there were strong suspicions that Mayor Daley's' political machine in Chicago was responsible for the Kennedy victory. Nixon, unlike Trump in 2020, did not claim that the election was stolen, although he was encouraged to do so. The liberal media never gave Nixon credit for that decision. There had been speculation that Kennedy's wealthy, ambitious father did everything he could to influence the vote in Illinois. The truth was never pinned down conclusively, and there never was a thorough investigation. There is certainly at least a possibility that the 1960 election was stolen. Robert Caro, in his books about Lyndon Johnson, says without equivocation that Johnson stole the election which made him a United States Senator. Absent that "win" he never would have become president.

A couple of years later, Nixon suffered another defeat when he lost his bid to become the governor of California. It looked like Nixon's political career was over. He told the press that they wouldn't have Nixon to kick around any longer. At that low point, he was no doubt considering joining a prestigious law firm where he could make a huge salary. But, by 1968, he was the president. No Clinton, you were not the comeback kid – Nixon was.

1972 was the opposite of 1968. Nixon's opponent was Senator George McGovern of North Dakota, probably the most liberal member of the Senate who had turned strongly against the Vietnam War. Nixon won 49 states. Had he decided to relax in California or on Key Biscayne, he still would have been reelected. McGovern won only Massachusetts and Washington D.C.

From the ecstasy to the agony! From Nixon's 1972 landslide victory to the agony of being faced with impeachment and a forced resignation on August 9, 1974.

Nixon resigned because of the idiocy of the burglary at the Democratic National Committee offices at the Watergate Complex in Washington, D.C. on June 17, 1972. Why do I say "idiocy"? Because by the date of the break in, it was obvious that McGovern was going to be the Democratic nominee. Nixon did not need spying or intelligence or dirt; he only needed to be breathing to defeat McGovern.

McGovern was nominated at the Democratic National Convention held in Miami Beach July 10-13. McGovern had been a fighter pilot in World War II; he was no peacenik but like so many of his fellow Americans, he came to believe that our role in Vietnam, resulting in the deaths of some 55,000 young Americans, was a huge mistake. Nixon's "silent majority" still bought into the myth of a peace deal with honor.

McGovern choice for vice president was Missouri Senator Thomas Eagleton who had been hospitalized for depression and electroshock therapy. How could McGovern and the bigwigs in the Democratic Party not have known this? How could their vetting process have been so shallow? Plenty of politicians in Missouri knew of Eagleton's history. In 1972, the public was far less tolerant about mental problems.

When the truth came out, Eagleton was dropped from the ticket. At first, McGovern tried to be loyal, saying he was still behind Eagleton 1,000%. In terms of political reality, he had no choice. Eagleton was replaced by President Kennedy's brother-in-law, Sargent Shriver, who had been the Director of the Peace Corps. That decision did not alter the electoral disaster.

Lyndon Johnson had a similar fall to Nixon's. In the 1964 presidential election, he had crushed Senator Barry Goldwater of Arizona defeating him by some 16 million votes, the largest popular margin in U.S. history. Johnson won the Electoral College with 486 against 52. But by 1968, he had become so unpopular that he decided to retire.

His excuse was that he was going to devote all his energy to achieving either victory or a peaceful and honorable resolution to the war. Years later, under Nixon and Kissinger, the war ended in a disaster for America. The North Vietnamese were totally victorious. America and our ally, South Vietnam, lost and there was nothing honorable about it.

Gerald Ford became president when Nixon resigned. He lost to Carter in a close election in 1976. 40 plus million as against 38 plus million. 50% to 48%. In the electoral vote it was Carter 297, Ford 240. Ford made a mistake which in all likelihood cost him the election. The decision was to grant Nixon a full pardon.

In a debate with Carter, Ford made a serious mistake by not conceding that the Soviet Union dominated its satellites in Eastern Europe. Stalin and the Soviets had dominated those countries since the end of World War II. They were recognized as being part of the Soviet Bloc – satellite countries including Poland, Hungary, East Germany, etc. How could a seasoned politician and sitting president not know that? Most 8th graders would know it.

When the two-term governor of California, Ronald Reagan, ran against Jimmy Carter in 1980, he won all but six states. His victory was the first time since the defeat of Herbert Hoover, in 1932 by Roosevelt, that an elected president was denied a second term. The same thing happened to the first President Bush, who lost to Clinton.

When Reagan ran for reelection against Senator Walter Mondale of Minnesota, his victory was even more impressive. Mondale, who had been Carter's vice president, only won his home state. Mondale's selection of Geraldine Ferraro as his running mate, the first woman to ever be on a presidential ticket, did not help.

In Reagan's win over Carter the electoral vote was 489 to 49. In the landslide over Mondale, the electoral vote was 525-13.

My guess is that when a McGovern or Mondale or Goldwater is crushed in a presidential election, they would regret that they ever got the nomination in the first place. I have the same feeling about a baseball team that wins their pennant but loses four straight in the World Series.

The 1920s was the decade of three Republican presidents – Harding, Coolidge and Hoover. The prosperous decade before the Depression of the '30s. The 1920 election – Harding vs. James Cox (Governor of Ohio)

1. Popular vote: Harding received 16,144,093 votes (60.4%) and Cox received 9,139,661 (34.1%)
2. Electoral College vote: Harding 404 – Cox 127.

Harding's abbreviated tenure (he died August 2, 1923) was plagued by multiple scandals. He was succeeded by his Vice President, Calvin Coolidge.

1924 election – Calvin Coolidge vs. John W. Davis (Democrat) vs. Robert M. La Follette (Progressive)

1. Popular Vote: Coolidge received 15,723,789 votes (54%), Davis received 8,386,242 votes (28.8%) and La Follette received 4,831,706 (16.6%).
2. Electoral Vote: Coolidge 382 – Davis 136 and La Follette received 13.

1928 election – Herbert Hoover vs. Al Smith

1. Popular Vote: Hoover received 21,427,123 votes (58.2%) and Smith received 15,015,464 (40.8%)
2. Electoral Votes: 444-87

1932 starts the Roosevelt Era – elected to 4 terms. No president had ever served more than 2.

Roosevelt was elected in 1932, and re-elected in 1936, 1940 and 1944. It wasn't until 1951 that a president was limited to two terms.

In 1932, Roosevelt received close to 23 million votes to Hoover's nearly 16 million. 57.41% against 39.65%. Roosevelt won 42 states against Hoover's 6. In the Electoral College vote it was 472 to 59. Hoover had been Harding's Commerce Secretary, and Coolidge retained him in that position.

In 1936, Roosevelt crushed Landon. 523 electoral votes for Roosevelt – 8 for Landon. In the popular vote Roosevelt – 27,752,648 (60.80%) – Landon 16,681,862 (36.54%).

In 1940, Roosevelt defeated Wendell Willkie, a Wall Street figure with a background in finance and business. He had never served in Congress or been a governor. He received over 22 million votes, as compared to Roosevelt's 27 million plus. Roosevelt carried 38 states – Willkie 10. In the Electoral College, it was Roosevelt 449 – Willkie 82.

If you were to ask Americans to name all four of Roosevelt's opponents, I would bet that less than 1% could do it. Alf Landon, close to zero. Willkie, close to zero. Many more would remember Thomas Dewey who had been governor of New York and who was Roosevelt's opponent in 1944.

Against Dewey, Roosevelt had 25,612,916 votes, 53.4% - Dewey 22,017,929, 45.9%. Roosevelt carried 36 states – Dewey 12. In the Electoral College, Roosevelt 432 – Dewey 99.

Early in 1944, it was obvious that Roosevelt was a very sick man. He looked haggard and weak, his complexion was grayish. You did not need to be a doctor to discern that. Many individuals said privately, some even publicly, that he could not survive a fourth term. So the selection of a vice president was particularly important. Roosevelt dumped Henry Wallace for Harry Truman.

But the liars prevailed, just like the liars prevailed following President Wilson's disabling stroke.

Vice Admiral Ross McIntire was Roosevelt's personal physician. He said the President's "health is perfectly okay" – that Roosevelt was proud "of his flat tummy" and there was – "nothing wrong with him organically at all."

The Democratic National Chairman Robert Hannegan said –

"That he was – very vigorous, the picture of health." There are almost never consequences for those who tell such outrageous lies.

Roosevelt won re-election in November 1944; he died on April 12, 1945.

Millions of Americans did not know that as an adult Roosevelt had been crippled by polio, that he could not walk or even stand unaided. When he was filmed standing, he would be supported by one of his tall strong sons, looking normal and vigorous. His powerful voice and excellent delivery projected an image of vitality. When Roosevelt had to be lifted from a car and carried, photographs were not allowed.

Roosevelt's Vice President, Harry Truman, served as president for nearly a full term since Roosevelt had died so early in his fourth term. In the 1948 election, Dewey had again secured the Republican nomination.

According to the polls and the media, Dewey was a heavy favorite. He was overconfident; he did not campaign nearly as hard as he should have; his speeches were uninspiring; he was playing it safe. Truman's campaign was the opposite: he was tireless; his followers repeated the line over and over again – "Give 'em Hell, Harry!" – and he did. His main target was the Republican "Do-Nothing Congress." Truman invigorated large and enthusiastic crowds as he traveled the country by train.

After his win, Truman in a very famous photograph held up the front page of the Chicago Daily Tribune with the headline – "Dewey Defeats Truman."

Truman surprised everyone. He was decisive, he was a take charge guy. He gave the order to drop atomic bombs on Hiroshima and Nagasaki on August 6 and 9 – 1945. He had only been president since April. Roosevelt would have loved to have survived until victory was won in World War II.

In the popular vote against Dewey Truman got 24,178,347 votes – 49.6% -- Dewey 21,991,292 – 45.1%. – Truman had 303 to Dewey's 189 in the electoral vote. Truman carried 28 states – Dewey 16. He also had to contend with Senator Strom Thurmond, Dixiecrat, who received 1,175,930 votes – 2.4%. Thurmond got 39 electoral votes from the Deep South.

THE SQUEAKER OF ALL TIME IS DECIDED BY THE SUPREME COURT

I refer to the 2000 election between Al Gore, Clinton's vice president, and Bush II. Everyone knows Bush became president. Few people remember that Gore received over a half-million more votes than did Bush.

The dispute was all about Florida where Bush had been certified as the winner. Supposedly, he won by one half of a percent. Florida had 25 electoral votes. The problem was with punch-card balloting machines which did not register an unknown number of votes. Because of that deficiency, the Florida Supreme Court on December 8, 2000 ordered a manual recount of ballots.

Days later, the United States Supreme Court reversed the Florida Supreme Court, saying the manual counting of ballots should stop. That decision made Bush II the president.

Had Gore carried his home state of Tennessee, he would have become president. That could have made him very bitter.

The opinion of the U.S. Supreme Court puts to bed the oft repeated cliche that we are a nation of laws, not men. Had the makeup of the court been different, Gore would have been president. Had the dissenters been in the majority, Gore would have become president. The dissenters were Ginsburg, Breyer, Stevens and Souter. Gore was one vote short. Rehnquist, Scalia and Thomas were in the majority.

One of the dissents clearly said – "The Court was wrong to take this case." The laws had not changed but the individuals on the Florida Supreme Court and the U.S. Supreme Court interpreted them differently.

The laws themselves reflect the preferences of thousands of individuals. All we need to do is consider the 5 to 4 decisions of the Supreme Court and other appellate courts to realize how misleading is the hallowed political assertion that we are a nation of laws. Yes, we are a nation of laws – laws passed and interpreted by men and women with different agendas and beliefs.

CHAPTER 28

ADDITIONAL REFLECTIONS ON PRESIDENTIAL ELECTIONS AND POLITICS

I am surprised by the number of times that a candidate who won his party's nomination for president, lost his home state. I would have thought that those voters would be proud to see a local boy become president. On the other hand, they are the ones who know the candidate best and would be most familiar with his weaknesses.

Gore lost his home state of Tennessee to Bush II in the election of 2000. When General Eisenhower defeated Adlai Stevenson in 1952, he won all but nine states. Stevenson had been the Governor of Illinois, but that state went for Eisenhower. In that same year, Truman was leaving the presidency. Eisenhower won Truman's home state of Missouri.

Al Smith had been the Governor of New York. He lost to Herbert Hoover in the election of 1928. New York went for Hoover. Smith also had to contend with much anti-Catholic sentiment.

The Catholic issue was still lurking when Kennedy ran for president in 1960. Those opposed to a Catholic president could not admit to their own prejudice, so they came up with an argument that a Catholic president would be taking orders from the Pope. Kennedy very effectively dealt with the issue directly and it was basically put to rest.

Alf Landon had been the Governor of Kansas. When he ran against Roosevelt in 1936, he only won two states – Maine and Vermont. Kansas went for Roosevelt.

George McGovern lost his home state of North Dakota when he ran against Nixon in 1972. He won only a single state- Massachusetts.

When Walter Mondale ran against Reagan, he won only a single state, but at least it was his home state of Minnesota.

Let's look at a few instances of hardball politics. In political circles, there is a very famous television ad that the advertising insiders admire. During the 1988 campaign between Bush I and Michael Dukakis, the ad was known as the Willie Horton ad.

Horton was a murderer and rapist imprisoned in Massachusetts. The very liberal Dukakis had a prison furlough program, which allowed prisoners, even prisoners like Horton, to leave prison temporarily. During such a break, Horton committed another rape and murder. Bush's campaign manager was Lee Atwater, known to be a tough practitioner, a master of dirty tricks. The ad showed a black man going through a turnstile.

Dukakis would have been doomed by an answer he gave during a presidential debate. Of course, Mr. Liberal was against the death penalty. He was asked the kind of question seldom asked by panelists. The substance of the question was – If your wife was raped and murdered, wouldn't you want the killer to be executed?

Instead of reacting like a normal man and showing some anger and fire, he gave a weak, longwinded answer, as though he was teaching a class in constitutional law. What he should have said was, "I would want to strangle that bastard myself." I can guarantee you that answer would have aroused the crowd into a standing ovation. Instead the answer he gave caused a lot of liberals to vote for Bush.

Bush received nearly 49 million votes – Dukakis close to 42 million. In the Electoral College it was Bush 426 – Dukakis 111.

Four year later (1992) Bush lost to Clinton – Clinton 44.9 million votes to Bush's 39.1 million. The entry of Ross Perot (a very rich and very strange guy) into the race probably helped Clinton. Perot got a huge number of votes – 19.7 million. But he did not win a single state in the Electoral College.

Third-party candidates like Wallace, Thurmond, Perot never have a chance of winning, but they can tilt the outcome. Even Teddy Roosevelt could not win as a third-party candidate. Ralph Nader was accused of making Bush president rather than Gore in 2000. He received 2,882,055 votes – zero electoral votes.

Timing is so important. At the height of his popularity, Nader might have had a chance to win the Democratic nomination. He had proved himself to be an effective consumer advocate. All Americans are consumers and he was fighting for them. He was highly intelligent, an excellent speaker. He would have done very well in debates. His lifestyle was frugal, he had no interest in becoming rich. His image was that of an honest, true believer.

By 2000, his most ardent followers were angry at his entry into the Bush/Gore contest. By 2000 his image was different – many saw his preaching as having become tiresome, even annoying. What could have prompted him to enter the 2000 race knowing he had zero chance of winning and knowing that many of his former admirers would become his enemies? Hard to figure!

During the contest between Lyndon Johnson and Barry Goldwater, a television ad was shown of a lovely young girl with a flower in her hand. The sound and music made it clear that if Goldwater were to win, that girl and millions of others could die in a nuclear war. When Goldwater called Johnson on it, saying that the ad was outside the boundary of even tough politicking, Johnson professed ignorance, which, of course, was a lie. The ad was pulled but it had already done its damage.

When Ed Koch, the Mayor of New York City, was running against Mario Cuomo for Governor of New York, the Cuomo camp came up with the slogan –

"Vote for Cuomo, not the homo" –

When Cuomo denied that he had anything to do with that slogan, Koch called him a "prick."

For many years, the United States had in place a crazy system as to when an elected president actually takes office. The election takes place in early November, yet the winner doesn't become the president until March 4 of the following year. So the president who lost or retired remains in office for 4 more months. During that time, the incumbent can be doing all sorts of things, issuing all kinds of orders and directives that the new president totally disagrees with.

That system changed, by virtue of the 20th Amendment to the Constitution, which was ratified by the states on January 23, 1933. The new date for when a winning candidate can take his seat in the Oval Office is January 20.

But hey, that is still nearly 3 months after the election. The newly elected president should be inaugurated 30 days after the election. Is the delay tolerated so that there will be enough time to prepare for lavish parties and the inaugural ball? It was the 22nd Amendment ratified on February 27, 1951 which limited a president to two terms.

Few Americans could name a vice president who never became president. Yet it is surprising as to how many did become president. Here's the list.

VICE PRESIDENTS WHO BECAME PRESIDENTS

This list provides strong evidence for never turning down the vice presidency.

1. **John Adams**—VP to George Washington, was elected president after Washington retired.
2. **Thomas Jefferson**—VP to John Adams, won against Adams in the election of 1800.

3. **Martin Van Buren**—VP to Andrew Jackson, became president after Jackson retired.
4. **John Tyler**—VP to William Henry Harrison, who became president after Harrison's death. Tyler served out Harrison's term for four years but was never himself elected president.
5. **Millard Fillmore**—VP to Zachary Taylor, assumed the presidency upon Taylor's death. Fillmore served out Taylor's term but was never himself elected president.
6. **Andrew Johnson**—VP to Abraham Lincoln, who became president after Lincoln's assassination in 1865. Johnson served until 1869, receiving very low marks. Why had Lincoln not chosen a higher quality candidate? Ulysses Grant became president after Johnson serving two terms.
7. **Chester Arthur**—VP to James A. Garfield, assumed the presidency upon Garfield's death. Arthur served out Garfield's full-term but was never himself elected president.
8. **Theodore Roosevelt**—VP to William McKinley, became president after McKinley's assassination, then was elected to a full term.
9. **Calvin Coolidge**—VP to Warren G. Harding, became president after Harding's death, then elected to a full term. Coolidge served as president from 1923-1929, to be followed by Herbert Hoover. Coolidge could have run for a second term but chose not to.
10. **Harry Truman**—VP to Franklin D. Roosevelt, became president after FDR's death, then elected to a full term. He served as president 1945-1953. Truman could have run for a second term but chose not to. He would have lost to Eisenhower just like Adlai Stevenson lost.
11. **Lyndon Johnson**—VP to John Kennedy, became president following Kennedy's death, then elected to a full term. 1963-1969. Johnson could have run for another term but his popularity tanked as a result of the Vietnam War.
12. **Richard Nixon**—VP to Dwight Eisenhower.

13. **Gerald Ford**—VP to Richard Nixon. Ford became President after Nixon resigned. In his one shot to be elected, he lost to Jimmy Carter.
14. **George H. W. Bush**—VP to Ronald Reagan. He was elected after Reagan's two terms. He served only one term 1989-1993, losing to Clinton.
15. **Joseph R. Biden**- VP to Barack Obama.

PRESIDENTS WHO DIED IN OFFICE

1. William Henry Harrison.
2. Zachary Taylor.
3. Abraham Lincoln. Assassinated.
4. James A. Garfield.
5. William McKinley. Assassinated.
6. Warren G. Harding.
7. Franklin D. Roosevelt.
8. John F. Kennedy. Assassinated.

There have been five presidential elections in which the successful candidate did not receive a plurality of the popular vote. Hillary Clinton got nearly 3 million more votes than Trump in 2016. Gore got over a half-million more votes than Bush in 2000.

How do they handle that psychologically? Winning, but losing! If Trump had ever won the popular vote and yet lost the electoral vote, I don't think he would have accepted the result. And that, hypothetically, would have been a real crisis.

Hillary remained politically active granting interviews, sounding off on various issues and continuing to blast Trump as a threat to democracy. Gore, on the other hand, dropped out of the political world – his new focus became the climate.

ABOUT THE AUTHOR

Stanley M. Rosenblatt is recognized as one of America's great trial lawyers. Along with his wife and law partner Susan, they challenged the Tobacco Industry's half- century of lies about the harms caused by their products. That case resulted in the single largest verdict in American history – $145 billion.

Stanley also achieved numerous record verdicts in previous personal injury and medical malpractice cases, and he successfully defended a first-degree murder charge in a groundbreaking euthanasia trial that made national headlines.

Somehow Stanley also found the time to author five books – "Trial Lawyer" – "Malpractice and Other Malfeasances" – "Murder of Mercy" – "Justice Denied" – "The Divorce Racket".

He also found the time to host two television programs on the Public Broadcasting Service – "Within the Law" and "Israel Diary". On "Within the Law" he interviewed some of the country's most prominent lawyers, judges, and civil rights leaders. On "Israeli Diary" he interviewed prime ministers and presidents and defense ministers including Ariel Sharon, Yitzhak Rabin, and Shimon Peres. Also, Arab leaders including the Defense Minister of Jordan.

Stanley and Susan are the parents of nine children and have been blessed with over thirty grandchildren. Susan, great mother and grandmother, brilliant lawyer, underwent 8 c-sections. To her the whole process of creating a human being was miraculous.

Milton Keynes UK
Ingram Content Group UK Ltd.
UKHW020211300724
446213UK00010B/135/J